TRANSLATING THEORY TO PRACTICE

TRANSLATING THEORY TO PRACTICE

Thinking and Acting Like an Expert Counselor

RICHARD D. PARSONS

West Chester University

Upper Saddle River, New Jersey
Columbus, Ohio

Library of Congress Cataloging in Publication Data

Parsons, Richard D.
  Translating theory to practice : thinking and acting like an expert counselor /
Richard D. Parsons.
      p. cm.
  ISBN-13: 978-0-205-56970-0
  ISBN-10: 0-205-56970-6
  1. Counseling.   I. Title.

  BF636.6.P37 2008
  158'.3—dc22

                                                                          2008017391

Vice President and Executive Publisher: *Jeffery W. Johnston*
Senior Editor: *Meredith Fossel*
Director of Marketing: *Quinn Perkson*
Series Editorial Assistant: *Maren Vigilante*
Senior Marketing Manager: *Krista Clark*
Production Editor: *Gregory Erb*
Editorial Production Service: *Progressive Publishing Alternatives*
Composition Buyer: *Linda Cox*
Manufacturing Buyer: *Megan Cochran*
Electronic Composition: *Progressive Information Technologies*

This book was set in Palatino by Progressive. It was printed and bound by Hamilton Printing.
The cover was printed by Phoenix Color Corporation/Hagerstown.

Pearson® is a registered trademark of Pearson plc
Merrill® is a registered trademark of Pearson Education, Inc.
Pearson Education Ltd.   Pearson Education Australia Pty. Limited
Pearson Education Singapore Pte. Ltd.   Pearson Education North Asia Ltd.
Pearson Education Canada, Ltd.   Pearson Educación de Mexico. S.A. de C.V.
Pearson Education—Japan   Pearson Education Malaysia Pte. Ltd.

      Merrill   10 9 8 7 6 5 4 3 2 1
   is an imprint of

   PEARSON   ISBN 13: 978-0-205-56970-0
                     www.pearsonhighered.com   ISBN 10: 0-205-56970-6

ABOUT THE AUTHOR

Richard D. Parsons is Graduate Professor of Counselor Education at West Chester University, West Chester, PA. In addition to teaching and directing the post-master's counselor licensing program at West Chester, Dr. Parsons does psychotherapy and provides consultation services to industry, schools, professionals, and religious communities in the tri-state area of Pennsylvania, New Jersey, and Delaware.

Dr. Parsons is a member of numerous national and state professional organizations and has been named a member of American Men and Women of Science, American Catholic Who's Who, and Pennsylvania's Counselor of the Year.

In addition to his numerous speeches and workshops, Dr. Parsons has authored or co-authored over 70 professional articles, books, and book chapters. His most recent books include the clinical training texts: *Counseling Strategies that Work! Evidenced-based Interventions for School Counselors* (Allyn & Bacon); *The Ethics of Professional Practice* (Allyn & Bacon); *The School Counselor as Consultant* (Brooks/ Cole); and *The Fundamentals of the Helping Relationship* (Waveland Press).

CONTENTS

CHAPTER FOUR
Behavioral-Orienting Framework   69

CHAPTER FIVE
Schemas: Cognitive Focus   101

Let me tell you about my home heating system. I know, this is probably not what you expected when you began reading—but stay with me! Anyway, I have a relatively new gas heater for my house. One evening this past winter, the house got very chilly and it was clear the heater wasn't working. Well, being the 'man' of the house and a relatively bright individual I figured I should go check it out. Well, I figured out how to take the front panel off the heater and when I did, I saw lots of wires, and pipes and what appeared to be a motor and I looked . . . and looked . . . and looked. The problem is I looked and saw everything in there but I really didn't know what I should be looking for or how to recognize that something was wrong.

Scene 2. The heater service man arrives. He walks up to the heater, puts his tool box down, looks for a second, disconnects one of the white PVC pipes that was going toward the motor area, and he extracts a leaf from the pipe. In less than two minutes the problem was diagnosed and resolved!

Feeling somewhat foolish and trying to defend my ego, I said to the repair man, "Wow that was simple!" His response to me was quite insightful and in a way serves as the theme of this book. He said, "Yep, it's really simple when you know what you're looking for!" While counseling may never be 'simple', it is much more efficient and clearly less draining on all involved when the counselor knows what he or she is looking for and, of course, recognizing it when he or she sees it!

COUNSELING: MORE THAN SKILLS AND TECHNIQUES!

More than 50 years ago, Pepinsky and Pepinsky (1954) recognized counseling to be, in part, a cognitive activity. As such, it follows that the process of becoming a counselor must involve the acquisition of cognitive skills and not just behavioral skills of social interaction. To be an effective counselor one needs to know what he/she is looking for and recognize it when he/she sees it! Being an effective counselor truly requires one to think like an effective counselor. Yet, a quick review of the literature on counselor training will highlight the fact that counselors-in-training are given a lot of theory, research, and micro-skill training but little preparation in learning how to think like an 'expert' counselor (Kleiner, A.J., 2006).

For those in training and those recently graduated, encounters with real clients are most often accompanied by apprehension and anxiety about knowing what to do and when to do it. It is an apprehension that is the hallmark of the novice counselor and one that distinguishes novice from expert.

LEARNING TO THINK LIKE AN EXPERT

Translating Theory to Practice is a text written in response to this void in counselor training—that is, training new counselors to **first think** like an expert and
then act accordingly. The text focuses on the development of the cognitive skills
necessary to reason through the vast amount of clinical information provided by
clients in order to provide purposeful and effective therapeutic responses.

Literature on the distinction of *expert-novice* spans a number of disciplines
and provides a rich base from which to identify the processes that need to be
developed if one is to move from being a novice to becoming an expert. Experts
and novices, regardless of discipline, differ in their encoding of information, the
organization of information in memory, and the use of this information in reasoning or problem solving. Consider the following.

Experts store knowledge in abstract, problem-relevant categories that are
connected by underlying conceptual principles relevant to problem solution.
In contrast, novices organize knowledge into categories based on superficial,
irrelevant cues that may not be pertinent to generating a problem solution
(Chi, Glaser, Farr, 1988). Thus, while gazing into the inner working of my
heater, I was often distracted by irrelevant cues such as size of parts and colors
of wires. However, the expert—understanding the principle of air flow, com-
bustion, and heat exchange—was quickly able to diagnose the source of the
problem and thus the problem solution.

Experts in counseling also have been identified as having organizational
cognitive structures—schemas—which help them quickly make sense of the
information that a client is presenting. Novices, however, often find themselves
in a state of buzzing-blooming confusion with all the influx of information
being shared by the client—information they are ill-prepared to organize or
comprehend (Etringer & Hillerbrand, 1995). This was certainly true for my
experience, as I stared into the complex of wires, pipes, and moving parts, I was
frozen in indecision. This was quite a contrast to the ease with which the expert
navigated these data, efficiently identifying the problem and the steps needed
to reach resolution.

In addition to these general characteristics, experts in counseling typically
employ elaborate systems of understanding of the process and problems being
presented within the helping relationship. They are able to discern important
information from that of less importance; they are able to find themes and trends
running through the client's story (i.e. pattern recognition); and they are able to
blend knowledge of research and theory with the reality of the client's needs and
resources in the delivery of their interventions (Mayfield, W.A., Kardas, C.M., &
Kivlighan, D.M.,1999).

Finally, the expert counselor uses procedural (versus declarative) knowledge. Rather than simply approaching the client with static declarative knowledge
(e.g., "Oh, the DSM IV characteristics of depression are . . . "), the expert counselor
approaches the client organizing data into "If . . . [condition phase], then . . .
[action phase]" statements. With such procedural knowledge, the expert counselor
views the data presented from the perspective of . . . "If the client presents with

this, then I'll do that." Such procedural knowledge of what to do and when to do it is essential if one is to be an effective and efficient helper.

FOCUS OF THE TEXT

Translating Theory to Practice is a text that assists students to employ four distinct organizing schemas (i.e., solution-focused, behavioral, cognitive, and transtheoretical) in their process of data reception, pattern recognition, and utilization. Emphasis throughout this text is on the importance of employing procedural knowledge ("if this then do that") to guide professional practice. *Translating Theory to Practice* will assist those in counselor training and those new to the profession to move them from being passive recipients of client information, to active agents of change, purposively utilizing the information received in the process of helping their clients.

Research suggests that procedural knowledge is acquired as the result of practice accompanied by feedback (e.g., Anderson, 1982; Byrnes, 1996; Kohls-Gatzoulis, et al., 2004). Practice and feedback will be central to this text. Case illustrations, case presentations with analyses of counselor 'thinking', and directed practice activities will be employed as teaching tools throughout the text.

Each chapter provides a blending of theory, practice, and guided personalized application. The chapters include:

- A description of the theoretical constructs presented with the chapter, along with the supportive research.
- Clinical illustrations of the concepts and constructs discussed.
- In depth cases, including sample counselor dialogue.
- Guided practice exercises.
- A list of web-based and literature-based resources of additional material.

AN IMPORTANT CAVEAT

While the hope and the intent of this text is to assist those in the early stages of their counseling careers to begin to think and act like an expert, it must be highlighted that the operative word in the previous sentence is 'begin'.

Becoming an expert in counseling or in most any professional field of endeavor requires continued training, personal reflection, supervision, and corrective feedback. Increasing our expertise in both knowledge and skill requires all of the above and certainly practice . . . practice . . . practice! Hopefully the current text provides a good spring board from which to start this process.

ACKNOWLEDGEMENTS

While this project is written under the authorship of my name, its completion is the result of the effort and support of many wonderful people.

To Virginia L. Blanford and Arnie Burvikovs at Pearson Longman/Allyn & Bacon, I say thank for you for the support and encouragement you provided, and to the staff at Progressive Publishing Alternatives and specifically, their editorial staff that took my words and shaped them into a text.

I would like to thank my colleagues, especially Dr. Wally Kahn and Dr. Lynn Spradlin for their reflections and insightful comments and suggestions. Finally, I would like to offer a very special thank you to my wife Ginny. Her acumen as a teacher and her probing questions and call to clarity helped to make what was just another text into a reader-friendly instrument of learning.

REFERENCES

Anderson, J.R. (1982). Acquisition of cognitive skill. *Psychology Review,* 89, 369-406.

Brynes, J.P. (1996). *Cognitive development and learning in instructional contexts.* Boston: Allyn & Bacon.

Chi, M.T.H., Glaser, R. & Farr, M.J. (1988). *The nature of expertise.* Hillsdale, NJ: Lawrence Erlbaum Associates, Inc.

Etrigner, B., Hillerbrand, E., & Clairborn, C.D. (1995). The transition for novice to expert counselor. *Counselor Education and Supervision,* 35 (1), 4-17.

Kleiner, A.J. (2006). Effects of counselor process change models and microskills training on counseling self-efficacy and treatment conceptualization ability. *Dissertation Abstracts International: Section B: The Sciences and Engineering,* 67(1-B), 549.

Kohls-Gatzoulis, Julie A.; Regehr, Glenn; Hutchison, Carol. (2004). Teaching cognitive skills improves learning in surgical skills courses: a blinded, prospective, randomized study. *Canadian Journal of Surgery,* 47 (4), 277-283.

Mayfield,W.A., Kardas, C.M., & Kivlighan, D.M. (1999). Differences in experienced and novice counselors' knowledge structures about clients: Implications for case conceptualization. *Journal of Counseling Psychology,* 46(4), 504-514.

Pepinsky, H. B., & Pepinsky, P. (1954). *Counseling theory and practice.* New York: Ronald Press.

PART I

COUNSELING AS REFLECTIVE PRACTICE

CHAPTER 1

COUNSELOR COMPETENCIES: MORE THAN SKILLS

In his masterwork, *The Principles of Psychology* (1890), William James described a baby's initial impression of the world as one of "... great blooming, buzzing confusion" (p. 462). While James was describing the stream of thought experienced when first introduced to this world, he may just as well have been describing the experience of most counselors when first introduced to a professional exchange with a client. Whether it is in a course titled "The Fundamentals of a Helping Relationship" or "Clinic 101," the first time a counselor in training is introduced to a "professional" interaction, or client interview, the experience is one best described as buzzing—if not blooming—confusion.

Trained in fundamental communication and relationship-building skills, the novice counselor or counselor in training often finds that his/her use of open questions, minimal encouragers, and skills of reflection invite a barrage of client disclosure. A simple question such as *"What brought you here?"* can elicit quite an overwhelming response and an abundance of information—especially when posed to a client exhibiting mania (see Case Illustration 1.1).

CASE ILLUSTRATION 1.1

"... AND WHAT BRINGS YOU HERE?"

Counselor: Mary, thanks for coming. Perhaps you could tell me what brought you here today?

Mary: Well, it has been a long time coming. I mean everyone has told me I need to talk to someone. My family, my friends, they've all been pushing me. It's been years. . . .

I guess it started when I was in elementary school. I mean, everyone made fun of me. You see, I was really fat as a child, my parents always said I was big-boned, but I was fat. Do you think

(continued)

I'm big-boned? Well, anyway, being teased liked this got me to the point where I didn't very much like myself and I always expected that people would make fun of me—I still do. And, so I started to withdraw from the other kids. I spent a lot of time in my room, playing with dolls and drawing and . . . now I know this will sound crazy, but I'm not! Anyway, I had this imaginary friend and we would have dress parties and tea parties and just hang out in my room. It's kind of strange but I miss her at times. I've even thought it would be nice to bring her back into my life. But, hey, 28-year-old women shouldn't have imaginary friends, right? Am I going too fast?

As in Case Illustration 1.1, many counselors, especially those in the early stages of their professional development, know how to acquire information, but may be unsure of how to use it. The counselor in our case illustration may have been flooded, not only by the client disclosure, but also by her own thoughts regarding what to do. Should she interrupt? Should she ask for clarification? Where does she go next? How does she use this information? These are just a few of the questions the counselor may need to consider as she proceeds in her work with Mary. In very simplistic terms, for many novice counselors, knowing what to say after "What I hear you saying is . . ." presents a major challenge.

Presented with client disclosure, counselors quite often attempt to register and record *all* that is conveyed in hopes that it may prove useful and directional at some point in the future. Sadly, this attempt at data reception is done without discernment of what is relevant and what is not; or what is essential for planning and what is only tangential. Without this ability to discern it is easy for a counselor to feel overwhelmed. Under these conditions, it is not unusual to find counselors who are unable to focus and are unsure of the direction they should take. It is at these moments that their experience can best be described as one of buzzing, blooming confusion — an experience that is often responded to with utterances of an "ummm" or "aahh," as the counselor bides time in hopes that somehow clarity will emerge.

When providing professional service to one in need, biding time in hopes that clarity and direction will emerge is insufficient. The competent counselor needs to know how to navigate through the mass of material and information presented in sessions in order to find the path that will best assist the client.

Perhaps the picture that is being painted is too harsh or too critical — that is not the intent. It is simply that this author's initial therapeutic encounters and his experience of more than 30 years of graduate training has provided him abundant illustrations, both observed and personally experienced, of the buzzing, blooming confusion one can experience if he/she is only armed with skills to unearth information but is lacking the means to organize these data and to make sense of the encounter. It is this idea of developing an effective, organizational framework, and of learning to think and act like an expert counselor, that serves as the focus of this and of all chapters to follow.

Specifically, after reading this chapter you will be able to:

1. explain the possible difficulty in using relationship-building skills indiscriminately;
2. describe what is meant by an "ill-structured" problem and its relevance to counselor training;
3. describe some of the differences in expert versus novice thinking; and
4. define "orientation framework" and explain its value to counselors.

KNOWLEDGE AND SKILLS OF A COMPETENT COUNSELOR

Defining and evaluating professional competence has been and remains a central issue in the field of psychotherapy and counseling (Overholser & Fine, 1990; Procidano, Busch-Rossnagel, Reznikoff, & Geisinger, 1995; Schöttler, Oliver, & Porter, 2005). Professional schools of education and counselor preparation programs are fully aware of the complexity and dynamic of the counseling relationship and the counseling process and the difficulty in defining components of competency. To this end, organizations such as CACREP (Council for Accreditation of Counseling and Related Educational Programs) and state licensing bodies have attempted to articulate specific competencies to serve as training outcomes and standards for competent professional practice (see Table 1.1).

Competence Requires Knowledge and Skill

A review of the literature in search of a listing of core competencies reveals that schools of professional education, while perhaps differing in their curricular emphasis, highlight similar competencies as core to the development of professional practice. Competencies most often highlighted as essential for effective, competent practice include: (a) *mastery of factual knowledge* such as that needed for assessment, diagnosis, and treatment; (b) competence in *generic clinical abilities* such as those involved in basic interviewing and the ability to establish and maintain a constructive working alliance and possession of adequate cultural competency; and (c) competence in *orientation-specific technical skills*, such as learning how to operationally define a behavior of real concern (BORC) from a behavioral orientation.

There is a long-standing debate over the degree to which emphasis is placed on the more academic elements (e.g., constructs, concepts, theories) as opposed to skill-based elements (see Schöttler, Oliver, & Porter, 2005). Many training programs would suggest that they seek to balance academic elements such as knowledge of theory and research with the more technical skill-based "nonacademic" elements. (Schöttler, Oliver, & Porter, 2005). However, others argue that training programs typically emphasize academic skills while neglecting those skills of clinical competence, relegating these assets to a practica or internship experience (Beutler, Macchiato, & Allstetter-Neufeldt, 1994; Sakinofsky, 1979). Support for

TABLE 1.1 Sampling of Specified Competencies

General Area	CACREP (Council for Accreditation of Counseling and Related Educational Programs)	State Licensing Agencies Example: Pennsylvania Licensed Professional Counselor
Human growth and development: Understanding the nature and needs of individuals at all developmental stages	Yes	Yes
Social/cultural foundations: Understanding issues and trends in a multicultural and diverse society	Yes	Yes
Helping relationships: Understanding the skills required for developing and maintaining a counseling and consultation relationship	Yes	Yes
Group work: Understanding group development, dynamics	Yes	Yes
Career and lifestyle development: Understanding career development theories	Yes	Yes
Appraisal: Understanding individual and group approaches to assessment and evaluation	Yes	Yes
Research: Understanding types of research methods, basic statistics	Yes	Yes
Professional orientation/professional identity: Understanding all aspects of professional functioning, including ethics and standards of practice	Yes	Yes

this allegation can be found in the stated outcomes for counselor training that are listed by CACREP (see Table 1.1).

The "academic" knowledge base of competency.   When considering the types of knowledge needed to function as a competent counselor, most would agree that counselor trainees need to acquire adequate levels of factual information concerning basic psychological processes, human development, professional ethics, and theories of intervention (Overholser & Fine, 1990). A review of the course description of typical graduate training programs provides insight into the types of knowledge targeted.

Most counselor programs provide courses in each of the following areas: theories of counseling, career development, adolescent psychology, sexuality, addictions, group principles, assessment, consultation, family and systems counseling, and supervision. The theory, research, constructs, and concepts provided in these courses typically serve as the knowledge base for competent professional counseling. Exercise 1.1 (Part A) provides you with an opportunity to identify the academic components of your training.

The technical/clinical skills.   In addition to providing this knowledge base, training programs attempt to teach the technical/clinical skills that must be employed in counseling. At its most basic level, competence in clinical skills involves the ability to foster productive therapeutic relationships with clients (Overholser & Fine, 1990; PSWAIT, 2001; Sakinofsky, 1979). Approaches utilizing microskills training approaches (e.g., Ivey & Ivey, 2003; Truax & Carkhuff, 1967) help counselor trainees develop and employ skills such as accurate reflections of content and feelings, clarification, questioning, summarizing, and confronting. These interpersonal communication skills are essential to the creation of a working alliance and thus play an essential role in counseling outcome (Horvath, 2001). If used effectively, these interpersonal skills elicit client exploration, reduce anxiety in clients, alleviate clients' experiences of isolation, and permit the counselor to become a personally potent reinforcement in clients' lives (Carkhuff & Berenson, 1967).

These fundamental relationship and communication skills often serve as the clinical "substance" of many counseling training programs (Kleiner, 2006). Students in counselor training are given the opportunity to learn, to practice, and to receive corrective feedback on these fundamental skills. In laboratory-type courses or clinics, persons in training can become quite proficient in these fundamental skills. Exercise 1.1 (Part B) invites you to reflect on your training and program of professional development.

■ ■ ■ ■ ■

EXERCISE 1.1

REFLECTIONS ON A PROGRAM OF TRAINING

Direction: As you continue your professional development, it is a good idea to reflect on the specific knowledge and skill you have developed and to identify areas in which you can have future professional growth. **Part A** of this exercise invites you to identify the courses or training experiences you have had that have increased your knowledge in each of the specific areas. **Part B** invites you to continue this self-reflection, but to now target your development of technical/clinical skills. In both cases, there is an opportunity for you to assess your competence—a point that may help you target future areas for growth.

(continued)

■ ■ ■ ■ ■ ▬▬▬▬

EXERCISE 1.1   (CONTINUED)

PART A: ACADEMIC KNOWLEDGE-BASED COMPETENCY

Knowledge Base	Training Experiences (including courses)	Level of Competency (mastery, beginner, absent)	Specific Areas of Professional Knowledge to Target for Future Development
Group work: Understanding of group development, dynamics			
Career and Lifestyle development: Understanding of career development theories			
Appraisal: Understanding individual and group approaches to assessment and evaluation			
Research: Understanding types of research methods, basic statistics			
Professional orientation/professional identity: Understanding all aspects of professional functioning, including ethics and standards of practice			
Human growth and development: Understanding the nature and needs of individuals at all developmental stages			
Social/cultural foundations: Understanding issues and trends in a multicultural and diverse society			
Other:			
Other:			

■ ■ ■ ■ ■

EXERCISE 1.1   (CONTINUED)

PART B: TECHNICAL/CLINICAL COMPETENCY

Clinical Skills	Training Experiences (including courses)	Competency Assessment (mastery, beginner, absent)	Specific Areas of Clinical Competency to Target for Future Development
Helping relationships: Understanding the skills required for developing and maintaining a counseling and consultation relationship			
Intervention strategies: Ability to employ specific intervention strategies and principles within a session or client contract			
Group process: Can successfully form and facilitate group process.			
Assessment: Able to employ formal and informal, individual and group assessments			
Other:			
Other:			

It must be noted, however, that it is not the blanket employment of these skills that makes one effective. Rather, it is the intentional, directional, and purposeful use of these skills not only to build a working alliance but also to therapeutically impact the client (see Case Illustration 1.2).

The counselor in Case Illustration 1.2 may have been trained in using skills of reflection, continuation, or confrontation, but it is employing each of these skills with purpose and anticipated impact that makes for effective counseling. The key ingredient to the effective use of these skills, therefore, is less in *knowing how* as it is of *knowing when* to employ a question rather than a minimal encourager or a summarization rather than a reflection. For those armed with only the skills to

■ ■ ■ ■ ■

CASE ILLUSTRATION 1.2

EMPLOYING COMMUNICATION SKILLS SELECTIVELY

> **Client:**   Well, I feel somewhat petty, but everything she does really annoys me!
>
> **Counselor:**   Everything she does?
>
> **Client:**   Well, not quite everything but, well, for example she invited us to her house for dinner and she knows we have teenage boys. Well, she served some fancy dish with a special sauce and did the whole formal dining room scene.

REFLECTION

At this point the counselor has options for responding. The counselor could simply remain silent and allow the client to continue. The counselor could use a reflection such as *"So she presented a somewhat formal type dinner?"* Or, the counselor could invite the client to continue to elaborate on the dinner by employing a minimal encourager such as "formal dining room scene . . .".

encourage client disclosure but without the ability to guide, direct, and control that disclosure, the resulting flood of information can lead to the previously described buzzing, blooming state of confusion.

Sadly, while most training programs competently deliver the knowledge base and fundamental skill base for counseling, training often stops there. Students are assisted in developing these skills and then often let loose in a practica or internship experience with the hopes that the theory and research taught will magically integrate with the skills developed and result in effective, competent counseling—a hope that often fails to come to fruition.

Skills of Judgment and Decision Making

Clinical judgment and decision making—knowing how to think as a competent counselor—are at the core of effective clinical practice (Gambrill, 2005). The competent professional—the expert counselor—does not simply know more than the novice, although that too may be true, but rather he/she thinks "differently" (Bereiter & Scardamalia, 1986).

Beyond understanding the theory and research of counseling or successfully employing effective communication and relationship-building skills, the competent counselor is one that *"thinks like an expert."* To be fully competent, counselor trainees need knowledge of theory and research, fundamental communication skills, and the cognitive skills and processes required to reason through clinical information presented by the client in order to formulate effective plans for change (Kleiner, 2006). The importance of learning to think like a counselor becomes even more obvious when one considers the nature of the work in which counselors are engaged.

Unlike professionals who work with problems that could be described as structured, counselors and others working in the mental health field are engaged with problems that are ill-structured (see Simon, 1973; Voss & Post, 1988). In counseling, the problems addressed typically lack clear end products, specific beginning points, and predictable, linear steps leading to resolution.

Consider the more structured problem or task confronting one who is attempting to assemble a new cooking grill. While there will be ample opportunity to make adjustments and to perhaps use some creative problem solving, the process is mainly clear. The parts needed for assembly are typically marked and easily identified, the sequencing of the steps to take to achieve the goal (i.e., assembly) are prescribed, and the outcome—once achieved—is obvious and easy to identify, since we can now cook those burgers! Contrast this with the type of problem presented to a counselor. Perhaps it is something as simple as a client who is seeking help with what he/she self-diagnosed as being "too stressed." What are the parts? Is there a diagram illustrating the specific sequence of steps? Is there even a clear, commonly agreed-on outcome or product? The answer to these questions is "No."

The type of problems presented to counselors fail to provide parameters defining the specific steps to be taken, or the timing and sequencing of those steps. Further, assessing progress is often difficult because of the lack of clarity about the desired endpoint or markers to observe along the way (Strupp & Hadley, 1979). Clearly, if the problem fails to provide a structure to follow it will be incumbent upon the counselor to organize the data and to provide structure to the encounter. This is the uniqueness of ill-structured problems and it is clear that it requires a different type of cognitive ability than what is called on in structured situations.

Even when labeled with words such as anxious, depressed, and stressed, each client, and thus each clinical presentation, is unique. Given this uniqueness, it is clear that training counselors cannot hope to teach trainees formulaic approaches to counseling. Counselors in training cannot be given templates to follow as they help move clients from problem presentation through to problem resolution. Rather, those in training need help in developing the cognitive ability to process client data in light of professional theory and research and then need to adapt interventions and clinical responses appropriately.

It is this fluidity and adaptability in thinking that is one of the hallmarks of "expert" counselors. Expert counselors are able to take the complexity and uniqueness of any client's presenting concerns and can decompose this ill-structured problem into subproblems, reconfiguring these in ways that allow for more meaningful resolution (Voss & Post, 1988).

While knowledge and skill are important to becoming a counselor, given the above, it is clear that learning to think like an expert may be just as important to effective counseling (Johnson & Heppner, 1989; Robinson & Halliday, 1987).

THINKING AND PROCESSING LIKE AN EXPERT

As previously noted, the competent professional—the expert counselor—does not simply know more than the novice, but rather, he/she thinks differently (Bereiter & Scardamalia, 1986). Understanding what differentiates the thinking of counseling experts and counseling novices is an essential first step in structuring counselor training and ongoing professional development (Etringer, Hillerbrand, & Clairborn, 1995).

Procedural Versus Declarative Knowledge

While it is probably obvious that experts possess more factual, domain-specific knowledge (i.e., declarative knowledge), including such things as the listing of diagnostic symptoms for major disorders or the criteria for differentiation of Asperger from autism, it is also true that experts possess greater procedural knowledge (Etringer, Hillerbrand, & Clairborn, 1995; Chi, Glasser, & Farr, 1988). Experts connect disparate areas of knowledge, allowing them to make more discriminating judgments about the information being presented and helping them to develop appropriate responses for novel situations (Chi, Glasser, & Farr, 1988). Thus, a passing comment by a client or perhaps a bodily response to a counselor's inquiry, while going unnoticed by a novice counselor, may be connected more readily to a piece of research or theoretical construct by the expert. With this understanding, the counselor's next response will be intentional and directive.

Experts have the ability to approach situations with a greater awareness of what to do if a particular condition exists. For example, the expert, knowing that a client was "sent" to counseling, as may be the case with a school-based referral or a court-referred client, may focus his/her interventions at first on helping the client increase awareness and ownership of the value of the counseling, rather than simply jumping into the resolution of the referred problem. The expert understands that under this condition of "other" referral, client's ownership takes precedence over problem resolution (see Chapter 6, transtheoretical issues). Or, perhaps when working with two separate clients who present with a major depressive episode, the expert may recognize that if a client has good social support, then he/she can proceed with outpatient counseling as opposed to assuming that all clients who present with major depression need to be hospitalized.

This same type of procedural knowledge is evident in the expert's employment of fundamental relationship-building skills. Expert counselors, like novices, understand that accurately reflecting a client's statements provides evidence that the counselor is attending. However, unlike the novice, an expert counselor also understands that such a reflection highlights that a particular disclosure has more value (to the counselor) than those elements that were not included in the reflection. As such, the expert employs reflection discriminately and purposively.

Experts will use reflections as interventions to direct clients toward elaboration on specific relevant information, to highlight a point and increase client awareness, or to test their own counselor hypotheses. Case Illustration 1.3 demonstrates this "If . . . then" procedural approach in which the counselor is attempting to help the client recognize his personal responsibility in the situations being discussed.

■ ■ ■ ■ ■ ▬▬▬▬▬▬▬▬▬▬▬▬▬▬▬▬▬▬▬▬

CASE ILLUSTRATION 1.3
SELECTIVE USE OF REFLECTION

Client: He's always on my case.

Counselor: Always?

Client: Yeah, like today. I come into class and I am two minutes late and he gives me this look.

REFLECTION

At this point the counselor could reflect on the entire client statement *"So you are two minutes late and he gave you a look,"* or the counselor could focus on the teacher's response and state *"So he gave you a look."* But if the hypothesis is that the client needs to take more responsibility for his actions, then the counselor may be selective and purposeful in the reflection, stating *"So you came to class two minutes late . . .".*

For the expert counselor, counseling interventions and strategies are not employed in a vacuum but are extensions of their operative framework or theory (Greenberg, Elliott, & Lietaer, 1994; Lebow, 1987). As noted in Case Illustration 1.3, even a simple reflection of feeling or a paraphrase of content is underpinned by some theoretical rationale that defines the purpose and intended impact on the client. It is this understanding and employment of procedural knowledge that distinguishes the expert from the novice. Exercise 1.2 is offered to clarify this point.

■ ■ ■ ■ ■ ▬▬▬▬▬▬▬▬▬▬▬▬▬▬▬▬▬▬▬▬

EXERCISE 1.2

AND WHAT WERE YOU INTENDING?

Directions: When I sit with students reviewing their video or audiotaped sessions with their clients, I will often stop the tape and simply ask: What was your goal for . . . (asking questions, employing a summarization, allowing the client to continue to repeat herself, etc.).

My goal isn't to suggest that students should or shouldn't have done that, or should have done something in its place. Rather, the goal is to help students to begin to view all that they do within the session as an intervention and, thus, begin to think about their goal for their actions.

For this exercise you should tape (audio or video) one of your simulated or actual clinical sessions. Using an alarm or some type of timer, stop the tape every three minutes and observe what is going on. What is happening with the client (in light of what has been happening)? Then, observe your next response. What type of response was it? Before you begin the tape, ask yourself, as best as you can remember: Why did you do that? What was my intent? My goal? Now, advance the tape and see if you were successful.

Again, the goal of this exercise isn't to demonstrate how effective you are in session; rather, it is to highlight the degree to which you are, or are not aware of the intentions behind your actions.

Pattern Recognition and Forward Thinking

Pattern recognition skills is another area in which experts appear to have the upper hand over novices (e.g., Charness, 1991; DeGroot, 1965; Patel & Groen, 1991). The recognition of meaningful patterns facilitates the recall of strategy-relevant information (Cunning & Stewart, 1983).

Unlike novices, experts can identify critical features of a problem. With an understanding of the critical features and the pattern they reflect, the expert counselor engages in forward thinking. That is, experts move quickly from identifying the "what is" to the articulation of the "what is desired" and the steps needed to move to that end goal. (Gick, 1986; Larkin, McDermott, & Simon, 1980; Simon & Simon, 1978). Perhaps it is too simplistic to cite as an illustration, but it is clear that my heater repair person (cited in the preface) not only was able to quickly recognize a problem of air flow but used the recognition to hypothesize the source of the blockage and, in that case, successfully tested the hypothesis by removing the leaf. This is the procedural and forward-thinking characteristic of an expert.

In a more clinical illustration, consider the clinician working with a client who states that she is "somewhat concerned about her spending habits." As the clinician begins to gather information about the definition and history of this habit, she learns that not only has this client seen numerous counselors, but that now in session the client begins to strongly criticize the "incompetence" of all of the other counselors. Further, the client is quick to note, she "is really pleased because [this counselor] is the best" she has ever encountered.

In a situation such as this, a novice counselor may feel encouraged and affirmed by the client's comments. With this sense of client acceptance, the novice may eagerly begin to attempt to identify goals and appropriate interventions to help the client with her spending habits. An expert, however, will process all the information, including details of the spending as well as the "style" with which the client presents this information. Being able to process and categorize all this information, the expert may now employ a question, a reflection, or a confrontation to test the hypothesis that the issue to be addressed is not one of habit (i.e., spending) but one of a personality pattern — specifically, the possibility of the existence of borderline personality disorder. If supported by additional data, this assessment would give shape to the nature of the treatment/intervention plan that should follow.

When engaged in a counseling relationship, experts process data presented by the client in a way that helps them regard the problem in terms of conceptual principles, and work from these data to meet goals and provide interventions. They are assisted in the process by their use of organizational frameworks.

THE NEED FOR AN ORGANIZATIONAL FRAMEWORK

Although there may be "nothing so practical as a good theory" (Lewin, 1951, p. 169), many counselors fail to embrace this premise. Counselors tend to be doers and are pragmatic in their approach, and therefore are a tad less concerned with the philosophical or theoretical aspects of counseling. However, if counselors approach their profession and their moment-to-moment interaction with a client, armed only with a set of skills or bag of disconnected interventions, they may find themselves applying technique after technique in a hit-or-miss fashion.

A counselor's theory or organizational framework provides a structure within which to understand the data being presented and the best path to follow. As used within this text, "organizational framework" (theory) refers to a systematic and organized set of propositions.

Educators and supervisors have emphasized the importance of helping counselors in training and entry-level counselors to embrace and articulate an organizing framework. Employment of such a organizing framework assures internal consistency in case conceptualization, treatment planning, counseling practices, and expected outcomes (Lebow, 1987; Magnuson, Norem & Wilcoxon, 2000; Neufeldt, Iversen, & Juntunen, 1995; Piercy & Sprenkle, 1988). The question is, however: Which model should be used?

Which Orientation Framework?

While there are numerous theories, models, and microtheories purported to explain human functioning and dysfunction, there is no single counseling theory, model, or framework that is totally valid and entirely comprehensive. And while some may have empirical research to supports their tenets, this does not automatically demand that those with little support be immediately rejected. The absence of empirical support may reflect the limitations of our research methods as much as it reflects the adequacy or inadequacy of a particular model or framework.

For this text, four specific orientations have been selected for discussion: **solution focused** (deShazer, 1985), **behavioral** (Hersen, 2006), **cognitive** (Beck, 1976), and **transtheoretical** (Prochaska, Redding, & Evers, 2002). The intent, however, is not to suggest that these are the best or only valid orientation frameworks in counseling; rather, these models have been chosen as the platform to depict how experts—regardless of theoretical model or orientation framework—employ that model to guide understanding, hypothesizing, and responding during counseling exchanges. It is not the goal of this text to provide you, the reader, with training in a specific model but rather to allow you to see, reflect, and practice "thinking like an expert" from various orientations. It should further be noted that this is not a one-size-fits-all profession in which the specific model or a specific intervention will always be employed and applied in the same way, regardless of the uniqueness of the client, counselor, or context. As such, the competent counselor will need to be adaptive and flexible in his/her approach to counseling and must evaluate theories and interventions employed (Tinsley, 1992). The importance of this issue of knowing what we are doing and why we are doing it, as well as assessing our success in doing it, cannot be understated.

In Chapter 2 you will see that this reflection—this evaluation—is not something that is assigned only at the end of a session or at the termination of a client contract. The effective counselor will truly be a reflective practitioner, reflecting both *"on"* practice and *"in"* practice.

REFERENCES

Beck, A.T. (1976). *Cognitive therapy and the emotional disorders*. New York: International Universities Press.

Bereiter, C. & Scardamalia, M. (1986). Educational relevance of the study of expertise. *Interchange*, 17(2), 10–19.

Beutler, L.E., Macchiato, P.P., & Allstetter-Neufeldt, S. (1994). Therapist variables. In A.E. Bergin & S.L. Garfield (Eds.), *Handbook of psychotherapy and behavior change* (4th ed., pp. 229–269). New York: John Wiley & Sons.

Carkhuff, R.R., & Berenson, B.G. (1967). *Beyond counseling and therapy*. New York: Holt, Rinehart, & Winston.

Charness, N. (1991). Expertise in chess: The balance between knowledge and search. In K.A. Ericsson & J. Smith (Eds.), *Toward a general theory of expertise* (pp. 39–63). New York: Cambridge University Press.

Chi, M.T.H., Glaser, R. & Farr, M.J. (1988). *The nature of expertise*. Hillsdale, NJ: Lawrence Erlbaum Associates, Inc.

Cunningham, N.J., & Stewart, N.R. (1983). Effects of discrimination training on counselor training response choice. *Counselor Education and Supervision*, 23, 46–61.

deShazer, S. (1985). *Keys to solution in brief therapy*. New York: Norton.

DeGroot, A. (1965). *Thought and choice in chess*. Hague, Netherlands: Mouton.

Etringer, B., Hillerbrand, E., & Clairborn, C.D. (1995). The transition from novice to expert counselor. *Counselor Education and Supervision*, 35(1), 4–17.

Gambrill, E.D. (2005). *Critical thinking in clinical practice: Improving the accuracy of judgments and decisions about clients*. Hoboken, NJ: John Wiley & Sons.

Gick, M.L. (1986). Problem-solving strategies. *Educational Psychologist*, 21(1/2), 99–120.

Greenberg, L.S., Elliott, R.K., & Lietaer, G. (1994). Research on experiential psychotherapies. In A.E. Bergin & S.L. Garfield (Eds.), *Handbook of psychotherapy and behavior change* (4th ed.) pp. 509–539 (Chapter). New York: Wiley.

Hersen, M. (Ed.) (2006). *Clinician's handbook of adult behavioral assessment*. San diego: Elsevier Academic Press.

Horvath, A.O. (2001). The therapeutic alliance: Concepts, research, and training. *Australian Psychologist*, 58(2), 170–176.

Ivey, A.E. & Ivey, M.B, (2003). *Intentional interviewing and counseling*. Pacific Grove, CA: Brooks/Cole.

James, W. (1981, [Originally published in 1890]). *The Principles of Psychology*. Cambridge, MA: Harvard University.

Johnson, W.C., & Heppner, P.P. (1989). On reasoning and cognitive demands in counseling: Implications for counselor training. *Journal of Counseling and Development*, 67(7), 428–429.

Kleiner, A.J. (2006). Effects of counselor process change models and microskills training on counseling self-efficacy and treatment conceptualization ability. *Dissertation Abstracts International: Section B: The Sciences and Engineering*, 67(1-B), 549.

Larkin, J., McDermott, J., & Simon, D.P. (1980). Expert and novice performance in solving physics problems. *Science*, 208(4450), 1335–1342.

Lebow, J.L. (1987). Developing a personal intergration in family therapy: Principles for model construction and practice. *Journal of Marital and Family Therapy*, 13(1), 1–14.

Lewin, K. (1951). *Field theory in social science*. Chicago: University of Chicago Press.

Magnuson, S., Norem, K., & Wilcoxon, A. (2000). Clinical supervision of prelicensed counselors: Recommendations for consideration and practice. *Journal of Mental Health Counseling*, 22(2), 176–188.

Neufeldt., S.A., Iversen, J.N., & Juntunen, C.L. (1995). *Supervision strategies for the first practicum*. Alexandria, VA: American Counseling Association.

Overholser, J.C. & Fine, M.A. (1990). Defining the boundaries of professional competence: Managing subtle cases of clinical incompetence. *Professional Psychology: Research and Practice*, 21(6), 462–469.

Patel, V.L. & Groen, G.J. (1991). The general and specific nature of medical expertise: A critical look. In K.A. Ericsson & J. Smith (Eds.), *Toward a general theory of expertise* (pp. 93–125). New York: Cambridge University Press.

Piercy, F.P. & Sprenkle, D.H. (1988). Family therapy theory-building questions. *Journal of Marital and Family Therapy*, 14(3), 307–309.

Procidano, M.E., Busch-Rossnagel, N.A., Reznikoff, M., & Geisinger, K.F. (1995). Responding to graduate students' professional deficiencies: A national survey. *Journal of Clinical Psychology*, 51(3), 426–433.

Prochaska, J.O., Redding, C.A., & Evers, K.E. (2002). The transtheoretical model and stages of change. In K. Glanz, B.K. Rimer, & F.M. Lewis (Eds.), *Health behavior and health education. Theory, research and practice*, (3rd ed, pp. 88–120). San Francisco: Jossey-Bass.

Psychology Sectoral Workgroup on the Agreement on Internal Trade (PSWAIT), (2001, June). Mutual recognition agreement of the regulatory bodies for professional psychologists in Canada. [Electronic version]. Retrieved September 17, 2003, from www.cpa.ca/MRA.pdf.

Robinson, V. & Halliday, J. (1987). A critique of the microcounseling approach to problem understanding. *British Journal of Guidance and Counselling*, 15(2), 113–124.

Sakinofsky, I. (1979). Evaluating the competence of psychotherapists. *Canadian Journal of Psychiatry*, 24(3), 193–205.

Schöttler, T., Oliver, L.E., & Porter, J. (2005). Defining and evaluating clinical competence: A Review. *Guidance and Counseling*, 20(2),46–55.

Simon, D.P. & Simon, H.A. (1978). Individual differences in solving physics problems. In R. Siegler (Ed.), *Children's thinking: What develops?* (pp. 325–348). Hillsdale, NJ: Erlbaum.

Simon, H.A. (1973). The structure of ill-structured problems. *Artificial Intelligences*, 4(2), 181–201.

Strupp, H.H. & Hadley, S.W. (1979). Specific vs. nonspecific factors in psychotherapy. *Archives of General Psychiatry*, 36, 1125–1136.

Tinsley, H.E.A. (1992). Psychometric theory and counseling psychology research. In S.D. Brown & R.W. Lent (Eds.), *Handbook of counseling psychology* (pp. 37–71). New York: John Wiley & Sons.

Truax, C.B. & Carkhuff, R.R. (1967). *Towards effective counseling and psychotherapy: Training and practice*. Chicago: Aldine.

Voss, J.F. & Post, T.A. (1988). On solving of ill-structured problems. In M.T.H. Chi, R. Glasser, M.J. Farr (Eds.), *The nature of expertise* (pp. 261–285). Hillsdale, NJ: Lawrence Erlbaum Associates.

SUGGESTED RESOURCES

Chi, M.T.H., Glasser, R., & Farr, M.J. (Eds.). (1988). *The nature of expertise*. Hillsdale, NJ: Lawrence Erlbaum Associates.

Etringer, B., Hillerbrand, E., & Clairborn. C.D. (1995). The transition from novice to expert counselor. *Counselor Education and Supervision*, 35(1), 4–17.

Gambrill, E.D. (2005). *Critical thinking in clinical practice: Improving the accuracy of judgments and decisions about clients*. Hoboken, NJ: John Wiley & Sons.

Prochaska, J.O., Redding, C.A., & Evers, K.E. (2002). The transtheoretical model an stages of change. In K. Glanz, B.K. Rimer, & F.M. Lewis (Eds.), *Health behavior and health education. Theory, research and practice* (3rd ed, pp. 88–120). San Francisco: Jossey-Bass.

CHAPTER 2

REFLECTIVE PRACTITIONERS: THINKING BEFORE AND WHILE DOING!

Chapter 1 highlighted the importance for a counselor to possess a fundamental body of knowledge and a set of clinical skills. It was also emphasized that skills and academic knowledge alone are insufficient and that to be effective as a counselor, one needs to employ an orientation framework. While this is true, it is essential that we remember that the counseling process is not static and, as such, cannot be translated into a fixed template to be applied to all clients across all sessions. The effective counselor is one who employs his/her knowledge, skill, and orientation flexibly to guide clinical judgments and decisions. In order to be flexible and responsive to the uniqueness of each encounter, a counselor must learn to employ reflective thought and reflective dialogue to think critically about his/her actions (Hoshmand, 1994). The practice of reflection has been identified as an essential component to effective practice (Hoshmand, 1994; Nelson & Neufeldt, 1998; Neufeldt, Karno, & Nelson, 1996) and, as such, is an important objective for counselor education (Fong, Borders, Ethington & Pitts, 1997; Nelson & Neufeldt, 1998). The value of reflection "in" and "on" practice serves as the impetus for this chapter, and the "what," "why," and "how" of reflective practice is the focus.

Specifically, after reading this chapter you will be able to:

1. explain what is meant by reflective practice;
2. describe the importance of reflection "in" and "on" practice;
3. identify elements involved in case conceptualization and treatment planning as a reflection "on" practice; and
4. experience the opportunity to review your own reflection "in" and "on" practice.

THE EXPERT—REFLECTING "IN" AND "ON" PRACTICE

In his classic work, *The Reflective Practitioner, How Professionals Think in Action* (1983), Donald Schon describes professional practice as both a consequence of science and artistry.

> Every competent practitioner can recognize phenomena . . . for which he cannot give a reasonably accurate or complete description. In his day to day practice he makes innumerable judgments of quality for which he cannot state adequate criteria, and he displays rules for which he cannot state the rules and procedures. (pp. 49–50)

While the scientist in each of us may feel uncomfortable with Schon's (1983) suggestion that decisions and judgments may be made without articulated rules and criteria, the truth is that in each of our professional encounters, adjustments to treatment plans and modifications of initial responses often occur truly in process or "on the fly."

Accepting that decisions are often made in process does not suggest that the science and technical rational foundation for our counseling is unimportant. Rather, it is simply to suggest that our orientation and perspective on practice needs to be expanded to include the recognition that ours is not a strict "formulaic" profession. Our strategies, interventions, and techniques—even when empirically supported (Parsons, 2007)—will need tailoring and fine tuning in light of the uniqueness of each client and each clinical encounter. But these adjustments, while appearing intuitive and unexplainable, are not unintentional. A counselor, through reflection and evaluation, will select behavior, response mode, technique, or interventions to use with a client *at any given moment* within a session (Hill & O'Grady, 1985, p. 2). These intentional adjustments may be difficult to identify or recognize since they are often embedded in the counselor's preconceived theoretical model (Gambrill, 1990). However, through the practice of reflection *"in"* and *"on"* the counseling dynamic, a counselor can increase his/her awareness of this intentional process of observing, hypothesizing, selecting, and testing all interventions and can thus increase the effectiveness of his/her practice.

The reflective counselor will be one that can take the "unexplainable, the seemingly intuitive, and by describing the elements and pieces of knowing and understanding that lead to the 'spontaneous, skillful execution of the performance'" (Schon, 1987, p. 25) increase his/her effectiveness. The effective counselor will employ thoughtful reflection and metacognition to: (a) attend to client information; (b) employ theory and research as the framework within which to understand this information; and (c) develop hypotheses about the client's needs and goals, which in turn provide the basis for selecting optimal intervention strategies given these data and counseling objectives (Hanna, & Giordano, 1996; Hill & O'Grady, 1985).

To be successful, a counselor has to have the ability to scrutinize the nature and impact of his/her interventions both at the macrolevel (e.g., in developing a treatment plan) and at the microlevel (i.e., with each interactive sequence in a counseling session). *Having the ability to adequately plan for each session in a reflection* **on** *practice, as well as to adjust "within" each session by way of reflection* **in** *practice is essential for making the innumerable judgments required of a competent counselor.*

CASE CONCEPTUALIZATION AS REFLECTION "ON" PRACTICE

Regardless of a person's theoretical orientation, it is important for a counselor to develop an understanding of the client and his/her presenting concern and desired goals. This process of conceptualizing a case and its importance to effective practice has been highlighted throughout the literature (e.g.,Wantz & Morran, 1994; Morran, Kurpius, Brack, & Brack, 1995; Falvey, 2001; Prieto & Scheel, 2002). But what is case conceptualization and what are the cognitive skills required to develop strategies for understanding and addressing client problems?

Case Conceptualization

Case conceptualization or case formulation can be defined as a set of "hypotheses about the causes, precipitants, and maintaining influences of a person's psychological, interpersonal, and behavioral problems" (Eells, 2002, p. 815). A counselor's case conceptualization is not only an appropriately comprehensive, yet flexible, account of a client's presenting concerns, it also serves as the scaffold that supports the counselor reflections "on" and "in" practice and the decision and directions that follow.

Effective case conceptualization demands the use of a complex set of skills, including the ability to (1) collect relevant client data, (2) integrate these data into a consistent view of the client's main issues, and (3) develop a coherent plan for change that follows logically from this conceptualization of the client's main issues (Eells, 1997; Shaw and Dobson,1988). Case conceptualization links client data to treatment plan and counseling interventions.

Given the uniqueness of each client and, by definition, the unique nature of each case conceptualization, counselors cannot simply approach the counseling process as if it were a recipe to be followed. Attending to relevant data, integrating that data and responding by way of selection and implementation of counseling interventions demands that counselors step out of the buzzing, blooming confusion of the counseling dynamic and reflect on what they know, where they are going, and how to get there. This is a reflection on and in practice. Exercise 2.1 provides an opportunity for you to engage in this process using simple clinical information.

■ ■ ■ ■ ■ ▬▬▬▬▬▬▬▬▬▬▬▬▬▬▬▬▬▬▬▬▬▬▬

EXERCISE 2.1

CASE CONCEPTUALIZATION

Directions: Case conceptualization is a process of linking client data to treatment plan and counseling interventions. The process requires that the counselor collect relevant data, which is integrated in a consistent view of the client and his/her main issues, which in turn lends to the development of a coherent plan of change. With these three factors in mind, consider the client information provided below, and by responding to the stimulus questions, create an articulated view of this case and treatment plan to be employed. It would be helpful to share your conclusions with a colleague or a supervisor and to discuss any variance in your perspectives.

CLIENT INFORMATION

1. Client is a 4-year-old male.
2. Client is the only child of two professional working parents.
3. Client has been exhibiting anxiety in attending daycare (crying, holding on to parents at time of separation, pleading to avoid separation from parents).
4. Parents report that the client is able to separate from parents in order to go with grandparents, his uncle, and the live-in sitter.
5. Parents, particularly the mother, express guilt about leaving the child, feeling that perhaps the mother should stay home until the child is ready for first grade.
6. School personnel report that once parents have left the school building and parking lot, the client typically calms and engages in play activities. This process rarely takes more than 30 minutes.
7. Mother noted that when she is at home, the client tends to follow her and demand her attention, requesting her engagement in play activities, often the same type of activities found at the day care to the point in which the mother noted it is hard to get anything done.
8. Both parents reported that the client exhibited normal development, reaching developmental milestones as expected. The client was described as a very "bright," "observant," and "engaging" child. The reported anxiety has just become apparent with the initiation of daycare.
9. Parents did note that the client tends to want a lot of attention at home and even attempts to interrupt the parents if they are engaged in conversation. Typically, while verbally correcting the client for such interruptions, the parents will pick the client up and sit him on their lap as they continue their conversation.
10. There is no reported history of depression, anxiety, or drug or alcohol abuse among the parents or extended family members.

Guided questions

- Do we feel we have enough information to begin to conceptualize the nature of the problem and a treatment approach?
- What, if any, additional information would you like to have? If you seek additional data, why? What hypotheses are you attempting to test?
- Is there any evidence to suggest that the anxiety is global? Specific? (Hint: see line 4 under client information.)
- Is there any evidence to suggest a biological basis for the anxiety? (Hint: see lines 6 and 10.)
- Are there any environmental cues or contexts that seem to stimulate the anxiety response? (Hint: see lines 3 and 9.)
- What resources does the client have that may be used as a resource in treatment planning? (Hint: see lines 4, 6, 9.)

(continued)

■ ■ ■ ■ ■

EXERCISE 2.1   (CONTINUED)

- What possible auxiliary issues may exist that need to be addressed? (Hint: see lines 5, 7, 9.)

Hypothesized client issue and approach to be used
- Is the focus of your initial hypothesis the client?
  If so, why or why not? What evidence leads you to the conclusion?
- If your focus is not the client, would you focus on the parents? The school?

Why? What evidence leads you to your conclusion?
- Would your strategy be one targeting affect? Behavior? Cognition?
  Why? What evidence leads you to your conclusion?
- What would be your goal for the next session?

Case statement. Write a sentence (or two) that would summarize the nature of the major issue and your (initial) plan for addressing the issue.

Treatment Planning

The approach or strategies employed within counseling reflect the counselor's best judgment of how to proceed given the case conceptualization and the counselor's experience and knowledge of research supporting treatment efficacy. Treatment planning is a complex process that clearly outlines a consistent relationship among problem definition, treatment goals, counselor philosophy, theory, and counseling research. The initial formulation of a treatment plan should also reflect the counselor's assessment of the client's adaptive functioning, readiness for counseling, and reflection on preferred treatment options.

The conceptualization of the "what is" in terms of presenting concerns and client resources and the "what is hoped for," that is, the goals and outcomes for the counseling, sets the framework for the consideration of strategies and techniques needed to move the client toward the desired outcome. With this conceptualization as the backdrop, the counselor will call on previous experience and knowledge of current research to begin the identification of intervention strategies that appear to offer the best hope for goal attainment. It is at this stage that the reflective counselor will need to assess his/her competency to provide the services identified or to embrace the need to refer or seek additional consultation and supervision.

While developing plans that are adaptable and responsive to the unique talents and needs of the client, treatment plans should not be loose or idiosyncratic and should not be based on the momentary whim of either the counselor or client. Decisions made as a result of reflection *on* practice should, when possible, have empirical support. Ideally, the counselor would have empirically validated rules at his/her disposal that match the "if" component of the rule (the elements of the client situation) with the "then" (i.e., actions to be taken) component of the decision. For example, when presented with a severely depressed client (i.e., the "if"), the standard of practice requires that the counselor assess the level of risk for suicide (i.e, the "then") or, if the client's presenting concern is one of a simple phobia (the "if"), research may lead the counselor to conclude that systematic desensitization is the treatment of choice (the "then").

There are those that outright reject all approaches without empirical support (Duncan, Hubble, & Miller, 1997) and others that object to a "slavish adherence" to tried-and-true models because they mitigate against developing a personal style (Efran, Luken, & Lukens, 1990, p. 142). The position taken here is simply, when possible, methods that have proven successful in the past with this counselor or with others, as evident by the research, are good places to start when conceptualizing one's case and formulating treatment plans. That is exactly what one counselor did in response to his client, Niajian (see Case Illustration 2.1).

Regardless of the source of one's intervention, be it research or personal experience, it is the process of employing procedural knowledge (i.e., if . . . then), which is responsive to data gleaned through reflection "in" and "on" practice, that is the hallmark of the expert counselor (see Chapter 1).

Using the "Eye" of an Experimenter

If we revisit Eells' (2002) definition of case conceptualization, it is important to note that it is defined as a set of "hypotheses." Thus, even when a counselor's case

■ ■ ■ ■ ■ ▬▬▬

CASE ILLUSTRATION 2.1
NIAJIAN—CHILDHOOD OCD

The client in this case is a 12-year-old Asian American male, Niajian. Niajian engaged in counseling because he was exhibiting the following symptoms: obsessions about germ-related contamination, fear of spreading such contaminants, ritualized hand wiping and washing, excessive seeking of reassurance from parents, disturbing sexual and violent images, excessive checking of schoolwork and homework for errors, and rereading until it felt "just right."

The client presented as a very bright, highly articulate, and motivated person. He identified his thoughts as "weird" and while stating that he was not embarrassed about his thoughts and repetitive actions, he "really wanted to learn a different way to deal with this stuff."

In beginning to plan a treatment regimen, the counselor in this case, while being trained in cognitive-behavioral treatment methods, referred to the research literature to see if any other interventions have been demonstrated to be effective. In addition to his initial inclination to provide psychoeducation for client and family, the counselor decided to develop a regimen of cognitive restructuring in which the client would be taught to recognize and relabel his obsessive thoughts and feelings in a more realistic fashion. Further, as a response to his reading of the literature, the counselor included a exposure-response prevention strategy within the treatment plan.

conceptualization is well developed and his/her treatment plans are empirically supported, the effective counselor realizes that both are reflective hypotheses and need to be tested. Counseling is not static, nor should planning for counseling be a one-time process. From intake to termination, counselors must continue to reflect on and in their practice, gathering and analyzing case information in order to reformulate hypotheses and to adjust treatment decisions (Makover, 1996; Mordock, 1994; Tillett, 1996). The reflective counselor approaches each interaction and each exchange with the eye of an experimenter. That is, the counselor employs the intervention with an expectation of a specific outcome and observes and collects data, either formal or anecdotal, in order to test the observed outcome against what was hypothesized. These data depicting the impact will then be employed to modify, adjust, or simply fine-tune treatment decisions.

What is Reflection "on" Practice?

While implied throughout the preceding discussion, **reflection "on" practice** refers specifically to the thinking that takes place following a session or an encounter, which allows the counselor to review what he/she did, what he/she anticipated would happen, and what in fact did happen. This type of reflection after the fact provides data from which to judge the direction the sessions are taking, the rate with which the client is moving in the desired direction, and even helps the counselor develop a set of questions, ideas, and propositions to test in the next encounter. Reflection on practice allows the counselor to refine the case conceptualization and the treatment decisions that follow. However, for this process to be of value, counselors must be open to information that may contradict initial clinical impressions and hypotheses.

It is essential to be mindful that the conclusions we draw, which in turn guide our actions, are truly based on our "best guess" hypotheses. As such, the effective reflective counselor will be open to revisiting and reformulating hypotheses and approaches as opposed to forcing validation of initial impression by selectively attending to some data at the expense of others. Because of the ease with which we can reshape reality to fit our assumptions, some have encouraged counselors to use both confirmatory and disconfirmatory strategies (e.g., Ridley, 1995; Morrow & Deidan, 1992). Other strategies, such as actively attending to seemingly less important details about the client or even taking a view of the client from a different theoretical orientation, may help to reduce the effects of counselor bias. When employed in the process of reflecting "on" practice, such procedures will open the counselor to data that may result in the reformulation of hypotheses and in a redirection of the intervention process.

This process of reflection should be employed throughout the entire counseling contract, starting with the initial contact. Beginning with the intake process, the counselor reflecting on practice will begin to consider questions such as: How comfortable am I with this type of client? This type of presenting concern? How confident am I that I have the training and experience to work with the client competently? What are my initial goals for this session? What is the basis (e.g., theory, research, experience) for my goals and my strategies? What data was I provided that suggested these goals are appropriate? How will I assess movement toward these goals?

These are just some of the questions that a counselor reflecting on practice may consider as they attempt to answer the question: What's next? Case Illustration 2.2 provides an example of one counselor's reflections on practice following an initial intake session.

■ ■ ■ ■ ■

CASE ILLUSTRATION 2.2
REFLECTIONS ON INTAKE

INITIAL REFERRAL DATA
The referral sheet provided only minimal information. The client was a 35-year-old woman currently going through a divorce after 10 years of marriage with no children. She worked as a pharmacist for the past 11 years and complained to her boss that she was having trouble focusing on work given the stress of the divorce. As part of her employee-assistance package, she was referred for short-term counseling.

ADDITIONAL INFORMATION GATHERED AT INTAKE
The client described that she has lost 12 lbs. in the past 3 weeks and is unable to sleep (difficulty getting to sleep and staying asleep). The client stated that she has difficulty getting to work since she simply thinks, "Why bother?" Further, the client shared that she has had problems with concentration and in fact has caught herself placing incorrect medications and/or incorrect amounts in prescription bottles that she is filling. When asked about suicidal ideation, the client noted that she is horrified about being the only person in her family ever to have gone through a divorce and that she is not sure she can face her family. She noted that while she sometimes "wishes" she would just disappear, her faith and the realization of the impact that hurting herself would have on her parents prevents her from ever thinking about killing herself.

POSTSESSION REFLECTION "ON" PRACTICE
The reflective counselor in this case found herself reflecting on practice guided by the following questions. The purpose for her reflections was so that she would know "what next?" and how best to approach the next session.

1. What is my diagnostic impression or problem formulation?
2. What client factors (readiness, motivation, levels of awareness, specific resources, etc.) would indicate good/poor prognosis?
3. Do I have enough information to start the case conceptualization and treatment planning? What else do I need to know?
4. How do I assess the nature of our professional relationship? Is the client giving evidence of trusting? Is there a sense of confidence? Is the relationship supportive of client disclosure and reception to feedback? What other factors or elements significant to a helping relationship are present? Absent?

(continued)

5. Given the initial impression, what treatment modalities do I need to consider? Is she a candidate for brief counseling? Outpatient? Does she need medical evaluation?
6. Given my knowledge, experience, and competency, how best can I assist this client? Do I serve as treatment provider? Is a referral-out required? What is my role now and in the future with this client?
7. What are my goals for the next session? How do I proceed? How will I assess the progress of the next session?

One of the key reflections illustrated by the counselor in Case Illustration 2.2 was her concern about a goal for this and future sessions and the way movement toward that goal could be assessed. Ridley (1995) stated that many counselors assume that their good intentions make them helpful clinicians. This assumption can lead to the use of bad, although well-intended, interventions. To avoid the good intentions–bad interventions scenario, Ridley (1995) urged counselors to evaluate the effectiveness of their interventions regarding their helpfulness. Reflecting on practice with questions such as "How do I know that I have been or will be effective?" or "What specific changes or client reactions do I expect?" can help focus reflective counselors on criteria (e.g., verbal or nonverbal client cues) to be used to evaluate the efficacy and efficiency of their counseling. Counselors may find it useful to more formally record their reflections in case notes using a format such as that found in Table 2.1.

TABLE 2.1 Reflections "on" Practice

Client Name: _____

Session Date	Hypothesis Being Tested	Intervention	Expected Outcome	Observed Outcome	Adjustment

The practice of reflection on practice increases counselors' awareness of what they do, why they did it, and the degree to which it was effective. Taking the time to review and analyze a session for client themes and counselor intentions behind each intervention and their effectiveness provides data that can be used to direct adjustment and to increase counselor effectiveness.

A Model for Reflection on Practice

As presented here, the effective, reflective counselor will systematically reflect on the implemented plan—making appropriate adjustments to goals and strategies. To be most useful, this reflective process should be systematic—not random or haphazard. The data are not arbitrary but are guided by hypotheses and assumptions about the strategies under investigation, with the goal being the increased effectiveness of the interaction.

The process is truly reflective in that it starts with planning, moves to strategic action, then to evaluation, and is followed by adjustment (Elden & Chisholm, 1993). The steps to be used when engaging in such reflection "on" practice can be found in Figure 2.1. Even though the process is presented here as involving clear, distinct, linear steps, the reality is that this is a dynamic process, moving back and forth across these steps as the data acquired continually reshapes practice decisions, additional questions, and the gathering of additional data. The use of this process in practice is shown in Case Illustration 2.3.

■ ■ ■ ■ ■ ▬▬▬▬▬▬▬▬▬▬▬▬▬▬▬▬▬▬▬▬▬▬▬▬▬▬▬▬▬▬▬▬▬

CASE ILLUSTRATION 2.3

IT SHOULD HAVE WORKED . . .

Maria presented with a concern about weight and sought the assistance of a counselor in hopes of developing a weight-loss program. After taking an extensive history and gathering data using a functional behavioral analysis, terminal goals were set, as were a number of subgoals **(Step 1: Identification of Goal or Subgoal).** In preparing to develop a treatment plan, the counselor relied on two sources of knowledge **(Step 2: Review of Knowledge Base/Experience).**

a. A review of Maria's record of eating patterns over a two-week period suggested that Maria tended to eat high, yet empty, calorie foods late at night when she was bored or when they were visibly presented (e.g., a box of candy sitting on the counter).
b. Second, the counselor reviewed the research and found techniques that addressed removal of the stimulus and provided an alternative response to employ in situations such as boredom were effective in reducing the undesirable snacking behavior.

With this information as the knowledge base, the counselor proposed a treatment program **(Step 3: Select Intervention)** that focused on stimulus control and alternative response training. The plan was enacted using the following steps **(Step 4: Intervention Implementation).**

a. First, Maria would not purchase any candy, cookies, or cakes (Maria's desired treats).

(continued)

b. Further, since Maria liked to have some snacks on hand for guests it was decided that these snacks would be placed in containers with a note stating: "Is this something you really want?" on the lid. The containers would all be placed out of sight in a cupboard.

c. Maria also agreed to the following "rule." If experiencing a craving while watching television, she will first perform 10 sit-ups (something she was doing each day in the morning), drink a glass of water, eat an allowable snack (celery, apple wedge) and wait 10 minutes. If the craving continued she would be allowed to take a low-fat, low-sugar snack.

Both the counselor and the client felt good about the program and thus it was implemented. Over the course of the next three weeks (while requiring some minor adjustments, for example, including "calling my friend" when the client was bored and about to eat), the client was successful in following the program. Data were collected over the next four weeks and it was clear that the client was embracing and employing the program and that all empty calorie snacks were eliminated from her late-night regimen (**Step 4: Observation and Data Collection**).

The problem was that the client continued to gain weight and abdominal girth (**Step 5: Comparsion of "What Is" to "What Was Expected"**). The program was implemented (**Step 6: Review of Application**) and it should have worked, given the counselor's experience and the extensive supportive research (**Step 7: Review Rationale**). The question, of course, is "Why wasn't it?" (**Step 8: Reset Goals and Recycle**).

As a result of consultation with the client, her physician, and a colleague, the counselor recommended that Maria undergo a full physical examination. While this step may have proved helpful in the beginning, it now appeared essential. The examination revealed two very significant findings. First, Maria was diagnosed with type II diabetes and she had fibroid tumors developing in her uterus. This data, while not negating the potential benefits of the original plan, clearly required adjustment to the goals, expansion of the treatment plan, and reconsideration of the measures of success.

REFLECTION "IN" PRACTICE

While it is essential to reflect "on" practice and adjust accordingly, reflection *in* practice is also essential to successful practice. This reflection "in" practice occurs in what may appear to be an intuitive, unconscious, spontaneous action. Consider the simple example of an individual ice skating. If you are new to the activity, you stand, you wobble, you begin to fall, but as all of this is occurring you are rapidly processing the data coming from your senses and adjusting muscle activity to regain your balance. This process of taking data in—contrasting the experience to the original expectations and goals—and then reflecting in order to think in new ways about the experience, all with the end result of an adjustment to hopefully bring "what is" in line with what "is hoped" for, is **reflection "in" practice.**

This process of reflection in practice is clearly a complex cognitive process that happens very quickly and most often below the immediate level of our awareness. But by identifying this process and bringing it to our conscious awareness as best as possible, we can learn to incorporate it more effectively within our moment-to-moment client interactions.

Identification of goal (or subgoal)

Review of

       Knowledge base (theory/research)

       Previous experience

Selection of intervention

Implementation of intervention (If...then, hypothesis)

Observation/data collection on impact

Reflection of "what is" to what "was expected"

Review of application of intervention

Review of selection rationale of intervention

Review–reset goals

Recycle

FIGURE 2.1   Reflection "on" Practice

Approaching the situation as a reflective conversation, the expert counselor views each exchange—each moment of interaction—as an intervention, an intervention that needs to be observed and assessed for effectiveness. The process is one in which the counselor is simultaneously involved in design and implementation of action, "while at the same time remaining detached enough to observe and feel the action that is occurring, and to respond" (Tremmel, 1993 p. 436).

Through this detachment and ability to reflect and feel the action occurring, the reflective counselor can utilize a repertoire of understandings, images, and actions to reframe a troubling situation so that problem-solving actions are generated. Consider the simple gesture of reaching out your hand to welcome a client to the counseling setting. What is the intent of such a gesture? Is it to reduce client anxiety? Is to begin to set the stage for the professional intimacy that the relationship will demand? If so, what happens when the counselor—with hand outstretched—sees that the client is an amputee? Or what if in response to the counselor's "warm, friendly gesture", the client manifests increased anxiety? The counselor who is **reflecting "in" practice** will rapidly process these data and attempt to adjust in ways that increase the possibility of achieving the initial goals. As such, perhaps when confronted with the amputation, the counselor continues to reach forward but now with two hands, embracing the client's forearm while verbally saying "welcome." Or in the case of the anxious client, perhaps the counselor simply moves his/her hand with a gentle sweeping motion, from the outreached position, to one pointing to a chair for the client, saying, "Welcome. Please make yourself comfortable." These are not actions that can be prescribed nor even anticipated, but require that rapid processing of data and comparison of what is to what was hoped for, with the result being an adjustment of counselor action. This last line needs to be repeated. *Reflection in practice is the process of comparing **what is** to **what was hoped for** or expected. The outcome of this comparison is an adjustment in the counselor's action geared to bring the* what is *closer in line with the* what is desired.

The illustration of the handshake is simple and clear in that what was expected is obvious. Since we have all employed an action such as extending one's hand in a gesture of greeting, we are clear as to what the counselor expects to have happen as a result of this action. Our experience sets up our expectation of what will be. Thus, at least in situation, when what we expect will be (i.e., a warm reciprocal outreach by the client) does not occur, we will experience surprise and even tension. It is this surprise and this tension that serve as the impetus for reflection and adjustment. But this occurs because we knew what to expect. How will the counselor who is new to the profession, or one who is still in training and thus by definition has limited experience with the counseling dynamic, know what to expect? How will he/she know what to expect when introducing an intervention, even one as small as the offering of a reflection or a summary or an open-ended question? If we are unsure of what we are expecting to occur, it will be hard to note the disparity of what is to what was hoped for, and as a result it will be impossible to make adjustments "on the fly."

Luckily, all counselors—even those new to the field or still in training—enter counseling knowing what to expect, as long as they employ operative models or orienting frameworks when engaging in counseling. It is this framework that sets up the expectations of impact and outcome and it is this framework through which they will process the current data and experience to match the what is to the what is expected (given that orienting framework). Consider Case Illustration 2.4, demonstrating this reflection in practice and the value of an orienting framework, which in this case was knowledge of relationship skills, to guide that reflection and adjustment.

■ ■ ■ ■ ■

CASE ILLUSTRATION 2.4

TO QUESTION OR NOT TO QUESTION, THAT'S THE REFLECTION

The following case illustration depicts an intake interview with the counselor's thoughts/reflection identified as the bases guiding his/her response "in" practice. As noted in the text, the reflective practitioner often experiences surprises in session as his/her expectations of what will conflict with the "what is." Look for that element of surprise within this case and see if you can anticipate the counselor adjustment.

Counselor: Well, Ellen maybe you could help me understand what it is that you wanted to talk about?

Ellen Oh boy, where do I begin? Well, I'm 45 years old and I guess this is an early midlife crises. I mean, look at me, well you didn't know me before but I'm 40 lbs. overweight, my hair is graying, although it's dyed now so you can't see it, and I hate my job. Don't get me wrong, I'm really good at it . . .

Counselor (reflection in practice)

Wow! Ellen is certainly verbal—I didn't expect such a flood of thoughts in response to my question. Now, I'm not sure if it is her style, or a response to initial anxiety or maybe evidence of possible hypomania?

Do I stop her and ask for clarification? What's wrong with the job?

Or do I summarize to try to gain some control over the dynamic?

Maybe let her continue and see if the pattern is just anxiety over the initial meeting and as such should slow down and focus.

Counselor: Hmmm . . . hmmm [with head nod as minimal encourager].

Ellen: Well, actually it's all of this stuff [becoming tearful, and sitting back in the chair]. [taking a breath] I think the real issue is that I'll be turning 45 in two weeks and I'm single. I've had relationships but nothing over the past year and to be honest I'm really lonely.

Counselor (reflection in practice)

Okay—Ellen's initial presentation appears to have been a result of some anxiety, but if this is her pattern it most likely would prove detrimental to developing new relationships. While she is noting her being lonely as the issue, I'm wondering if there is something else with the reference to turning 45? Perhaps, poor self-image? Feeling devalued? Does she believe she "needs" someone in order to be worthwhile?

Maybe I should help her focus as a way to provide structure and direction and reduce her anxiety?

Perhaps she could benefit from being affirmed, maybe she would relax if she realized she was not going be evaluated within our relationship.

(continued)

Counselor: [using a summary and a question]

Well Ellen, I really appreciate your honesty and willingness to share. It seems like you have given a lot of thought about the issues that you want to work on, including your weight gain and job dissatisfaction, but if I understand you correctly, it's the feelings of loneliness that are most concerning to you at this time?

Ellen: No, not at all. I mean sure that's an issue, but I'm really frustrated at work!

Counselor (reflection in practice)

Yikes, didn't expect that. Was I incorrect in my summary? Or maybe the timing was off. Okay, what to do?

Counselor: [reflecting and affirming]

So, while there are a couple of things that we could work on, the most pressing issue for you right now is your work and the frustration you are experiencing. Could you tell me a little about the nature of your work?

Counselor (reflection in practice)

Need to allow the client to set the agenda, focus on strengthening the relationship, and if it seems appropriate, reintroduce the loneliness issue.

As evident in the previous illustrations, reflection in practice begins with the recognition of a dilemma and an experience of emotional discomfort in response to a professional experience (Harvey, Hunt, & Schroder, 1961). Whether it is the counselor with hand outstretched or one receiving a strong negative response to what was expected, the process of catching oneself in emotional discomfort or cognitive dissonance from experiencing a "what is" (which is different from "what was expected") is necessary for reflection. This emotional awareness provides a bridge to critically (although nonjudgmentally) analyze the initial assumptions and beliefs about the client and the processes being employed. Our counselor in Case Illustration 2.4, while surprised by the client's response, did not process the experience with self-criticism (e.g., "Boy I screwed up") or client attack (e.g., "What's up with her?") but rather objectively evaluated the possibilities of what was happening and the options available for moving the encounter to a positive outcome.

As noted, counselors operating from reflection in practice often experience surprise when their interventions fail to elicit the expected response or outcome (see Case Illustration 2.4). This surprise requires that the counselor first have an expectation of what "will be" to contrast with the "what is." This expectation is created by the counselor's use of a model or orienting framework, which not only places the client's issues within a meaningful context but establishes what to expect when stimuli for change are introduced (Irving & Williams, 1995). While this process of employing specific orienting frameworks (e.g., solution focused, behavioral, cognitive, or transtheoretical) serves as the focus for the remaining chapters, the following case illustration shows how it may occur in practice (see Case Illustration 2.5).

■ ■ ■ ■ ■ ▬▬▬▬▬▬▬▬▬▬▬▬▬▬▬▬▬▬▬▬▬▬▬

CASE ILLUSTRATION 2.5
LESS RESOLVING, MORE RELATING

The client is a 56-year-old woman who came to the counselor in a state of "depression" and "panic." The initial intake revealed that the woman had been married to a physician for 36 years and had successfully raised three adult children, but was now faced with the reality that her husband was filing for divorce. The panic experienced by this client revolved around issues such as:

- being unable to support herself;
- having been a housewife for so long that she no longer had marketable skills;
- unsure of all that needed to be done—paying bills, checking insurance, etc—since that was all previously handled by her husband; and
- being totally isolated since all of her "friends" were couple friends.

On gathering the data, the counselor, using a cognitive orienting framework, hypothesized that the issue at hand was one of distorted catastrophic thinking. The client's anxiety was stimulated by her belief that these problems, while difficult, were irresolvable. With this as the case conceptualization and operative context, the counselor began to gently confront the "catastrophic thinking" presented by the client while moving to some very practical problem solving.

Hypothesizing that the "panic" was created by her belief that she was helpless over the various issues confronting her, the counselor began to pose questions geared toward challenging the client's perspective. For example, the counselor stated the following:

- Linda, I'm a little confused. You noted that you would not be totally isolated since all of your friends were couple friends? How about your boys?
- I can see how concerned you are about being able to support yourself. Do you know the conditions of the divorce and what financial responsibilities you husband will have?
- While I know you have been a homemaker for the past 30 or more years and that you feel as if you don't have the skills needed to move into the market place, do we assume that you will need to begin working right away? Or will you have time for a transition and training?

These questions were posed in hopes of reducing anxiety and allowing the client to see that while this situation was certainly one requiring many adjustments, they were all "doable." The counselor's intent was worthwhile, and the strategies (i.e., employing confrontation as intervention) were reasonable given the cognitive-orienting framework, but the client continued to grow increasingly anxious and upset within session. *Not what the counselor had expected!*

The client's increasing level of distress served as the data for the counselor to conclude that the approach was incorrect. With this information, the counselor moved back from the original approach and stated, "Linda, it's clear that you are getting more upset as I ask these questions. That is not my intent. Would you share with me what it is you are experiencing now?" This question, this invitation to share her experience, was what the client needed. Rather than being asked questions and engaging in interactions geared toward problem solving, she wanted and needed to simply be heard. Given the context of losing her life partner, this client needed to tell her story, and to feel as if someone understood and cared. The problem solving could come later. She needed to relate, not resolve!

(continued)

In response to the counselor's invitation to share, the client responded, "You don't get it. For most of my life I was a Mrs! Now I'm not. I'm not sure what or who I am."

The client was correct. The counselor didn't get it. But being a counselor who reflected "in" practice and who was open to testing and reshaping initial hypotheses, he received this new data and now did "get it." With the client's comment, the counselor's map changed. No longer were issues of bills and friends and careers of importance. The concerns far exceeded these and reflected fundamental issues of identity, security, and personal worth. With this as the context, the counselor shifted from intervention geared to problem solving to interventions that would facilitate the client's sharing, relating, and experiencing genuine, unconditional valuing. With the client now placed within this context, the interventions of choice were no longer confrontation and problems solving, but rather those of attending, reflecting, and encouraging client disclosure while providing evidence of the counselor's unconditional positive regard.

Clearly, as illustrated, the process employed is one that helps the counselor become aware of the data provided by the client at any one moment and helps him/her integrate that data into his/her cognitive schema and thinking strategies. As illustrated in the case, a counselor's reflection in practice facilitates the formation of goal intentions (e.g., desired end states) and implementation intentions (e.g., goal-directed behaviors and plans to achieve one's goals) by directing the counselor's attention to situational and client cues that serve to guide relevant responses (cf., Gollwitzer, 1999).

For this process to occur the counselor needs to (a) actively attend to information received from the client, (b) apply theoretical knowledge to the situation, and (c) decide on optimal interventions to meet counseling objectives (Hanna, & Giordano, 1996). Perhaps if our counselor working with Linda (Case Illustration 2.6) was more empathic he would have been attentive to the impact that being married and a homemaker for 30-plus years had on the formation of her self-identity. With this awareness and an understanding of the theory and research resounding female identity development (e.g., Gilligan, 1993), he would have realized that the optimal intervention would be that which addressed this devastation and not the presumed distortion of normal adjustment issues. Such a reflection occurring "in" practice or even following a session as reflection "on" practice will lead to better planning and treatment efficacy (Van Der Zee & Oudenhoven, 2000). It is this ability to be reflective both "in" and "on" practice that serves as the hallmark of the effective counselor.

Developing Reflection "In" and "On" Practice

Reflective thinking involves identifying the facts, formulas, and theories that are relevant for solving complex and ill-defined problems (King & Kitchener, 1994), including the clinical judgments made throughout the counseling process. Those in counselor training and all in practice should think critically about the assumptions that guide their practice decisions. A number of strategies have been employed to facilitate the development of reflective thinking for counselors in practice (see Table 2.2).

TABLE 2.2   Strategies for Developing Reflection "In" and "On" Practice

METHOD	DESCRIPTION	SOURCE
Journal Writing	Keeping a record of a session that targets ■ Description of the events and experiences ■ Hypotheses about why it occurred ■ Personal responses and reactions to the experience—both within the session and following the session (including feelings, images, and thoughts) ■ Impact of reflection and planned next step	Stickel & Trimmer, 1994
Interpersonal Process Recall (IPR)	IPR is an instructional method that uses videotaped sessions of previous counseling sessions as the focus for reflection. In supervision, students are guided toward increased awareness of their feelings and attitudes that may have been operative at various points in the session and which may have influenced their decisions and responses. The process employed is to allow the clinician to review the taped session and the freedom to stop the tape at any point they recall a thought, feeling, impression, or internal dialogue that may have occurred at the point and which may have been active in the formulation of their response. Through such reflection the counselor becomes more aware and sensitized to his/her attitudes and patterns that may be activated within the session and that impact treatment decisions and effectiveness.	Kagan & Kagan, 1991
Reflective Teams	Uses a group of counselors (professionals or students) to share observations of a session. This strategy has often been used to assist a counselor who feels "stuck" in practice. The method has been used in family therapy and group work and requires the counseling to be suspended while the team discusses what was observed. Following this observation, the family or the group under investigation then processes or discusses the observations made by the observers. The process not only provides stimulus to move the session but models the value of multiple perspectives for understanding and conceptualizing clinical experiences.	Anderson, 1991

Finally, before leaving this chapter, it may be helpful to step into the world of a reflective practitioner. Exercise 2.2 provides an initial step into the process of development as a reflective practitioner.

■ ■ ■ ■ ■

EXERCISE   2.2
AND WHY DID I DO THAT?

Directions. Throughout this chapter, the importance of reflection **on** and reflection **in** practice has been highlighted. For this exercise, you will need to engage in a simulated counseling session with a friend or a colleague. You will need to tape (audio or video) the session.

Step 1: Prior to meeting with your client, write down two goals you hope to achieve as a result of the session. Be as concrete as possible in describing how you would know that the goals were achieved.

Step 2: Following the session, you are to sit and review your tape recording. Stop the tape at any five points in which you, as counselor, are responding or intervening within the session. Write down what you said or what you did, even if it was to remain silent.

Step 3: Answer the following questions.

1. Compare your responses (listed in Step 2) to the goals you established in Step 1. Are they goal related? Do they help move you and your client in the desired direction?
2. As best as you can remember, what exactly was your intent (your goal) for this specific response or intervention at that specific point in the interaction? Were you successful?
3. Knowing your intended goal at these points in the session, how else could you have responded or intervened to be more effective?

This is a process that should be repeated as a way of practicing **reflection on** and **reflection in**.

REFERENCES

Anderson, T. (Ed.). (1991). *The reflecting team: Dialogues and dialogues about the dialogues.* New York: Norton.

Duncan, B.L., Hubble, M.A., & Miller, S.C. (1997). *Psychotherapy with 'impossible' cases: The efficient treatment of therapy veterans.* New York: W. W. Norton & Co.

Eells, T.D. (1997). Psychotherapy case formulation: History and current status. In T. D. Eells (Ed.), *Handbook of psychotherapy case formulation* (pp. 1–25). New York: Guilford Press.

Eells, T.D. (2002). Formulation. In M. Hersen & W. Sledge (Eds.), *The encyclopedia of psychotherapy* (pp. 815–822). New York: Academic Press.

Efran, J.S., Luken, M.D., & Lukens, R.J. (1990). *Language, structure, and change: Frameworks of meaning in psychotherapy.* New York: W. W. Norton & Co.

Elden, M. & Chisholm, R.E. (1993). *Emerging varieties of action research: Introduction to the special issue. Human Relations,* 46(2), 121–142.

Falvey, J.E. (2001). Clinical judgment in case conceptualization and treatment planning across mental health disciplines. *Journal of Counseling and Development,* 79(3), 292–303.

Fong, M.L., Borders, L.D., Ethington, C.A., & Pitts, J.H. (1997). Becoming a counselor: A longitudinal study of student cognitive development. *Counselor Education and Supervision,* 37(2), 100–114.

Gambrill, E. (1990). *Critical thinking in clinical practice.* San Francisco: Jossey-Bass.

Gilligan, C. (1993). *In a different voice: Psychological theory and women's development.* Cambridge, MA: Harvard University Press.

Gollwitzer, P. (1999). Implementation intentions: Strong effects of simple plans. *American Psychologist,* 54(7), 493–503.

Hanna, F.J., Giordano, F.G., (1996). Theory and experience: Teaching dialectical thinking in *counselor* education. *Counselor Education and Supervision,* 36(1), 14–24.

Hanna, F. J. & Giordano, F. G. (1996). Theory and experience: Teaching dialectical thinking in counselor education. *Counselor Education & Supervision*. 36(1), 14–25.

Harvey, O.J., Hunt, D.E., & Schroder, H.M. (1961). *Conceptual systems and personality organization*. Oxford: Wiley.

Hersen, M. & Porzelius, L.K. (Eds.). (2002). *Diagnosis, conceptualization, and treatment planning for adults: A step-by-step guide*. Mahwah, NJ: Erlbaum.

Hill, C.E. & O'Grady, K.E. (1985). List of therapist intentions illustrated in a case study and with therapists of varying theoretical orientations. *Journal of Counseling Psychology*, 31(1), 3–22.

Hoshmand, L.T. (1994). Supervision of predoctoral graduate research: A practice-oriented approach. *Counseling Psychologist*, 22(1), 147–162.

Irving, J.A. & Williams, D.I. (1995). Critical thinking and reflective practice in counselling. *British Journal of Guidance & Counselling*, 23(1), 107–116.

Kagan, N.I. & Kagan, H. (1991). Interpersonal Process Recall. In P.W. Dowrick (Ed.), *Practical guide to using video in the behavioral sciences* (pp. 221–230). New York: Wiley.

King, P.M. & Kitchener, K.S. (1994). *Developing reflective judgment: Understanding and promoting growth and critical thinking in adolescents and adults*. San Francisco: Jossey-Bass.

Makover, R.B. (1996). *Treatment planning for psychotherapists*. Washington, DC: American Psychiatric Association.

Mordock, J.B. (1994). Treatment planning in counseling. In: J.L. Ronch, W. Van Ornum, & N.C. Stilwell, (Eds.), *The counseling sourcebook: A practical reference on contemporary issues* (pp. 227–233). New York: Crossroad Publishing Co.

Morran, D., Kurpius, D.J., Brack, C.J., & Brack, G. (1995). A cognitive-skills model for counselor training and supervision. *Journal of Counseling & Development*, 73(4), 384–389.

Morrow, K.A. & Deidan, C.T. (1992). Bias in the counseling process: How to recognize and avoid it. *Journal of Counseling & Development*, 70(5), 571–577.

Nelson, M.L. & Neufeldt, S.A. (1998). The pedagogy of counseling: A critical examination. *Counselor Education and Supervision*, 38(5), 70–88.

Neufeldt, S.A., Karno, M.P., & Nelson, M.L. (1996). A qualitative study of experts' conceptualization of supervisee reflectivity. *Journal of Counseling Psychology*, 43(5), 3–9.

Parsons, R.D. (2007).*Counseling strategies that work! Evidenced-based interventions for school counselors*. Boston: Allyn & Bacon.

Prieto, L.R. & Scheel, K.R.(2002). Using case documentation to strengthen counselor trainees' case conceptualization skills. *Journal of Counseling and Development*, 80(1), 11–22.

Ridley, C.R. (1995). *Overcoming unintentional racism in counseling and therapy: A practitioner's guide to intentional intervention*. Thousand Oaks, CA: Sage.

Schon, D.A. (1983). *The reflective practitioner: How professionals think in action*. New York: Basic Books.

Schon, D.A. (1987). *Educating the reflective practitioner*. San Francisco: Jossey-Bass.

Shaw, B.F. & Dobson, K.S. (1988). Competency judgments in the training and evaluation of psychotherapists. *Journal of Consulting and Clinical Psychology*, 56(5), 666–672.

Tillett, R. (1996). *Psychotherapy assessment and treatment selection. British Journal of Psychiatry*, 168(1), 10–15.

Tremmel, R. (1993). *Zen and the art of reflective practice in teacher education*. Harvard Educational Review, 63(4), 434–460.

Van Der Zee, K.L. & Oudenhoven, J.P. (2000). The Multicultural Personality Questionnaire: A multidimensional instrument of multicultural effectiveness. *European Journal of Personality*, 14, 291–309.

Wantz, D.W. & Morran, D.K. (1994). Teaching counselor trainees a divergent versus a convergent hypothesis-formation strategy. *Journal of Counseling & Development*, 73(1), 69–73.

SUGGESTED RESOURCES

Caspar, F. (1995). *Plan analysis: Toward optimizing psychotherapy*. Seattle: Hogrefe & Huber.

Eels, T.D. (Ed.). (1997). *Handbook of psychotherapy case formulation*. New York: Guilford Press.

Hill, C.E. & O'Grady, K.E. (1985). List of therapist intentions illustrated in a case study and with therapists of varying theoretical orientations. *Journal of Counseling Psychology*, 31(1), 3–22.

Schon, D.A. (1983). *The reflective practitioner: How professionals think in action*. New York: Basic Books.

PART II

MAKING MEANING—
FOUR VIEWS

CHAPTER 3

A SOLUTION-FOCUSED ORIENTING FRAMEWORK

Counseling is certainly a dynamic process. A skilled competent counselor can, through a process of reflecting "on" practice, approach a session with a well thought out, empirically supported set of interventions. However, as noted in the previous two chapters, to be effective, one must be willing to be surprised by session material and be able to respond to that surprise in a reflective way "in" practice. A counselor's particular frame of reference or orientation serves as the foundation for these reflective practices. It is a counselor's operative model that acts like a "looking glass" through which data are processed—plans emerge and reflections "in" practice result in effective adjustments.

The current chapter will introduce you to one such looking glass, one such frame of reference—Solution Focus Theory. While the basic tenets of the theory will be presented and discussed, it must be noted that the emphasis of the chapter is not on a full explication of the theory, nor a discussion of its validity and utility. Rather, the focus of this chapter—as is the focus of the book—is to highlight the process of reflection "on" and "in" practice as applied by counselors employing specific orienting frameworks.

The goal for this chapter is to demonstrate not only how a solution-focused operative framework comes alive in practice, but also how it gives life and direction to the counseling process. Specifically, after reading this chapter you will be able to:

- describe the basic tenets of a solution-focused model of counseling;
- explain how the utilization of constructs such as goal setting, goal scaling, and identification of exceptions guides the counselor's reflection on and in practice;
- employ a solution focus orienting framework to respond to simulated case material.

SOLUTION FOCUS: A DEPARTURE FROM CLASSIC MODELS

Solution-focused brief therapy first appeared in the early 1980s, and its title and specific steps have been attributed to Steve de Shazer and his wife, Insoo Kim Berg, and their team at the Brief Family Therapy Family Center in Milwaukee, Wisconsin. Solution-focused brief therapy extended on the earlier work of a number of therapists who practiced "brief therapy," most notably Milton Erickson (1977) and Jay Haley (1981, 1994). Since its inception, this solution-focused approach has been reported as an effective intervention for a variety of presenting concerns (e.g., de Shazer, 1988; Miller, Hubble, & Duncan, 1996, Jacob, 2001; Sharry, 2001).

The solution-focused model is a significant departure from the more classic, problem-focused therapeutic approaches. While most therapies involve clients coming to counseling with problems and seeking help, those operating from a solution-focused orientation involve clients coming into the relationship with solutions seeking expression. Solution-focused counselors enter the relationship as collaborators in the solution finding and solution-incorporating processes. The counselor takes an active role conducting the counseling and taking responsibility for the unfolding of the therapeutic process. The therapist's role in the solution-focused process is to continually encourage clients to explore what they want different in their lives (goals) and what resources and strengths they can bring to help make the goals reality (Berg & DeJong, 1996).

EPISTEMOLOGY THAT UNDERPINS SOLUTION-FOCUSED THEORY

Chapter 2 emphasized the importance of *thinking* like an expert and utilizing orienting frameworks to guide a counselor's reflections "on" and "in" practice. With this as the backdrop, it becomes clear that it is not just the strategies and techniques of any single theory or model that one should understand and employ, but rather, it is the fundamental philosophy and nature of the theory being discussed that must be understood and embraced. It is this elemental view of the world that will serve as the lens through which client data are filtered and decisions are made with counselor action.

While all counselors can step into a set of actions as if putting on a role or can perhaps follow a step-by-step recipe to interventions, the expert counselor assimilates rather than merely puts on their orienting framework. It is not simply what they do but how they are doing it that distinguishes the expert from the novice. In order to appreciate, value, and assimilate the solution-focused model, one must be fully aware and committed to the fundamental epistemology that underpins this theory.

O'Connell (1998) aligned solution-focused therapy with a constructionist, narrative approach to psychotherapy (e.g., White & Epston, 1990). Constructivism is a philosophical position that posits all of our knowledge is "constructed." What we present as fact and reality does not necessarily reflect any external "transcendent" realities; rather, it is all contingent on perception, social experience, and convention. This position holds that categories of knowledge and reality are actively created by social relationships and interactions. That is, we do not have direct access to objective truth and reality, but we are dependent on our linguistically constructed versions of reality. Consider even something as serious as identifying and labeling pathology. There was a time not so long ago that the American Psychiatric Association eliminated a specific "pathology," that of homosexuality! By the mere creation of a new statistical and diagnostic manual that no longer classified one's sexual orientation as serving as a base for diagnostic pathology, the American Psychiatric Association created a new reality. This is the potential of constructivism. By the singular act of redefining that which constituted pathology, an entire population of people who had previously been identified as "abnormal" or even "sick" were no longer viewed or treated that way.

The counselor operating from a constructivism point of view posits that the language employed in counseling co-constructs problems and solutions, thus creating reality rather than merely reflecting it. As such, the meaning of a client's experience can be renarrated in a way that works better for the client. As O'Connell (1998, p. 18) put it:

> The epistemological basis of [solution-focused therapy] offers the therapist a rich and varied access into a client's world. Its sensitivity to the power of language in socially constructing the problem creates many possible therapeutic conversations. Its acknowledgement of the presence of many different "truths" and standpoints validates the world view of clients, while providing a basis for "reauthoring" (White, 1995) the client's narrative.

The counselor who can appreciate the power of language and constructed realities will approach his/her counseling relations believing that no single person possesses more of the truth than any other. With this belief, the counselor respects the client-experienced "truths" as his/her own and gives precedence to the client's perceptions and experiences rather than digging for the "facts" or absolute "truth." Further, with an appreciation of the power of language and constructed realities as the framework, the solution-focused counselor will direct discussion and dialogue to the issues of *solutions* rather than *problems* (see Table 3.1).

By focusing the encounter on solutions and hopeful futures as opposed to becoming mired in a discussion of the client's unsuccessful problematic history, a reality of hope and positive expectations is created. Finally and perhaps most importantly, embracing a constructionist point of view positions the solution-focused counselor to approach client problems as neither fixed nor immutable truths, but rather as constructed realities that can be changed. It is this lens, this perspective, and this set of fundamental philosophical beliefs that are given form in the following operating principles and techniques.

TABLE 3.1 A Shift in Language and Constructed Realities

TRADITIONAL LANGUAGE OF COUNSELING—CREATING PROBLEM REALITIES	SOLUTION-FOCUSED LANGUAGE—SHIFTING THOUGHTS, CREATING NEW REALITIES	SOLUTION-FOCUSED COUNSELOR'S INQUIRY
I don't want this . . . that . . . or to be . . .	I want . . .	If we were successful, what would change or be different?
Everything is going wrong	Some things are going right and have gone right	When have you experienced these differences recently? Or in the past?
It's only going to get worse . . . more problems on the horizon	Movement toward goals is possible	What would a little piece of this change look like?
I'm a victim to factors outside my control	I have resources and can enact these, focusing on resources within my control	How did you do that? (i.e., achieve a piece of your desired state of change)
It's hopeless—I'm stuck	Small steps but progressing!	On a scale of 0–10, where 10 is reaching your goal 100% . . . where are you now and how would you know you moved up one step?

FUNDAMENTAL PRINCIPLES

While there are a number of specific techniques that will be discussed in the next section of this chapter, it is important to understand the fundamental principles that serve as the foundation of the practice of solution-focused therapy/counseling. It is by way of embracing and assimilating these fundamental principles that the counselor's reflection "on" and "in" practice become geared toward solution, rather than problem.

Start with the End in Mind

Assisting the client to focus attention and thus his/her reality on a future, desirable point that is possible to achieve will prove more productive than rehashing and re-experiencing nonproductive pasts. The counselor uses respectful curiosity to invite the client to envision his/her preferred future and then together, the counselor and client begin to target changes, regardless of the size, that help to bring this future to fruition. As such, a solution-focused counselor entering an intake session may ask the client "What would you like to change?" Or, "What would you like to see happen that would help you know or feel that this was a productive session?" The future, goal-oriented focus of such a question is evident, especially when contrasted with a more traditional inquiry such as: "Can you tell me about your problem?" or even, "How can I help you?" Knowing where the client wishes to be, whether it is in reference to a specific session or the counseling process, is essential for the articulation of strategies aimed at changing the "this" to the desired "that."

Meet the Client at His/Her Model of the World

Being able to understand how the client makes sense out of his/her life is important in the establishment of trust, as is hearing "goals" that are meaningful to the client. With this principal in mind, the solution-focused counselor will accept the first goal that a client presents, even if it seems not as important or a bit out of sequence when viewed from the counselor's perspective. For example, consider a counselor working with a client who is homeless and abusing drugs. While the counselor may want to address the drug utilization, the client's priority may be housing. Working from this principle, the counselor will join the client in the process of working toward his/her goal of finding housing, trusting that in time other goals, including reducing drug use, will emerge.

Transform the Client into a Customer

While some clients come to counseling because they were "told to attend" or because they wish to complain about the others who are the sources of their problems, the goal for the solution-focused counselor is to transform all clients into active, hopeful participants or "customers" (Berg & Miller, 1992; de Shazer, 1988). The client, who is a customer actively participates in therapy, appreciating what he/she brings to the encounter (Berg & Miller, 1992). The ideal client, as described by O'Connell (1998), would be the one that presents with statements such as: "I am very clear with what I would like to change in my life and I am willing to invest a lot of effort into making those changes. I have already begun to make progress and I would like to build on my strengths to develop those solutions" (p.28).

The solution-focused counselor uses the fundamental skill of helping (e.g., reflections clarification, open questions, etc.) to clarify goals and to foster the client's belief in the presence of (his/her) self-as-resource. This is often an important goal, especially when working with clients who arrive at counseling as a result of the mandate (i.e., adjudicated) or at the direction of another (e.g., students sent by teachers).

If It Ain't Broke (in the Client's Mind), Don't Fix It

Solution-focused counselors believe that not only is it important to respect the rights and wishes of clients as goals are formulated, but also to respect the way they see their lives and the way they wish to approach solutions. Thus, the solution-focused counselor is not concerned with imposing strategies or enticing the client to learn new things or develop new skills. Rather, the solution-focused counselor attempts to find and utilize those resources and strategies that are in the client's repertoire and can continue to be effective. In an attempt to build on that which is healthy and functioning in the client's life, the solution-focused counselor may ask: "Are there times or occasions when this situation was somewhat different?" rather than the more typical question, "Could you tell me more about these problems?" Through efforts to understand these times of 'exception" (i.e., when the client experienced the situation or his/her life as closer to that desired), both the counselor and the client will begin to envision the resources available to the client, which support the desired change.

Small Change Can Lead to Bigger Changes

The solution counselor recognizes the value of approaching the process of change in small, manageable steps. According to Rosenbaum, Hoyt, and Talmon (1990) such an approach:

- reduces pressure off both the counselor and the client that often accompanies having to work hard to bring about major changes;
- appears more enticing to a client who may be more willing to invest in making a small change rather than a big one (at least initially); and
- provides an opportunity to experience success and thus flame a client's hope for successful outcome to the relationship.

Helping the client identify an ideal state or terminal goal, articulating where they currently see their life in relationship to that goal, and then developing a meaningful first step toward the ultimate goal is a hallmark of a solution-focused counselor and his/her utilization of a technique called "goal scaling." This technique and others emerging from these fundamental principles are the focus of the next section of this chapter.

STRATEGIES AND INTERVENTIONS

With the fundamental philosophy and operational principles in mind, the question that now needs to be addressed is: "How are this philosophy (i.e., constructionist) and these principles given form in the counselor's reflection 'on' and 'in' practice?" The answer can be found in a review of the strategies employed by solution-focused counselors, specifically: goal setting, the miracle question, goal scaling, and finding exceptions.

Goal Setting

A major focus for the solution-focused counselor is in helping the client transform his/her issues of concern into specific goals. This shifting of focus from what is or what was to what is desired sets the foundation for the action plans necessary for goal achievement. The solution-focused counselor, through reflection "on" and "in" practice, attempts to assist clients to articulate goals that are well-formed, achievable, and viable within the counseling dynamic. Solution-focused problem solving relentlessly pursues the positive (Thompson & Rudolph, 2000). A number of researchers (e.g., Berg & Miller, 1992; deJong & Miller, 1995) have identified guidelines for the creation of these well-formed goals.

1. *The goal must be important to the client.* As noted previously, it is important for the counselor to join the client "where they are," and enter into their perspective. As such, identifying goals that are important to the client helps build on the cooperative atmosphere needed for successful therapy. Consider the situation of the high school counselor who is working with an 11th grade student, Jamal, who is failing in mathematics and science. In the initial exchange, the counselor discovers that the student's dream is to become a veterinarian. While a review of the student's academic records and aptitude tests may reveal that the student has a very small chance of getting into a school of veterinary science, at this stage in counseling, it is important to embrace the "dream" as the beginning of a place to dialogue. Thus, in session, the exchange may go something like the following:

> **Counselor:**   Jamal, you mention you always wanted to become a veterinarian.
>
> **Jamal:**   Yeah, I love animals and I've worked at the SPCA for the past two years.
>
> **Counselor:**   What is it about what you do at the SPCA that you really enjoy?
>
> **Jamal:**   I don't know. I like working with the animals—you know, washing them, taking care of them, feeding, walking. Things like that.
>
> **Counselor:**   You really sound like you enjoy that and I can see how excited you get talking about it.
>
> **Jamal:**   Yeah, my family thinks I'm nuts 'cause I love to be around dogs and hang out at the SPCA.
>
> **Counselor:**   Well this is something we want to keep in mind as you think about what you may want to do after you graduate. I know you said that you may want to become a veterinarian and we can look at what that would involve, but while we are at it, we may also want to look at all the other types of jobs that someone like you—who loves animals—would enjoy doing. How does that sound?
>
> **Jamal:**   Like working at the SPCA?
>
> **Counselor:**   Well, that is one thing but there are lots of others. Why don't we go over to the career center and use the computer discovery program to check it out?
>
> **Jamal:**   Okay.

2. *Keep goals small and achievable.* Within a counseling session, clients often begin with very large, vague goals. The counselor may find it helpful to refocus the client on small signs of success or "subgoals" that may be achieved on his/her way to the larger goal (Berg and Miller, 1992). Focusing on smaller goals, as markers toward some larger outcome, helps both client and therapist recognize progress. Skilled therapists help clients name and accomplish a series of small goals, which contribute to a bigger whole, since it is "easier to 'fill out a job application' than to 'get a job'" (de Jong and Miller, 1995, p. 730).

If we continue with our case of Jamal, the future veterinarian, we will see that the counselor assists Jamal to first become familiar with the career search program and move on to reading and discussing the descriptions of various careers along with educational requirements, salaries, and employment outlook. It will only be after finding success in these tasks that the counselor may have the client interview those in the field, or go and observe a professional who is working in the field. There will be much more to do in terms of looking into training and education, finding support and funding, and even going back to the original referral developing strategies to improve on Jamal's current achievement levels. There is much to do and, when viewed in totality, it can seem overwhelming and undoable. However, with the counselor's assistance, the client will be able to break the preferred future into smaller, more manageable goals, which in turn lends to the creation of doable tasks and achievable steps.

3. *Make goals concrete, specific, and behavioral.* As most of us move through our day-to-day functioning, we do so with an eye to achieving very concrete goals and objectives. Some of these goals may be quite significant, such as the case of a surgeon who is planning to complete a complicated operation, while others may be more matter of fact, such as stopping and picking up the laundry. Moving from our morning coffee to take our shower, drive our typical route to work, check our messages through to meeting our significant other for dinner that evening, we fill our days with goal identification and goal achievement. As we review our day, we will most likely find that we tend to be successful and feel as if we have accomplished something when our goals are clear, specific, and concrete.

Berg and Miller (1992, p. 37) noted that nonbehavioral goals, such as having more self-esteem, living a sober lifestyle, and getting in touch with feelings are difficult to achieve, mainly because success and progress are difficult to gauge. Yet, quite often, a client presents goals as vague, ill-defined dreams and wishes. The counselor operating from a solutions-focused orienting framework will employ his/her communication skills (e.g., reflection, clarifying, summarization), to help the client move from a statement of the vague wishes of life to the establishment of concrete, observable, behavioral forms of that wish. Consider the dialogue that ensued during the initial session between the counselor and Laura, a 52-year-old woman, who entered counseling "feeling useless."

Counselor: So, Laura, let me see if I understand. You are feeling that since the children are grown and the house is well established there really isn't much for you do, or at least, not much that gives you a sense of being of value—having some use.

Laura: I mean, I'm happy with my life, it's just . . . I don't know . . . I just would like to feel like I'm doing something worthwhile.

Counselor: Well, it seems understandable that since your previous responsibilities—caring for the children, establishing a household—no longer are as pressing, that you may want to find something else to do with your time and talent. But when you say you would like to "do something worthwhile," I am not real sure what "doing something worthwhile" means. Could you give me an example of something which for you would be a worthwhile endeavor?

Laura: You know I think that's part of the problem . . . I don't know what I mean. I mean, I know there are people making lots of money, but that's not what I'm really interested in doing. Don't get me wrong, that would be nice . . . but not the real important thing. And, I'm not looking to save the world, or solve the problem of world hunger or AIDS, but something that I feel gives me a chance to learn new things and use my talents and interests.

Counselor: Maybe you would try this little exercise. Let's pretend that tonight you go to bed being a mom and housewife—having completed all your chores and activities for the day just as you have been doing for the past 20-plus years. But then during the night a miracle happens, and when you awake you realize that things are dramatically different and that you are now free to use your time any way you wish . . . that all house details are taken care of and the children are self-sufficient. Given this miracle, what are some of the things you could imagine doing from that day on . . . big or small?

Laura: Wow, if miracles could happen! You mean anything?

Counselor: Mmm hmm, anything. Remember, a miracle has occurred.

Laura: Well, I love children, so maybe I would be working at a daycare or volunteering at the children's hospital. And, I've always enjoyed doing hand work—knitting, quilting etc., so. . . . .

Certainly, with additional support from the counselor this client that was "so unclear" may begin to see a pattern emerging, one pointing to her interest in working with children or the elderly in a teaching capacity. This increased concretization of a goal, while still broad and needing additional clarification, will at least serve as a starting point for some researching and further clarification.

4. *Goals stated in positive terms.* Counselors should consider the "dead person" principle when working with the client in identifying and setting goals. This principle is simply that if a dead person can do it, it is most likely not a useful goal.

Quite often, clients approach counseling stating what they don't want: "I don't want to be angry," "I don't want to be fat," "I don't want to get in trouble." Each of these statements reflect worthwhile goals but are phrased in ways that focus the counseling on what will not be rather than what will be. Placing goals in such a negative light similarly places the client in a passive role. With this negative, passive construction of a goal, the client is left with a sense of impotence about what it is that he/she needs to do to achieve these goals. As noted by Berg and Miller (1992), "Goals must be stated in positive, proactive language about what the client will do instead of about what she will not do" (p. 38).

To engage the client as an active agent in his/her own solution finding and implementation, the solution-focused counselor needs to help the client identify what it is that he/she wants in place of being angry, being overweight, or getting in trouble. Consider the brief dialogue between Carl, a recent employee who is speaking to the employee assistance counselor about what he perceives is a bad relationship with his manager.

> **Carl:**   I hate that I am such a wimp. Howard barks out orders—most of time he has no clue what we are doing or what needs to be done and often he is asking us to do things that would be unproductive. But I'm such a wimp, I just take it. I hate it. I hate being a wimp. I want to stop it!
>
> **Counselor:**   So, there are times when Howard is telling you to do something that you know is not the most productive thing to do and yet you seem to go along with what he is saying?
>
> **Carl:**   Yeah, I'm such a wimp . . . I can't believe it. I really want to stop it.
>
> **Counselor:**   Well, if we assumed that you did stop acting, as you say, like a "wimp," what would you be doing instead? How would you act? What would you do or say?
>
> **Carl:**   Well, I would tell him where to go. No, not really, but I would try to explain to him why his idea isn't a good one. I guess I would just speak up, tell him what I think and feel.
>
> **Counselor:**   So, if I understand your goal, it sounds like you would like to act more assertively, expressing what you think and feel, especially when it comes to Howard?
>
> **Carl:**   Yeah that's the word—I would be assertive!

While the concept of assertiveness needs to be more concretely described, at least the counselor has helped the client reconceptualize his goal from one that was negative and passive ("stop being a wimp") to one that is positive and engaging ("to become assertive").

5. *Goals are expressed as beginnings rather than endings.* The solution-focused counselor believes that the therapy, like life, is a process, one that can and should continue even when the formal counseling contract is completed. With this view of therapy as an ongoing process, the solution-focused counselor attempts to focus on the beginning and progress toward goals, rather than waiting for total goal attainment.

Throughout the sessions, the solution-focused counselor will seek information about small improvements, make small movements toward ultimate goals, and will encourage the client in their continued efforts. For example, the counselor may ask: "What would be the first small signs of change?" or "What small step could you take over the next week that could begin to move you towards your goal?" With ongoing encouragement, the counselor will help the client incorporate not just the specific interventions discussed in regards to this one goal but also incorporate the entire process of setting achievable, positive goals and using a reflection of his/her own strengths and abilities to sculpt actions that can be taken to move toward any of his/her identified goals.

6. *The goals are realistic and achievable within the context of the client's life.* Recognizing the multiple pulls, demands, and opportunities presented within one's life at any one time, the solution-focused counselor helps the client place his/her goals within the larger context of his/her life. For example, let's return to the case of Laura, the client seeking to do something of value with her life now that her children are grown and out of the house. While Laura may discover that she wants to work full time or return to school or become an active volunteer, the solution-focused counselor, while being supportive and encouraging, will want to help Laura recognize the potential impact of these decisions on her lifestyle. For example, by asking, "How might others notice that Laura has changed her life and the decisions she makes?", the counselor may help her to recognize that a decision to return to school may necessitate her dropping out of her book club or necessitate a change in the time that she and her husband eat dinner together or even require the re-allocation of savings in order to pay for tuition. This is not to suggest that she should not consider pursuing her goal but rather that she should do it with a realization of the impact it may have on the balance of her life and life activities.

7. *The client sees the goal as involving "hard work."* The solution-focused counselor respects the fact that while these goals are important to the client, they are not easily attainable, for if they were, the client would not be engaging in this working alliance. By helping the client see the goal as one involving hard work, the solution-focused counselor helps the client build a positive "face" and protects and promotes the client's feelings of dignity and self-worth (Berg and Miller, 1992, p. 43). Approaching the goals from the perspective that they will require "hard work" allows the client to internalize personal responsibility for achieving the goal while having a self-respecting place to fall back to in case of failure. This process leaves the client and therapist in a win-win situation. If they fail to reach the goal, it is still possible to achieve it if they can find how to work a little harder. If the client quickly gets to the goal, he/she can be complimented on being able to figure out such a difficult solution in a short period of time. Slow, steady progress can be accepted as normal and the client can be praised for his/her hard work (Berg and Miller, 1992, p. 42).

The Miracle Question: Stimulating Goal Identification

One strategy for goal identification for which the solution-focused model has received some attention is the use of the "miracle question." The purpose of this question is to assist the client (and counselor) to refocus the counseling on the construction of new behaviors for the near and extended future. The posing of the miracle question is a designed interview technique that helps move the client from the past problem and focus toward the future and solutions (Berg & Miller, 1992). In its generic form, the miracle question would look like the following:

> Suppose that one night, while you are asleep, there is a miracle and the problem that brought you here is solved. However, because you are asleep you don't know that the miracle has already happened. When you wake up in the morning, what will be different that will tell you that the miracle has taken place? What else? (Berg and Miller, 1992, p.13)

It is important to understand that the solution-focused counselor is not promoting the belief in miracles. Rather, the counselor is using this technique to remove constraints, such as the need to identify specific details, from clients' thinking and provide them with the permission to think broadly as to the ideal solution to their situation and concern.

Providing the client with the opportunity to think abut the unlimited possibilities a miracle would afford, helps to move the focus to the future (deJong & Berg, 1998). As presented, the miracle question is general and somewhat ill-defined. This format provides clients with the maximum freedom to structure their desired future. The miracle question can also be framed to lend to a more specific response. When a more concrete and targeted response is desired, the miracle question may look like the following:

> Imagine a miracle sorted out your problem. What ten differences might you notice about yourself the next morning? In providing your response focus on what you would be doing . . . rather than not doing. That is, rather than saying "I wouldn't be as down," focus on what you would feel, think, and do in contrast to being "down." For example, maybe you would feel more energized and smile more often.

Clearly, the form of the miracle question and its phraseology needs to be appropriate to the specific background and developmental level of the client. For example, when employed with younger children, a more concrete, magical form may need to be employed (Skalre, 1997). Thus, the question may be posed as the following: "If I were to wave a magic wand or rub a magic lamp and wish all your problems away, what would we see you doing if we could videotape you for one day?"

In posing the question, the solution-focused counselor needs to be ready to accept the client's first response, which may need some prodding and inviting to shape into a workable goal. Similarly, it is important to realize that sometimes the initial goal, as presented in this miracle scenario, needs to be reshaped so that it is positive in construction and clear enough to begin to serve as a reasonable target for client movement. For example, if a client suggests that in the future "their uncle would leave them a ton of money in his will," the counselor might probe and ask:

"And if that were to occur, what would that allow you to do that would make your current situation more desirable?" This reframe provides the client with an invitation to reformulate the goal that is phrased with a passive voice to one that shifts focus to clients on ability and the power to actively do something that would make the current situation more desirable. This process is illustrated by Aisha (Case Illustration 3.1).

■ ■ ■ ■ ■ ▆▬▬▬▬▬▬▬▬▬▬▬▬▬▬▬▬

CASE ILLUSTRATION 3.1
I WOULDN'T BE YELLED AT!

Context: Aisha, a sixth-grade student at J.R.F. Middle School, stood in the doorway of the counselor's office looking a bit sad and confused.

Counselor: Aisha . . . hi. Would you like to come in and talk?

(Note the counselor doesn't ask, "Aisha, what's wrong?" or "Can I help?" both of which focus the client on problem talk rather than goal and solution speak. The invitation to come in and talk is a solution response to her presence within a doorway.)

Aisha: (Entering, starts to cry.) I hate Mr. Zhang! He's always hollering at me. He makes me feel like a loser!

Counselor: I can see how upset you are, but I am proud of you for coming to talk about it . . . that's a start!

(Counselor is encouraging and supporting while also identifying a client resource, that is, her ability and willingness to "work" on the situation.)

Aisha, would you be willing to try something for me?

(Counselor respecting the client and inviting her as collaborator.)

Aisha: I guess.

Counselor: Let's pretend that you go home after school today having had some tough times in class, and some fun in others, but you go home and later when you go to sleep something happens—something like a miracle happens.

Now, you don't know a miracle has happened, so when you wake you just prepare for school like you usually do. But this time when you come to school you start to notice something is really different. In fact, school is exactly like you dreamed it could be—that during the night your dream has come true! Tell me Aisha, what would you notice?

(Counselor using the miracle question to refocus client on goals, rather than problems, framing the dialogue as one of hope and direction rather than problems and victimization.)

Aisha: Yeah, if only miracles could happen.

Counselor: I know this is just a little exercise and that miracles don't just happen. But just so we could get an idea of what it is that you are hoping for, maybe you could just describe what it is that you would notice that would indicate that a miracle happened?

(Counselor needing to reground client by rephrasing the miracle question.)

Aisha: Well, first of all Jamal would know I liked him (smiling), and I would be wearing that sweater I've wanted, and, yeah, and Mr. Zhang would get off my back. Yep, that would happen.

Counselor: Aisha, that's great. You said that Jamal would know you liked him. How would you know he knew?

(Counselor accepting client goal as a starting point.)

Aisha: He would sit with me at lunch and I could talk with him.

Counselor: Cool! You really know what to look for to see if you got what you wanted!

(Counselor, introducing the need to concretize goals.)

And, in addition to Jamal sitting with you at lunch, what else would be different following this miracle?

(Counselor grounding client.)

Aisha: Mr. Zhang would bug off . . . stop hollering at me!

Counselor: If Mr. Zhang stopped hollering at you, what would he be doing instead?

(Counselor attempting to reframe goal as a positive goal.)

Aisha: I don't know. Maybe he would treat me like the other students. You know, call on me when I have my hand raised and say nice things when I got an answer.

Counselor: Wow. That sounds nice. Let's pretend he, Mr. Zhang, was doing that. What would you notice about yourself? How would you be feeling? What would you be doing?

(Counselor attempting to expand the goal and begin to look for client resources.)

Aisha: Well, I guess I would feel more relaxed and happier in the class, and I guess I would be more active—you know, raising my hand and keeping my head up and looking at the material on the board.

Counselor: Wow. That's super. You really seem to know what you would like and even how you would like to be. Maybe we could figure out how to make this happen?

As illustrated in the case, the counselor was able to employ the "miracle question" to quickly move the client, Aisha, away from a problem focus to a more productive articulation of her goals.

While the miracle question is often used during the initial session, it can also be of value in a subsequent session as a way to ground the client who begins to move away from goals back toward a focus on problems.

FINDING SOLUTIONS

The solution-focused counselor views the client as a competent human being who, while experiencing difficulties and disappointments, has also experienced success and goal achievement. With this perspective, the solution-focused counselor seeks to identify those client resources that can be called on to assist in the current situation, and if effectively configured, will assist the client to move toward his/her preferred future. Two strategies, in particular, have special importance for the solution-focused counselor. They are finding exceptions and goal scaling, both of which are discussed in the next section.

Looking for Exceptions

When working with client data, the solution-focused counselor processes these data through two filters or "screeners." First, the counselor wants to help the client specifically identify what it is that he/she wants to be different in his/her life (i.e., goal setting). Second, the counselor wants to help identify what it will take to make this happen. When looking for these "interventions," the solution-focused counselor believes that the answer can be found within the client and the client's past successes.

Proponents of a solution-focused approach insist that there are *always* times when the problem is less or nonexistent for the client. deJong and Berg (1998) described exceptions as "those occasions in clients' lives when their problems could have occurred but did not—or at least were less severe." These times represent an exception to the current situation and as such, approximate the desired goal state. The counselor seeks to encourage the client to describe these exceptions and to identify what different circumstances exist in that case or what the client did differently. If the exceptions can be reviewed and analyzed, they can provide the materials for the creation of a solution to the presenting concern (Thompson & Rudolph, 2000).

In looking for exceptions, the focus is placed on the who, what, when, and where of exception times rather than focusing on problems. Clients are often questioned about what and how they did it when things were different (deJong & Berg, 1998). Consider the case of Nicole, a third-grade student who was identified by her teacher as being somewhat shy, socially withdrawn, and isolated from her peers.

Counselor: Nicole, can you tell me about a time when you were able to make a friend or to be with someone in a friendly way?

Nicole: Well, Lisa and I are friends. I asked Lisa to play with me when we were at recess and that was fun.

Counselor: Wow, that's super! How did you do that?

Nicole: Do what?

Counselor: Go up to Lisa and ask her to play. I mean, that was special and I was wondering what were you thinking about or what did you do to be able to go up to her and ask her to play?

By helping the child identify what she did and how she did it, the counselor lays a foundation for identifying ways that she could make it happen more often and thus would serve as a "solution" to her current experience of social isolation from her peers.

Throughout this process, the counselor will employ basic communication skills, especially those of paraphrasing and summarizing, to crystallize the elements contributing to this exception. As exceptions are identified, strengths are also uncovered and affirmed (deJong & Berg, 1998). By eliciting and constructing the exceptions to the problem and encouraging the exceptions to occur more often, the counselor invites the client to develop a sense of control over what had seemed to be an insurmountable problem. Let's return to the case of Aisha and observe how the use of fundamental communication skills helped move this client to the conceptualization of "interventions" that could prove effective for moving her toward her goal (see Case Illustration 3.2).

■ ■ ■ ■ ■ ▬▬▬▬▬▬▬▬▬▬▬▬▬▬▬▬▬▬▬▬▬▬▬▬▬▬▬▬▬▬▬▬▬▬▬▬▬

CASE ILLUSTRATION 3.2
AISHA'S EXCEPTIONS

In returning to Aisha (Case Illustration 3.1), we can see how the counselor uses active listening, reflection, encouragement, and questions to identify an exception, affirm the client, encourage Aisha to analyze the exception, and employ these data to formulate a possible "strategy" to move forward.

Counselor: Aisha, I know you say that Mr. Zhang is on your back and always mean to you. Has there ever been a time when you felt he was more positve with you? You know, a time when he called on you and praised you for your response?

Aisha: No. Never!

Counselor: Well, maybe it wasn't perfect like in your "miracle" but was there a time when it was a little better than it is now?

Aisha: Well, when we were discussing different cultures, I brought a story my great-great-grandmother wrote on slavery in North Carolina. Mr. Zhang was really excited. I remembered he wanted me to talk about it and show it to the class. And he said I did a super job and that I should be very proud of my family and the strong women like my Grannie. Boy, that was great.

Counselor: It sounds super. I bet you were really smiling?

Aisha: Yeah, that was a good week. I remember coming in and asking questions about other cultures that we were discussing. I really liked to know more about the Chinese culture and Mr. Zhang actually let me be the class recorder for our group.

Counselor: So Aisha, I can see that Mr. Zhang was really different during that time, but what was it that you were doing differently? How were you acting in class?

Aisha: Well, I liked what we were talking about . . . so I guess I was paying attention.

Counselor: That's great, but if I were in the class, how would I know you were paying attention?

Aisha: Well, I was looking up to the front and watching Mr. Zhang and I was raising my hand when he asked a question, and when I answered I really spoke loudly . . . I know sometimes I put my head down and mumble.

Counselor: Wow! You did some really neat things, Aisha. I wonder what would happen if we tried a little experiment? I wonder what would happen if tomorrow when you went into class, if you made sure you looked at Mr. Zhang? Also, when you answered a question, maybe you could keep your head up and speak loudly like you did in the past? I wonder if you did, what would Mr. Zhang do?

Coping questions.   There are times when a client fails to realize that he/she has experienced exceptions or understands that he/she possesses the resources needed to activate solutions. In these situations, the solution-focused counselor may employ *coping questions.*

An example of the use of a coping question was presented in the *Harvard Medical Health Letter* (2006). The case was of a woman with agoraphobia who was afraid to leave her house. However, the client shared that she had attended the funeral of an aunt whom she loved. The therapist expressed admiration and curiosity about how she coped with her intense anxiety.

While the client sees this event as one reflecting her anxiety (her problem), the therapist attempts to reframe the experience as one demonstrating exception. In a case such as this, the therapist praises the client for coping and attempts to identify the specific resources called on that allowed for this successful coping: "I can hear how difficult it was for you to get ready and leave the house to attend the services for your aunt . . . but somehow you did. That's amazing. How were you able to do that?" (That is, how did you cope?)

The effective use of coping questions and seeking exceptions provides the counselor the opportunity to commend the client on his/her strengths and true abilities (Davis & Osborn, 2000). This process not only unearths client resources but allows him/her to realize that the problems he/she is encountering have been and can be resolved.

Goal Scaling

A counselor employing a solution-focused orienting framework will see the client as most likely stuck because he/she is having trouble seeing the issue as solvable. As such, the counselor will attempt to employ strategies that help the client see things in ways that make change more likely to happen. One of these strategies is the use of goal scaling. Miller (1997) described these scaling questions as "the work horses of solution-focused therapy because they are frequently asked . . . to achieve a variety of therapeutic ends" (p. 12).

Goal scaling and scaling questions are used to help the client place his/her current experience in relationship to the desired goal. Scaling is a process by which the counselor reiterates a specific goal, and then having descriptively and concretely presented this goal at the far end of the scale (for example, at 10 on a 10-point scale), asks the client to identify where he/she feels presently in relationship to that goal (see Figure 3.1).

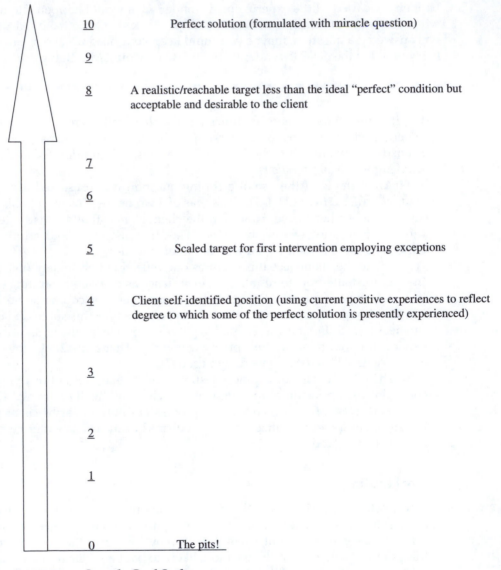

10   Perfect solution (formulated with miracle question)

9

8   A realistic/reachable target less than the ideal "perfect" condition but acceptable and desirable to the client

7

6

5   Scaled target for first intervention employing exceptions

4   Client self-identified position (using current positive experiences to reflect degree to which some of the perfect solution is presently experienced)

3

2

1

0   The pits!

FIGURE 3.1   **Sample Goal Scale**

Using visual aids such as a picture of a scale line or large thermometer (for children), the counselor will ask the client to place his/her current experience on the scale in relation to the desired ideal state. Once the client has marked on the scale, he/she will be asked to identify what he/she thinks it would take to move one or two steps up the scale toward the ideal. For example, a client who has a self-identified placement of 3 may be asked: "What would it look like if you were at a 4 or a 5? What do you think you would have to do to be at 4 or 5?" These questions are intended to encourage the client to see that movement is possible if taken in small steps, and with this refocusing on a manageable goal, the client will be more able to identify those behaviors and strategies that he/she has and can employ to make this movement.

Davis and Osborn (2000) believe that scaling questions are especially useful because they:

- quantify thoughts, motivation, and attitudes to aid client and therapist understanding;
- aid the client in his/her ability to explain challenging attitudes and feelings;
- help define the steps important to reaching goals and clarify the actual goals;
- assess progress and what needs to happen for progress to continue;
- develop an awareness that change is happening and a hopeful awareness that problems are subsiding; and
- aid in relationship assessment (e.g., students can be asked about how family members would answer the question so that a comparison is possible).

Remember, in establishing a scale, the counselor is not concerned with creating an "absolute" scale or even interrater reliability (i.e., client and counselor agreement). The task is simply to develop reference points against which the counselor and client can begin to strategize steps to facilitate client movement from this base point toward the ultimate goal.

If the circumstances presented have multiple parts or the client presents with multiple concerns, separate scales would be made for each concern or elements of a concern. For example, let's assume that a client presents with a concern about his/her finances, current career, and the failure to have a meaningful, intimate relationship. In dialogue with the counselor, the client prioritizes his/her goals to : (1) have a zero credit card balance, (2) have an updated resume, and (3) go on a date. In this case the counselor would help the client develop separate goal scales for each of the goals.

The Solution-Focused Counselor Reflecting "In" and "On" Practice

As described in the previous sections, solution-focused therapy is an approach based on solution-building rather than problem identification. It explores current resources and future hopes rather than present problems and past causes. As the

TABLE 3.2   Tasks for Initial Session(s)

TARGETS FOR INITIAL SESSION(S)	STRATEGIES
Identify client's desired outcome of the counseling process.	Ask specifically how the client might feel differently if this counseling session were successful.
Identify impact on day-to-day life experience if client achieves desired goals.	Employ the miracle questions. If tonight while you were asleep a miracle happened and it resolved all the problems that bring you here, what would you be noticing differently tomorrow?
Identify exceptions to the problems experienced. When in the past has the client experienced some of the desired goals and how did he/she do that?	After reiterating the ideal outcome/goal, ask the client when some of this goal has been experienced in the past . . . even slightly. Maybe it's a part of the goal or the entire goal to a lesser degree.
Identify what one small step would look like and what it would take to move in that direction.	Scaling. Placing the client's current experience of the goal on a scale . . . invite the client to describe what a small step in the direction of the ultimate goal would be like and what it would take to make that move.

practice of solution-focused therapy has developed, the problem has come to play a lesser and lesser part in the interviewing process (George, Iveson, & Ratner, 1999), to the extent that it might not even be known. Iveson (2002) noted that in solution focus, attention is given to developing a picture of the solution and discovering the resources to achieve it, and that this begins even during the initial contact. Table 3.2 depicts some of the tasks that a solution-focused counselor may seek to accomplish during the initial contact. Each of these points serve as a focal point for the solution-focused counselor as he/she prepares for an upcoming intake session in a process of reflection "on" practice.

The difficult part for many counselors, especially those trained in traditional problem-focused strategies, is to see the interaction as one focusing on hopes, goals, and successes. This directive to seek goals and solutions rather than to engage in elaborate analyses of problems and their history of development can be experienced as a difficult directive to embrace and employ. And yet, it is this construct of valuing a solution that drives this orienting framework.

Iveson (2002) provided a rather simple schemata of this guiding framework. It is presented in slightly modified form in Figure 3.2. Each of the components identified in the flow chart serve as minigoals and markers of progress identified by the solution-focused counselor as he/she reflects "on" practice. As depicted in this flow chart, the anticipation is that the session will start with a client entering with a sense of some preferred future state and hope in achieving. With that as the starting point, the solution-focused counselor will attempt to assist the client to fully develop and articulate that preferred future and times when some of this goal has been experienced. Once an experiential base has been identified, the counselor

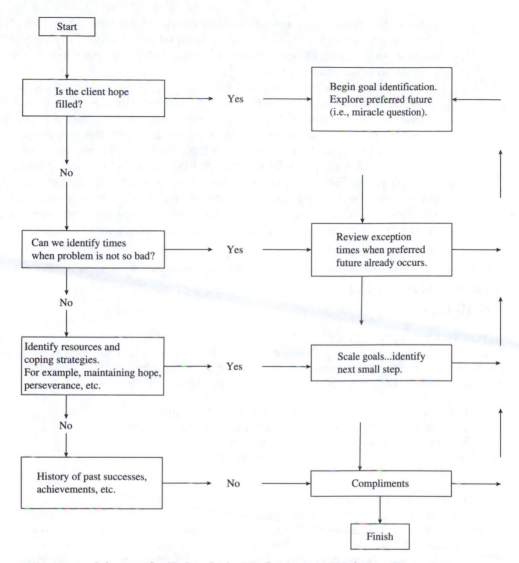

FIGURE 3.2   Schemata for "In" and "On" Reflections with Solution-Focused Framework

will assist the client in analyzing this exception to his/her current difficulty so that the skills, the attitudes, and the conditions surrounding that exception may be recalled and employed in the current situation. In order to establish the most hopeful base for the work to be done, the ideal state or preferred future will be scaled with the client investing energy to move one or two steps up the scale in order to experience success and bring his/her experience more in line with the preferred future. In subsequent sessions, identification of movement along the goal scale will take center stage. As such, the counselor, in subsequent sessions, may open with a questions such as "What is better since last we met?" Or, "How have you experienced your desired state over the course of the time away from session?" These improvements serve as the data from which to more fully understand the client's resources and to encourage continued utilization of these resources for the promotion of additional gains.

This process of reflecting "on" and adjusting by way of reflecting "in" practice is highlighted in this chapter's final case illustration—the case of Kathleen. It is suggested that prior to reading this case you review the underlying philosophical framework (assumptions and values) employed by a solution-focused counselor, along with the specific processes that develop from this orientation. These values, assumptions, processes, and strategies will then come to life as you read the case of Kathleen (Case Illustration 3.3). Further, as you will note, there are counselor's reflections identified prior to each counselor response. It may be helpful to your own assimilation of the solution-focused orienting framework for you to attempt to tie the counselor's reflections and responses to the solution-focused philosophy, assumption, and strategies.

■ ■ ■ ■ ■ ▬▬▬▬▬▬▬▬▬▬▬▬▬▬▬▬▬▬▬▬▬▬▬▬▬

CASE ILLUSTRATION 3.3
KATHLEEN

REFLECTIONS "ON" PRACTICE
Kathleen called to set up an appointment, noting that she wanted to come in and work on her problem with anger. When preparing for the initial session, the solution-focused counselor, **reflecting "on" practice,** established the following as the goals for the session.

1. To establish a working collaborative alliance with the client.
2. To establish a climate that is hopeful and productive for change.
3. To clarify, at least initially, goals for counseling.
4. To begin to uncover the client's strengths and resources.
5. To set homework.

REFLECTIONS "IN" PRACTICE
The work actually began with the initial phone call. Often, clients are unsure about the potential benefit of counseling or even the possibility of experiencing change. In addition, it is not unusual for the client to present self as defective, needing to change. The solution-focused counselor believes that the client need not change. Instead, the solution-focused counselor believes that what is helpful is for the client to reconsider choices in his/her interactions. As such, the counselor is sensitive to any evidence that the client is feeling defective and hopeless.

Kathleen: Well, I really need to see someone. I'm pretty screwed up and out of control.

Counselor: Well Kathleen, you certainly are in control at this moment and making a choice to do something about your current experiences. That seems pretty hopeful to me!

(Counselor is affirming, but also highlighting the resources the client has called on to enable her to take a step toward her goals.)

Kathleen: Thanks, but I don't know if I can do this—I've been like this all my life.

Counselor: Do you mean that every minute, every day, you're angry?

(Counselor asking for clarification but also gently challenging the client to look for exception.)

Kathleen: No . . . I know that was extreme. Actually, I'm pretty laid back a lot of the time, but it seems like I'm flipping out a lot.

Counselor: That's super! Not that you flip out sometimes, but that it is sometimes—not all the time. When we get together, it may be useful to look at those times when you don't flip out . . . that sounds like the way you want to respond?

(Counselor being encouraging, engaging client as collaborator—using client words and beginning to ground the client in goal and solution focus.)

Kathleen: Absolutely . . . I just get frustrated I'm not always calm.

Counselor: Well, Kathleen, thank you. You really do have a sense of what you want and the fact that you've experienced that in the past can be very useful. I look forward to meeting with you next Thursday.

(Counselor conveying a sense of hope and direction.)

Kathleen: Yeah, me too, I wasn't sure but I think this will be good.

Counselor: That's great . . . me too! Kathleen, I was thinking since you mentioned that there are times when you are calm and "laid back," maybe it would useful if during the time before we meet, you could notice if you experience any times when you are more or less "laid back" or any other changes that may take place since this telephone conversation.

(Counselor redirecting client to look for movement toward goal.)

DURING THE INITIAL SESSION

Counselor: Well, Kathleen, did you notice any changes, any differences, since our telephone conversation?

(Counselor, focusing on goals/forward view and small changes.)

Kathleen: Well, after our conversation, I felt happy I had called and actually I felt pretty encouraged, but that was short lived and I freaked out shortly thereafter. I'm a mess.

Counselor: I'm sure it feels "messy" at times and when you have expectations it can be discouraging when these don't come through. But if I understood you, you did feel hopeful when you felt as if we would focus on the times when you weren't "freaking out" (*using client language*). Kathleen, what is it you would like to see happen as a result of you coming here today (*goal focus*)?

(Counselor recognizes that the client is constructing herself as a problem and seeing this as a long-standing deficit. Counselor invites client to refocus toward goal setting.)

(continued)

Kathleen: I would be thrilled if I could just feel a little like I did when we spoke on the phone. You know, thinking that things could be better.

Counselor: So, one goal for our session would be to help you reclaim that hopeful feeling and expectation that things can change in the direction you would like, is that correct?

(Joining the client where she is and embracing her goal.)

Kathleen: Yes, that would be great!

Counselor: Well, it would help me if we could talk a little about what that would look like? What would it look like if change occurred and things were as you really wished them to be?

(Counselor is attempting to make the goal positive, concrete.)

Kathleen: Well, first of all I won't freak out anymore! I mean, I wouldn't lose my cool.

Counselor: Okay, but I'm wondering if you weren't freaking out or losing your cool, what would you be doing instead?

(Counselor using client words, but encouraging a reframing of the goal as a positive one rather than a negative.)

Kathleen: Well, when things weren't going my way I would just take a breath and remind myself that I did the best I could and then move on.

Counselor: That's great, so rather than freaking out, you would take a breath and after accepting things as they are move on?

(Counselor using a reflection to check for accuracy of understanding as well as to join client in "goal.")

Counselor: Kathleen, I wonder what else it would be like for you if things were the way you hoped they would be. Kathleen, I would like you to try something that I have found helpful. Imagine that you go home and tonight you go to bed but during the night a miracle happens so that when you wake in the morning you no longer had this problem that you have been discussing. Now you didn't know that a miracle had occurred, so what would you notice that was different?

(Counselor posing miracle question to more fully develop the client's goal.)

Kathleen: Well, things would be better. I'd be calm.

Counselor: That's a good start, but maybe we could develop it. So what would you be seeing or doing in addition to feeling calm?

(feeling the presentation is a bit vague, counselor accepts it as the client's goal, inviting clarification and development.)

Kathleen: Well, first I wouldn't be rushing around worried that I was going to be late for work and the fact that my husband left his coffee cup on the counter and dishes were in the sink wouldn't throw me into a rage.

Counselor: That's a pretty clear description. I wonder, what do you think others, like your husband, might say would be different?

(Counselor using encouragement and genuine praise.)

Kathleen: He would notice that I just put his dishes into the dishwasher without a sarcastic comment and that I wasn't slamming the cabinet doors and that I wasn't yelling.

Counselor: So he would notice that things were different, like the way you handled the dishes and cabinets . . . that's clear . . . but I wonder what would he say you were doing instead of yelling or being sarcastic and slamming doors?

(Counselor helping client to describe goals in positive terms.)

Kathleen: Well, he would say that I was simply reminding him that I appreciate when he places his dishes in the dishwasher and probably he would say, I just closed the cabinet and spoke to him in a conversational tone.

Counselor: That's really clear to me. Would this be what you mean when you say you would like to stop "freaking out"?

Kathleen: Yeah, I'd like to be calm inside, as well as sound, and look calm outside—even when I wanted to assert myself.

Counselor: Well, Kathleen, that is a pretty clear goal. That sounds like a really good start.

(Counselor offers genuine compliment.)

So, let's imagine we were creating a goal line or scale that went from 0 to 10. At 10, that would be the ideal, we would see that no matter what is happening in the kitchen you go in, you remain calm, place things in the dishwasher, and close doors, and yet express your desire for your husband to do the same thing and you do that in a firm, yet calm, conversational tone. Where on this scale would you see yourself presently?

(Counselor using goal scaling.)

Kathleen: I've been horrible. I guess I'd say at a 2 or 3 . . . lots of yelling and sarcasm and banging of doors.

Counselor: So, you see yourself at a 2 or 3, yelling sometimes and banging doors. What would it look like if you were at a 4 or 5?

(Counselor redirects client from negative self-evaluation and blaming to future by looking up the scale and establishing a possible real target for change—a small step!)

Kathleen: Well, maybe I would be sarcastic but I wouldn't sound like a wild woman yelling. I would just have a conversational tone.

Counselor: Okay, so a step in the desired direction would be when you can address your husband in a conversational tone rather than in a loud, yelling tone.

(continued)

Have you ever been able to do that?

(Counselor checking resources/looking for exceptions.)

Kathleen: Yes sometimes, or at least I've had mornings when I don't yell—even if I'm sarcastic about the dishes or bang a door or two.

Counselor: Really, that's great. When was the most recent time you were able to do that?

(Counselor using a tacting lead to help client reflect on an exception that can be analyzed.)

Kathleen: Actually, it's funny . . . it was last Saturday morning. I remember this 'cause it was our anniversary. I came down and he was already awake. He made pancakes as a surprise and the kitchen was a disaster, but I just cleaned up, thanked him for the surprise, though I did suggest that perhaps a maid would have been a great anniversary gift, but I kissed him and we had a great day!

Counselor: Wow, that's fantastic. How did you do that?

(Counselor beginning an analysis of the exception and identification of client resources.)

Kathleen: How did I do it?

Counselor: Yes, I mean, here you present a pretty clear goal of how you would like it to be and now you tell me that you actually have experienced that kind of morning. It might be helpful if we could figure out how you did it. What did you do—what choices did you make—to create this scenario?

Kathleen: Well, first of all, I was excited when I came to breakfast. I mean it was Saturday and our anniversary and Tom (my husband) let me sleep in. So I guess I started my day being relaxed, not rushing. And when I saw the mess I also saw the pancakes and his goofy expression and I thought, "He's a good guy . . . he loves me . . . he's just a klutz!"

Counselor: And that's all it took? To start your morning relaxed and then saying to yourself, "He's a good guy . . . just a klutz!"

Kathleen: Well, I think it helped me realize he wasn't doing these things to irk me, or stick it to me. I just figured that the things I think are messy and get me all worked up, just don't bother him. So, I guess that's why I wasn't angry.

Counselor: So, in addition to you simply saying to yourself "he's a good guy," you also reminded yourself he wasn't trying to make your life miserable but that he simply doesn't see the mess as you do?

Kathleen: I think so!

Counselor: Kathleen, it seems to me that this is something that if we could repeat or hold on to, that is, the thought that he loves you and simply has a different view on messiness, that it may help you to remain calmer even when asking him to help with clean up?

Kathleen: Yeah, that would be nice.

Counselor:

(In ending the session the counselor poses a formula first session task.)

Your memory of this exception to how things have been has been very helpful. I was wondering if in the time between now and when we meet next week if you would just observe what is going on with you and your life that you would like to see continue, and then, when we get together we can look at this as a part of your goals for our work together.

Kathleen: Sure, but you know I think I'm going to try to keep that thought in mind about Tom loving me . . . the big klutz!

Counselor: Wow, that's great. Great idea. You are really ready to get moving on this! So how about placing a little reminder next to your nightstand that maybe you would see first thing in the morning and it would help you to remember to go slow, stay relaxed, and remember that regardless of the state of the kitchen Tom loves you and he is a good guy!

Kathleen: He gave me the sweetest anniversary card that's right there . . . that should do it! But I can't promise you anything, but I'll try.

Counselor: No need to promise. You've already shown that you are willing to try and I appreciate that.

Before moving on to another operational framework, it may be useful for you to try Exercise 3.1, which provides you with an opportunity to step into a solution-focused schema as you reflect "on" and "in" a counseling session.

EXERCISE 3.1

I DON'T WANT TO BE HERE!

Context: The case involves an 8th grade student who was "dragged" into counseling by his mother. The initial presentation (by mom) was, "Here I've done everything I can—you fix him!" Bill (the student), sat there, arms crossed, frown on face, firmly stating, "I don't want to be here!"

Directions: With a colleague/classmate, discuss the following:

1. What two goals would a solution-focused counselor have for this initial encounter?
2. When reviewing Bill's initial comment we might be able to anticipate that a counselor operating from a more traditional problem-focused orientation might say something like, "I can see you are unhappy, why don't you tell me what the problem is between you and mom?" How would a solution-focused counselor respond to Bill's exclamation?
3. Where would the solution-focused counselor most likely attempt to engage the client? (Hint: Join the client in his goal?)

4. Given Bill's mom's comment, how would a solution-focused counselor reframe the issues in order to help empower the client and assist him to feel hopeful? (Hint: Is *he* broke?)
5. Working with a classmate or colleague, engage in a role play with the goal to move this client from a resistant, passive posture, to become active in the articulation of a terminal goal for this session, scaling that goal, and planning a strategy to move one step toward that goal.

REFERENCES

Berg, I.K. & DeJong, P. (1996). Solution-building conversations: Co-constructing a sense of competence with clients. *Families in Society: The Journal of Contemporary Human Services*, 77, 376–391.

Berg, I.K. & Miller, S.D. (1992). *Working with the problem drinker: A solution-focused approach*. New York: W.W. Norton.

Davis, T.E. & Osborn, C.J. (2000). The solution-focused school: An exceptional Model. NASSP Bulleting, 83, (603), 40–46.

deJong, P. & Berg, I.K. (1998*). Interviewing for solutions*. Pacific Grove, CA: Brooks/Cole Publishing Company.

deJong, P. & Miller, S.D. (1995). How to Interview for Client's Strengths. *Social Work*, 40(6), 729–736.

de Shazer, S. (1988). *Clues: Investigating solutions in brief therapy*. New York: W.W. Norton.

George, E., Iveson, C., & Ratner, H. (1999). *Problem to solution: Brief therapy with individuals and families*. London: B.T. Press.

Harvard Mental Health Letter. (2006). Solution-focused therapy. *Harvard Mental Health Letter*, 23(3), 4–5.

Iveson, C. (2002). Solution-focused brief therapy. *Advances in Psychiatric Treatment*, 8, 149–156.

Jacob, F. (2001). *Solution-focused recovery from eating distress*. London: B.T. Press.

Miller, G. (1997). Systems and solutions: The discourses of brief therapy. *Contemporary Family Therapy*, 19, 5–22.

Miller, S., Hubble, M., & Duncan, B. (Eds.). (1996). *Handbook of solution-focused brief therapy*. San Francisco, CA: Jossey-Bass.

O'Connell, B. (1998). *Solution-focused therapy*. Thousand Oaks, CA: Sage Publications.

Rosenbaum, R., Hoyt, M., & Talmon, M. (1990). The challenge of single session therapies: Creating pivotal moments. In R. Wells & V. Gianetti (Eds.), *The handbook of brief therapies*. New York: Plenum.

Sharry, J. (2001) *Solution focused groupwork*. London: Sage.

Sklare, G. (1997). *Brief counseling works: A solution-focused approach for school counselors*. Thousand Oaks, CA: Corwin Press, Inc.

Thompson, C. & Rudolph, L. (2000). *Counseling children* (5th ed.). Belmont, CA: Wadsworth/Thomson Learning.

White, M. (1995). *Re-authoring lives: Interviews and essays*. Adelaide: Dulwich Centre Publications.

White, M. & Epston, D. (1990). *Narrative means to therapeutic ends*. New York: W.W. Norton.

SUGGESTED RESOURCES

deJong, P. & Berg, I.K. (1998*). Interviewing for solutions*. Pacific Grove, CA: Brooks/Cole Publishing Company.

Guterman, J.T. (2006). *Mastering the art of solution-focused counseling*. Alexandria, VA: American Counseling Association.

Miller, S., Hubble, M., & Duncan, B. (Eds.). (1996). *Handbook of solution-focused brief therapy*. San Francisco, CA: Jossey-Bass.

Murphy, J.J. (1997). *Solution-focused counseling in middle and high schools*. Alexandria, VA: American Counseling Association.

O'Connell, B. (1998). *Solution-focused therapy.* Thousand Oaks, CA: Sage Publications.

CHAPTER 4

BEHAVIORAL-ORIENTING
FRAMEWORK

Reward and punishment systems have been used throughout recorded history, from child rearing to the criminal justice system, all in an attempt to influence behavior. Behaviorism as a model for therapy appeared in the 1950s with the early work of Skinner (1953), Wolpe (1958), and Eysenck (1958). Since that time, behavioral techniques have been demonstrated to be effective for depression (Beck, Rush, Shaw, & Emery, 1979; Martell, Addis, & Jacobson, 2001), anxiety disorders (Wolpe, 1981), obsessive-compulsive disorder (Foa, Steketee, & Oazrow, 1985), alcohol dependence, eating disorders (e.g., anorexia nervosa or bulimia nervosa), hyperventilation, attention-deficit/hyperactivity disorder, and conduct problems.

The current chapter provides a look inside the minds and practices of counselors who employ a behavioral-orienting framework to guide their reflections "on" and "in" practice. The fundamentals of a behavioral-orienting schema along with detailed illustrations of two specific forms of behavioral interventions will be presented. The emphasis of the chapter is on the way a counselor employing a behavioral-orienting framework reflects "on" and "in" practice. Those seeking a fuller explication of the history, rationale, and research supporting a behavioral model are referred to the additional resources cited at the end of this chapter.

The goal for this chapter is to provide the reader with the opportunity to experience the impact that assuming a behavioral-orienting framework has on the counselor's processing of client information and the resulting formation and implementation of intervention strategies. Specifically, after reading this chapter, you will be able to:

- describe the basic tenets of a behavioral model of counseling;
- explain how the utilization of constructs such as operationalized goals, functional behavioral analysis, and operant and respondent conditioning guide the counselor's reflection on and in practice and result in the creation and implementation of specific intervention strategies; and
- employ a behavioral-orienting framework to respond to simulated case material.

THE PHILOSOPHICAL UNDERPINNINGS
OF BEHAVIORAL THEORY

Behavior therapy, an approach that is grounded in the philosophy of behaviorism, emphasizes the observation, analyses, and focus on overt behavior, without discussion of affect or internal mental states. Behavioral therapy is based on the premise that specific, observable, maladaptive, or self-destructive behaviors can be modified by learning new, more appropriate behaviors to replace them. The strategies that emerge from this orientation are rooted in learning theory and the laboratories of Ivan Pavlov's (1960) classical conditioning and the work of B. F. Skinner (1953). Counselors with a behavioral-orienting framework employ the following philosophical assumptions as lenses through which to process client information.

Behaviorism Is Naturalistic

A fundamental assumption undergirding a behavioral orientation is that everything, including all human behavior, can be explained in terms of natural laws. The behavioral model does not concern itself with the existence of "soul," "psyche," or "mind" but targets behavior and a brain that responds to stimuli. Behavioral therapy, or behavior modification, is based on the assumption that emotional problems, like any behavior, are learned in response to the unique conditions of a person's environment and as such, can be unlearned. This principal guides the counselor to target his or her efforts in session to the clarification of goals, the collection and analyses of data that result in the creation of interventions. The entire process is approached with the mindset of a researcher.

Working collaboratively with the client, the counselor attempts to develop hypotheses about those factors maintaining the undesired behavior or elements that need to be present in order to develop the desired behavior. These hypotheses are then tested by way of the introduction of an intervention strategy, and data are collected to assess the impact of these interventions.

Humans as Conditioned Beings

While accepting genetics and the role they play, individual differences are believed to be a reflection of differences in experiences. The assumption is that human behavior is the product of our conditioning. This perspective posits that humans simply react to stimuli and our behavior is best understood as a function of the associations we have made, along with the reinforcement contingencies we have experienced. For example, what we deem as socially appropriate behaviors, including respecting the personal space of another person, raising one's hand in school to seek recognition prior to speaking out, and even employing verbal, rather than physical, means to resolve conflicts, are all the results of our social training. Thus, a client presenting with what has been labeled as inappropriate or dysfunctional behavior is simply manifesting a behavior—learned like any other behavior—and not exhibiting a symptom of an underlying disease.

Behavior Therapy—Data Driven

Counselors operating with a behavioral frame of reference assume that client behavior is functional and responsive to stimuli or in response to a history of consequential learning. As such, any attempt to modify that behavior must start with an understanding of the nature and context of this behavior. Behavioral therapy is data-driven. Interventions that are created are in response to the data, which demonstrates the what, when, and why of the current behavior of real concern (BORC).

Consider the situation in which a student is referred to the counseling office because he "refused to complete his desk work." The counselor with a behavioral-orienting framework will want to more fully understand the context of this behavior. The counselor will systematically observe the student within the context of the classroom and allow that data to give shape to an intervention plan. For example, let's assume that the student who is failing to complete desk work has severe attention-deficit/hyperactivity disorder (ADHD) and is seated next to the window that overlooks an active construction site. The data collected suggests that the amount of time on-task is related to the amount of activity going on at the construction site. With these data as the basis, the intervention strategy may be to simply move the student away from window and ease of visual distraction. Contrast this to the situation in which data reveal that the student's "refusal to complete the desk work" resulted in the teacher approaching his desk, bending down to eye level and spending up to two minutes encouraging the student to do his work. Further observation reveals that these are the only times students receive such individualized and extensive teacher attention. In this context, the failure to complete desk work appears to be a behavior that is in fact reinforced by way of teacher attentiveness. The intervention that is developed as a result of these data may include both extinction processes as well as differentially reinforcing the student, with teacher attention, only when the student is doing seat work and ignoring when not.

Behaviorism Moves from Understanding to Controlling

Those employing a behavioral-orienting framework seek not merely to understand a client's concern or stimulate insight. Rather the intent is to understand, predict, and control this behavior. The approach to intervention planning and implementation is somewhat experimental. That is, baseline data are collected by way of systematic observations, variables are then manipulated, and impact is observed. The manipulation of antecedent conditions and consequences are the experimental interventions introduced in an attempt to control the BORC. Consider the following brief exchange between a counselor and a client experiencing intrusive, anxiety-provoking thoughts.

Liz: It is amazing when I get into the image, I can almost smell the ocean and feel the sun . . . and I'm so relaxed!

Counselor: Well Liz, you really have a super ability to create that image and clearly it helps you to relax.

Liz: I love our beach house and the beach . . . so it's easy.

Counselor: Okay, Liz . . . so let's try this mini-experiment. Looking at your data it appears that your anxiety is generally around a 4 or 5 when you are at department meetings and a 7 or 8 when you do the presentations. So let's start with the department meetings. Are there any meetings coming up this week?

Liz: Every week!! We have one Monday, Wednesday, and Friday.

Counselor: Great! So let's try something. Prior to going into your meeting, could you take a couple of minutes, let's say three, to practice your relaxation breathing and get into your beach image? Then when you go into the meeting and find that your anxiety is up around 4 or 5 on your scale . . . how about trying to take one deep cleansing breath and as you breathe out, close your eyes just for a moment, and see yourself on the beach?

Liz: But what happens if I can't get the image back or stay on it when I'm in the meeting?

Counselor: Well, remember I said this was a mini-experiment. Whatever happens will be useful information and we can look at it and then adjust our plans in response to it. How's that sound?

Liz: Okay, I'm game!!

The counselor in the above scenario is not only inviting the client to approach the utilization of the intervention as a reflective researcher but the goal of the intervention is one of control—that is, controlling the client's anxiety. As will become evident in our discussion of intervention strategies, the techniques employed by the behavioral counselor are done with one purpose in mind—to change, modify, and control the client's behavior.

Dysfunctional Behavior—Contextually Defined

If all behavior is the result of learning, then qualitative distinction between normal and abnormal behavior is inappropriate. The behavioral model views the appropriateness of a particular behavior as a function of its adaptive quality and functionality within a particular context. For example, while a person living in New York City who decided to hunt down members of a competing advertising firm, kill them, and take and mount their heads as trophies in his game room would clearly be considered disturbed, that same behavior performed in a headhunter culture would be praised and prized. In each case, the behavior is identified as adjusted (i.e., normal) or maladjusted as a function of the context within which it is applied. From the behavioral frame of reference, behaviors are situation-adaptive or maladaptive.

The implications of this position are that there is no discontinuity between behavior we label healthy and that which we term pathological. The same principles that explain the formation and operation of so-called healthy behavior are those that have created and maintained that which we deem as pathological. Maladaptive behavior, like adaptive behavior, is learned (Chambless & Goldstein, 1982), and while not necessarily appearing so on first glance, does serve some purpose for the client.

The behavioral counselor attempts to identify the elements within the client's context that support the functionality of the BORC and either helps the client remove these elements and/or develop other, more effective ways of functioning within that context. The focus of the counseling is on the maladaptive behavior, not possible underlying causes. The goal for the counseling is to change this behavior rather than simply assist the client to gain insight or experience a catharsis.

FUNDAMENTALS OF REFLECTING "ON" (BEHAVIORAL) PRACTICE

While there are a number of specific techniques that will be discussed in the next section of this chapter, if we are to think like an expert with a behavioral-orienting framework, we must understand the fundamental paradigm that guides a behavioral counselor when reflecting "on" and operating "in" practice. Figure 4.1 provides a schematic of the steps considered and employed by counselors operating from a behavioral-orienting framework. Because of the importance of each of these steps in shaping the reflection "on" and "in" practice for the counselor with a behavioral orientation, they will be discussed in detail.

Developing a Working Alliance

Behavioral counselors utilize the same relationship and communication skills employed by all effective counselors. Behavioral counselors demonstrate warmth, acceptance, genuineness, and unconditional positive regard for their clients.

The initial session in behaviorally oriented counseling targets not only the explanation of the basic tenets of behavioral counseling but also the development of a working alliance. This alliance is essential in that it creates a condition in which accurate data are collected and interventions are employed (e.g., Kohlenberg & Tsai, 1991). Clients in behavioral counseling are expected to disclose important information as well as share their expertise (about themselves) to help shape interventions. The behavioral counselor emphasizes the client's role in interpreting all advice and encourages the client to view all interventions as that which should be explored and tested for effectiveness.

Therefore, while a behavioral counselor is data and technique driven, he/she values the need to adapt all techniques to the uniqueness of the client and the client's situation. The exchange found in Case Illustration 4.1 clearly depicts both

Identify who is to be involved in assessment and intervention

Identify the BORC (behavior of real concern)

Review history and context

Data collection–Functional-behavioral analysis

Contract–Set goals

Develop/implement intervention strategies to facilitate change

Monitor and adjust

Plan for maintenance and relapse prevention

FIGURE 4.1   **Behavioral-Orienting Framework: Guiding steps to reflection "on" practice.**

the need for the establishment of a working alliance and the value of the client's input into intervention formulation.

Identifying the BORC

During the initial session, the counselor operating from a behavioral-orienting framework will want to take a client history and identify the problem that the client is bringing to counseling. The counselor will employ basic communication skills to assist the client in describing his/her BORC. For those operating with a behavioral-orienting framework, the key to this initial exchange is the desire to assist the client in presenting the concern in specific, concrete, and measurable form as possible. Exercise 4.1 provides both an example of this reframing of a

■ ■ ■ ■ ■ ▬▬▬▬▬▬▬▬▬▬▬▬▬▬

CASE ILLUSTRATION 4.1

HOWARD—CONCERNED ABOUT PREMATURE EJACULATION

Howard: . . . . and I've tried things like distracting myself during intercourse, you know, thinking about the names of the Pittsburgh Pirates, but it doesn't work. I still get too excited too fast and it's frustrating.

Counselor: I'm sure it has been frustrating. There are a number of other techniques that have been helpful to others and that we may want to consider and even experiment with.

Howard: Such as . . .?

Counselor: Well, one technique, is the "stop and start" method. The idea here is that often the premature response is a result of hypersensitivity and difficulty in controlling your response. So, in this technique you literally train yourself to control the response by engaging in sexual stimulation until you recognize that you are about to ejaculate. You need to stop the stimulation for about 30 seconds and then you can resume. You would want to do this sequence of stop and start until ejaculation is desired, the final time allowing the stimulation to continue until ejaculation occurs.

Howard: I don't think that would work, that may frustrate my wife.

Counselor: Well, some men have used this technique, using self-stimulation.

Howard: Ah . . . I'm not into masturbation.

Counselor: Okay, there are other strategies we could try, if you think you would be okay trying them. For example, there is another technique that seems to have good results—a technique called the "squeeze" method. If you think your wife would be okay with this strategy it involves becoming sexually stimulated to the point of near ejaculation, and at that point, either you or your wife simply squeeze the end of the penis for several seconds, withholding future sexual stimulation for about 30 seconds, before resuming stimulation. Repeating this process will help you learn to engage with your wife while at the same time learning to stop/relax before continuing to ejaculation.

Howard: You know we tried something like that before but I guess we didn't stick with it. So I think Joan would be fine trying it. I'm just not sure if it is going to work.

Counselor: As we said, these are all "mini-experiments." You can try it and we can discuss what happened and what needs to be done to fine tune it in the future.

BORC as well as an opportunity to practice "operationalizing" typical presenting complaints. Remember the focus is on translating the presenting complaint into a concrete, observable, and measurable format.

■ ■ ■ ■ ■

EXERCISE 4.1

DEVELOPING OPERATIONALIZED DEFINITIONS

Directions: Below you will find a number of "typical" presenting complaints. Your task is to translate them into concrete, observable, and measurable definitions. It is helpful to share your operationalized definitions with a classmate or colleague as a way of checking the degree to which the concerned, as redefined, could be observed and measured.

Presenting Concern	**Operationalized Definition**
(Sample 1) Ramon is disruptive in class.	During class-challenge rounds, Ramon calls out answers without first raising his hand and waiting to be recognized.
(Sample 2) Trish is mean.	During recess, when classmates refuse to let Trish join in the game, she hits them on the head and runs.

Dan is hyperactive.

Tina has a drinking problem.

Louise has difficulty with anger.

Jose is self-destructive.

Review History and Context

In addition to developing an operational definition of the presenting concern, the behavioral counselor will take a client history in an attempt to identify antecedent stimuli that may be eliciting the behavior under consideration, as well as any consequential elements that may come into play in supporting the BORC. The counselor uses the history taking to assist the client in recognizing the development of the BORC and the realization that just as the BORC is a learned pattern, it can be unlearned or alternatives to it can be learned. This awareness facilitates the development of a collaborative and hope-filled relationship.

Data Collection—Functional Behavioral Analysis

Perhaps one of the most important steps for a counselor with a behavioral orientation is the gathering of data that depicts the conditions eliciting and/or maintaining the BORC. The behavioral counselor assumes that counseling will not be effective unless the behaviors to be changed are understood as they occur within a specific context. The behavioral counselor wants accurate understanding of the client's problems, the conditions, or context of their occurrence and the client's goals, before interventions are developed and employed. An in-depth understanding of the

BORC is acquired through a systematic process of data collection, called a functional behavioral assessment. While there are a number of different strategies that can be employed in collecting these data, one approach is to have the client collect information on those times when the BORC is exhibited. Specifically, the client records the appearance of the BORC, along with data reflecting the antecedent conditions that preceded the behavior as well as the consequences that followed (see Figure 4.2).

The client, with the counselor's assistance, will attempt to gather data that will help them to answer the following questions: "What comes directly before the behavior?", "What does the behavior look like?", and finally, "What comes directly after the behavior?"

The client and counselor will analyze these data, looking for patterns and possible relationships among antecedent, consequences, and behaviors. This reflection "on" practice will provide the targets for manipulation in order to modify the behavior. Consider the case of a client concerned about his habit of eating sweets. In reviewing the data, he and the counselor may notice that his eating of candy seems almost predictable when two conditions appear to be in place: he is under a lot of stress and he has ready access to and is visually stimulated by candy (e.g., a box sitting on his counter). With these data as the focus point, the client and counselor in reflecting "on" practice may decide to attempt to modify this sweet eating behavior by removing, or at least making less accessible, the box of candy that appears to serve as a trigger to his eating behavior. Futher, since the eating of sweets appears to occur when the client is experiencing stress, the counselor may assist the client to learn alternative response to stress management as effective replacements for the eating of sweets. While the illustration is simple and straightforward, it highlights the value of the functional behavioral assessment and the use of data in the process of reflecting on practice in order to create interventions. It is important to remember that no matter how the data are collected, the method is both user (i.e., client) friendly and provides meaningful and useful information. The counselor operating from a behavioral orienting framework

Functional-behavioral assessment

Antecedents (including slow triggers)	Behavior or SUDS (subjective units of discomfort)	Consequences

FIGURE 4.2   **The A-B-Cs of a Behavior of Real Concern (BORC)**

reflecting "in" practice may realize the need to make adjustments to the original plan in order to help the client collect the needed information. Consider the counselor in Case Illustration 4.2. The counselor in this illustration, while expecting to be able to review data, soon comes to realize that some adjustments need to be made.

■ ■ ■ ■ ■ ▪

CASE ILLUSTRATION 4.2
ADJUSTING "IN" PRACTICE—USER FRIENDLY DATA COLLECTION

What follows is a portion of the interaction between Maggie (the client) and her counselor. This is the second session together and Maggie had accepted the homework assignment of recording the frequency and conditions of her BORC.

Counselor: Hi, Maggie. How are you?

Maggie: Fine, I guess. I have to confess something. I didn't do any of my homework.

Counselor: That's okay. Let's talk about what happened.

Maggie: Well, when I left here last time, I really thought I knew what I was going to do but somehow when I started I don't know . . . it just wasn't working.

Counselor: Wasn't working?

Maggie: Well, I mean it was like . . . taking too much time to write everything down.

Counselor: Oh, okay. So you understood what you were going to keep in your log but when you started it just seemed like a lot of work?

Maggie: Yeah. I know I was going to try to describe every time I got really angry and tell you what was happening before I got angry, how angry I got, and what happened afterwards, but I would probably still be writing. [laughs]

Counselor: Actually, Maggie that's very useful information. The method we were going to use to collect information—using a running narrative or anecdotal report—maybe isn't the best way to do this. How about if we try something else? If we could identify the types of conditions that seem to accompany your angry behavior—you know, let's think back over some previous situations—what I could do is write down a couple of these and your reactions and even what happened afterwards and maybe make a checklist that you could use?

Maggie: I'm not sure what you mean.

Counselor: [taking out a large index card]

Let me see. You told me that when people ask you questions before you had a chance to take off your coat in the morning it makes you mad. And you also said that when people interrupt you when you are speaking it makes you mad. And when you get angry you sometimes yell or make a hostile gesture or push others. So, we could make up a series of cards that you could use like a menu and just check off what happened. So, for example, maybe Card 1 would look like this:

Antecedents	Behavior of Concern	Consequence
✔ Asked a question before had a chance to take coat off	Yelled at them	✔ People shut up
Interrupted in conversation	✔Made a hostile gesture	Got into verbal altercation
Somebody grabbed my seat at lunch	Pushed them	Got sent to the principal
Somebody butted in front of me in line	Spit on them	Got my seat/place back

And at another time the card may look like this.

Antecedents	Behavior of Concern	Consequence
Asked a question before had a chance to take coat off	Yelled at them	✔ People shut up
✔ Interrupted in conversation	✔ Made a hostile gesture	Got into verbal altercation
Somebody grabbed my seat at lunch	Pushed them	Got sent to the principal
Somebody butted in front of me in line	Spit on them	Got my seat/place back

Do you think that might be easier to use?

> **Maggie:**   Yeah, I could try that!
>
> **Counselor:**   Okay, but it would help if we could think of as many situations and responses as possible to list in the three columns. Okay?
>
> **Maggie:**   Yep . . . got it!

Contract—Set Goals

The challenge for many behavioral counselors is to balance his/her need to gather data and/or institute interventions with the client's need to be supported and understood. Assuming that a working alliance has been established and the client

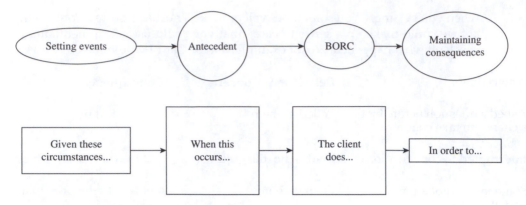

FIGURE 4.3   Constructing Hypotheses

feels empowered and hopeful about the data collection, then the behavioral counselor will take an active, directive role in formulating the behavioral analysis and the intervention processes to be employed. Using the data collected in the functional behavioral assessment, the counselor will begin to make decisions involving testing hypotheses regarding variables or events most strongly related to the occurrence of the BORC.

The schema employed as the counselor guides the client through the process of data analyses and intervention planning is presented in Figure 4.3. Case Illustration 4.3 demonstrates this process in action.

■ ■ ■ ■ ■ ▬▬▬▬▬▬▬▬▬▬▬▬▬▬▬▬▬▬▬▬▬▬▬▬▬▬▬▬▬▬

CASE ILLUSTRATION 4.3

CONSTRUCTING THE HYPOTHESIS

Background: The client, Thomas, is a 22-year-old college freshman who presented with concerns about social relationships. This general concern was redefined more specifically as Thomas displayed anxiety, shaking voice, and sweating when attempting to introduce himself to any girls on his dorm floor (BORC).

Data collection: Thomas and the counselor agreed to employ a simple narrative, log type format for data collection. The focus was on recording all of his social interactions in his dorm during the hours of 4 P.M. to 7 P.M. (times designated as the typical large group gathering times). Thomas was to describe the situation, his behavior, his SUDS (subjective unit of discomfort) score (i.e., number reflecting his discomfort on a scale of 1–10) and what followed once the encounter terminated. Thomas collected data on 11 specific encounters, four of which had SUDS scores of two or less (low anxiety), and the other encounters had SUDS scores over seven (moderate to high anxiety). A sampling of these data are provided in the table below.

Time/Date	Antecedent Conditions	Behavior and SUDS	Consequences
Friday, 6 P.M.	Alex, my roommate, said that he was going to meet up with Alicia and Tanya for dinner and wanted me to come. As I was showering I could feel my stomach getting into a knot. When we got on the elevator to meet them in the lobby I thought I was going to throw up. I kept saying, "What am I doing? This is stupid. I'll screw everything up."	When we got together I smiled like a dork all through dinner and could hardly eat. I was so nervous. I was jittery sitting at dinner, I hardly said a word . . . just smiling. My SUDS was at 8 . . . I wanted to run.	As we left the dining hall Alex asked if I was feeling okay and so did Tanya. They were really nice to me. I told them I must be coming down with something. Alex went back to Alicia's room but I begged off, saying I didn't feel well.
Sunday, 4 P.M.	I was going to connect with Bill and Maria, my lab partners to go over our chem lab. I was running a little late and was getting a little nervous. I got to the lab and we started on the work. These guys kind of rely on me since I really understand what's going on in class and they are struggling.	I spent most of our two hours explaining things to them. My SUDS was a 1 or 2 . . . real low.	Went to dinner together afterwards.
Sunday, 6 P.M.	Going to dinner with Bill and Maria— laughing about Chem class and cutting up on the professor.	SUDS 0 I was talking . . . felt really good . . .	Bill had to leave right after dinner, Maria and I hung out for a little while just talking about school and stuff.

Counselor: Well Thomas you certainly did a nice job with the data gathering. How do you feel it went?

Thomas: Actually, I was kind of surprised how many times I had to write about. I didn't think I was that socially active...and truthfully I really didn't expect to see many low SUDS scores. I guess I was focused only on the bad times.

(continued)

Counselor: I bet that's true for most of us . . . the typical experiences seem to go unnoticed but those that cause us discomfort leap out!

But it is kind of interesting in that as I look through your log, I notice there were four times where you seemed to be relaxed and enjoying interacting with a girl . . . like here on Sunday at 6 with Maria!

Thomas: Yeah, but that's just Maria!

Counselor: I'm not sure I understand?

Thomas: Well, we're in the same class together and we get to talk about that stuff and I guess cause I'm kind of into chem, I know what I'm talking about so it seems easy.

Counselor: So it is easier talking to Maria since you feel competent with the things you talk about?

Thomas: Yeah, I guess so.

Counselor: How about here [pointing to another positive interaction in the log] when you were out with Helen.

Thomas: Well, we weren't out . . . I mean we happened to go to the mall, she asked me to help her pick out a computer. It's kind of the same thing . . . I know computer stuff so I felt relaxed.

Counselor: Well, if we hypothesize that when you feel confident in your knowledge about the content of your interaction you seem relaxed, then can we assume that here, when you were with Alex and the two women from your dorm that you were not confident about the content of the interaction?

Thomas: Confident? I felt I would barf!

Counselor: Well, what was the content—the focus of the interaction—that you felt poorly prepared to handle?

Thomas: I don't know, actually, it wasn't that . . . I mean we were talking about school and cafeteria food and stuff, nothing major. You know, I think it was more the image I had in my head, even when I was getting on the elevator. I just kept seeing myself saying something stupid and the girls laughing at me.

Counselor: So, if we go back to your experiences with Maria and Helen, not only were you comfortable with the topic of conversation but was it also true that you did not create an image of you being rejected and laughed at?

Thomas: Yeah. I mean they are really nice and even if I was a total fool, they wouldn't laugh at me . . . they probably would laugh at what I did.

Counselor: That's great insight. So, it looks like a couple of things could be operating. First, the image—of being laughed at—seems to start the feelings of anxiety and your shy, withdrawing behavior.

Thomas: I think so.

Counselor: But, if we go back to the illustration with Alex, it looks like once you begin to get quiet and withdraw people respond? Like your withdrawal actually works!

Thomas: Works?

Counselor: Well, if the concern is that you will be laughed at it looks like your behavior actually disarms the others and rather than laughing at you they show real concern. That's what I meant by it works—it results in you getting what you want—both avoiding being laughed at and getting some positive attention from these girls. What do you think?

Thomas: I hadn't thought about that [looking at his data]. But, you may be right, look here on Wednesday when I was with Simone . . . the same thing happened.

Develop/Implement Intervention Strategies to Facilitate Change

It is important to remember that prior to employing any intervention, a counselor has the knowledge and skill necessary for systematic employment of the selected intervention. Further, the strategies selected for implementation need to reflect the client's and counselor's understanding of the data collected during the functional assessment and should reflect a sensitivity to uniqueness of the client and client's context. Thus, if we return to Thomas (Case Illustration 4.3), the data may suggest that Thomas's negative image prior to a social encounter renders him both anxious and relatively incompetent in conversation. The experience of incompetence further increases the anxiety and he begins a withdrawal process, one which apparently works to both reduce anxiety and elicit desired attention. If it is hypothesized that the anxiety and withdrawal is in response to the aversive, negative images, the counselor may introduce strategies to eliminate or change these antecedent negative imagery. However, if the counselor and client decide that the anxiety and withdrawal are actually reinforced by the supportive attention he receives, then Thomas, our client, may be assisted in developing alternative, more effective ways to elicit the support and care of the females with whom he is engaged. Either strategy appears justified given the data. The selection as to the target and the strategy will be a joint effort between counselor and client.

A brief sampling of behavioral interventions can be found in Table 4.1. As noted at the beginning of the chapter, it is not the purpose of this chapter to provide a step-by-step look at all behavioral intervention. Readers interested in such an explication are referred to the suggested readings found at the end of the chapter.

Monitored and Adjusted

The behavioral counselor appreciates the fact that a client does not live and operate within the sterile confines of a laboratory, and as such, the strategies that are clearly efficacious under controlled situations may need fine tuning and adjustment when attempted within the context of the client's life. It is important for the counselor to help the client embrace a researcher's mindset when attempting to employ interventions. With such a mindset, both the counselor and the client will approach the employment of a particular strategy as a "mini experiment," one in

TABLE 4.1   **Sampling of Behavioral Interventions**

INTERVENTIONS TARGETING CREATION OR INCREASE IN BEHAVIOR

- **Conditioning.** The counselor/client use reinforcement to encourage a particular behavior. For example, a child with Attention Deficit Hyperactive Disorder (ADHD) may get a gold star every time he stays focused on tasks and accomplishes certain daily chores. The gold star reinforces and increases the desired behavior by identifying it with something positive.
- **Token economy.** A procedure, based on operant conditioning principles, in which clients are given tokens, such as poker chips, stickers, check marks, etc. each time they exhibit the desired behavior. These tokens can later be exchanged for any one of a variety of tangibles or privileges listed on an exchange menu.
- **Modeling.** Assists the client in developing a new behavior through observation of a demonstration of the desired behavior.
- **Rehearsed behavior**. The counselor and client engage in role-playing exercises in which the counselor acts out appropriate behaviors. The client attempts to model that behavior and corrective feedback is provided.
- **Skills-training techniques.** The client undergoes an education program to learn and practice a variety of skills such as social communication, assertiveness, negotiating conflict, etc. Programs can be offered one-on-one in counseling sessions or as part of counselor-led group sessions.

INTERVENTIONS TARGETING REDUCTION/ELIMINATION OF BEHAVIOR

- **Extinction.** The process in which the frequency of a learned response to a conditioned stimulus decreases and ultimately disappears due to lack of reinforcement or the absence of the unconditioned stimuli.
- **Flooding.** A procedure in which a client is intensively exposed to the feared object, in reality or via imaging, for extended periods of time and without opportunity for escape, until the anxiety diminishes.
- **Systematic desensitization.** A procedure in which a fearful person, while deeply relaxed, imagines a series of progressively more fearsome situations. The two responses of relaxation and fear are incompatible, and the fear is dispelled by way of "counterconditioning," in which a stimulus that because of previous conditioning now elicits an undesirable response is associated with a new response that is incompatible to that which was originally conditioned.
- **Response costs.** Often used in conjunction with a token economy (see above), this procedure is a punishment procedure in which the client loses previously earned reinforcement (e.g., tokens) as a result of performing an undesirable behavior—one targeted for reduction and/or elimination.

which the strategy is employed, data reflecting the impact is gathered, and in subsequent session strategies is adjusted. This monitoring and ongoing adjustment of intervention strategies serves as the focus for subsequent sessions.

Plan for Maintenance and Relapse Prevention

Prior to ending the counseling contract, the behavioral counselor will want to help the client review the goals of the counseling, the strategies employed, the current state of the BORC, and the degree to which the positive results can be maintained and the relapse prevented. As the client and counselor move toward termination, a major focus of the reflection "on" practice will be on the identification of strategies that will facilitate the maintenance of the new behavior.

Quite often, relapse occurs simply because the client failed to anticipate the possibility of relapse or setback situations. For example, James had to work hard to break his smoking habit. While having now gone without smoking for over two months, James forgot that he had scheduled a cross-country bus trip with friends who smoked. His introduction into the intimate surroundings with smokers proved too seductive and James found himself once again engaging in smoking behaviors. If this trip had been discussed in session, the client and the counselor could have identified strategies that may have helped reduce the likelihood of the relapse, including the decision not to go until a later date when James' habit of not smoking was more fully entrenched.

Just as it was essential to analyze the antecedent conditions and consequences of the BORC when formulating an intervention, it is important to reconsider these factors because they may contribute to the maintenance of the client's gains and help to prevent relapse. As illustrated by James, sometimes the reintroduction of the client to the antecedent conditions (i.e., seeing and smelling cigarettes) can elicit the undesired behavior, so the failure to plan for ongoing reinforcement of the new behavior results in its weakening. It is important that the counselor assist the client in incorporating everyday rewards into the program as a way of maintaining the desired response. Therefore, while a student may have been earning points for learning to raise her hand before calling out a response in class, now as the use of these points is reduced, other rewards such as teacher praise or even self-affirmation (e.g., I'm doing great!), need to be employed.

STRATEGIES AND INTERVENTIONS

As noted in Table 4.1, there are a number of specific techniques used in behavioral therapy to help clients change their behaviors; readers are encouraged to refer to the references listed at the end of the chapter in order to learn more about the specifics of these strategies. However, for purposes of illustrating the impact that employing a behavioral-orienting framework has on the counselor's reflections "in" and "on" practice, two strategies will be discussed in some detail: (1) the use of operant conditioning and (2) systematic desensitization.

Operant Techniques: Developing and Strengthening Desired Behaviors

It is possible that a client will present with a concern regarding a behavioral deficit or deficiency. For example, a client may be interested in increasing the frequency of their exercising, study time, or even hand raising in class. When the goal is to develop a new behavior or increase the frequency of an existing behavior, the counselor with a behavioral orientation reflecting "on" practice knows the behavioral treatment of choice is to use reinforcement and contingency management procedures.

Consider the case of Alfonso, a self-described "couch potato." Alfonso came to counseling seeking assistance with the development of a weight reduction program. As noted previously, the counselor with a behavioral orientation approaches case conceptualization and treatment planning by performing a functional behavioral assessment. In the case of Alfonso, analyses of the baseline data led the counselor and client to conclude that targeting his lack of exercise was a good way to address the desired weight loss. Alfonso stated that he would like to be able to jog around his neighborhood for at least 20 minutes each day. As the counselor reflected "on" the conditions of the case, it became apparent that while this was a desirable goal, the fact that the client hadn't exercised in quite a while made that goal not readily achievable. As such, the counselor introduced subgoals and a process of shaping (i.e., reinforcing successive approximations of this desired goal) in order to identify realistic targets for behavioral change. The following were identified as subgoals.

Week 1: Spend 20 minutes walking the neighborhood each day
Week 2: Walk for 5 minutes, jog for 5 minutes, walk for 5, jog for 5
Week 3: Walk for 5 minutes, jog for 10 minutes, walk for 5 minutes
Week 4: Walk for 3 minutes, jog for 15, walk for 2 minutes
Week 5: Jog for 20 minutes.

Even though the client was motivated to lose weight, the reflection "on" practice led the counselor to hypothesize that "if the client were to engage in these behaviors, behaviors which were previously viewed as noxious, than some form of payoff or reinforcement may be needed." Alfonso initially suggested that if he reached his goal for the day, then he could eat a bowl of ice cream, something he really loved. While wishing to support the client in his active engagement in the process, the counselor making an "in" practice reflection was able to help the client see that the use of ice cream as a reinforcement may be counterproductive given the terminal goal of weight loss. Alfonso also enjoyed playing video games, so it was decided that he would agree (and his mother would serve as a reminder) that he would only play the video game following successfully engaging in the 20-minute exercise program as outlined. In this case, the use of a highly desirable activity—playing video games—was made contingent on the performance of the less-desired behavior (i.e., exercise), with the expectation that it would act as a reinforcement for the exercise and thus increase the frequency with which Alfonso engaged in exercise.

Sometimes the selected reward, while initially appearing to both counselor and client to be of value, simply does not work. In reviewing the data, the counselor may conclude that behavior required to receive the reinforcement was simply too costly, or perhaps the client had simply satiated to the reinforcement. In either case, the data collected during the intervention phase, just like the data collected during the problem identification phase, will provide valuable information for "on" practice reflection and treatment adjustment.

Returning to our case, the counselor noted that Alfonso started out well but soon became lax in his exercise program. In reviewing the data reflecting the frequency and duration of exercise, it became apparent that the reward of being able to play his video game was not working. In session, it was discovered Alfonso and his friends were going to a local video arcade and so he was less interested in engaging in his own video games found at home. With these data as the basis, an adjustment was made to the treatment plan. The counselor, in collaboration with the client, created a "token economy system" that afforded the client multiple reinforcement options. A brief outline of the system developed is

1. each time Alfonso met his exercise goal for the day, his mother would give him a bingo chip;
2. if Alfonso elected to do more exercise than the goal specified he could earn an additional bingo chip for each additional 20-minute segment of exercise performed within the day; and
3. each Saturday, Alfonso could exchange his tokens by giving them back to his mom in exchange for both "goods" and "privileges," a sampling of which is listed below.

- The purchase of a new video game (cost = 40 tokens)
- The rental of a video game (cost = 20 tokens)
- The ability to have his friend for a sleepover (cost = 10 tokens)
- The ability to pick a fast food dinner for Saturday night (cost = 5 tokens)
- A one-to-one exchange of a token for a quarter

With this adjustment to the operant program, Alfonso re-engaged in his exercise routine and lost the weight desired. It should be noted that the counselor, using the behavioral orienting framework, continued to monitor the effectiveness of the program, making additional adjustments, including the inclusion of "purchasing new clothes" to the exchange menu and the introduction of selfpraise for the client's exercising. This last modification was introduced as a way to support the new behavior in a more natural format so that it would be maintained once the token system was removed.

Systematic Desensitization—Modifying Undesirable Behavior

While the use of reinforcement is effective for the development of a new behavior, sometimes the focus of counseling is on the reduction or removal of an undesirable behavior. A number of strategies have proven effective in reducing the frequency of undesirable behaviors (e.g., extinction, flooding, implosion). One strategy that has extensive empirical support for its effectiveness is systematic desensitization (Wolpe, 1958).

In the late 1950s, Joseph Wolpe (1958) found that anxiety symptoms (i.e., undesirable behavior) could be reduced when the stimuli to the anxiety were presented in a graded order and systematically paired with a relaxation response.

The process will involve the following steps: (1) training the client to become proficient with some form of relaxation induction; (2) the development of a fear hierarchy; (3) the systematic presentation of a fear stimuli with a client in a state of relaxation; and (4) progression through the hierarchy. The use of systematic desensitization highlights the importance of reflection "on" and "in" practice. The counselor will need to collect and analyze data (reflection "on" practice) that support the utilization of this technique with this client. Further, throughout the development and application of the intervention the counselor will be called on to make adjustments as a result of reflections "on" and "in" practice. Consider the reflections required for each of the following steps in the employment of systematic desensitization.

Step 1: Relaxation training. While almost any method that results in the induction of a deeply relaxed state can be employed, one strategy often employed for relaxation training is progressive muscle relaxation. The progressive muscle relaxation procedure teaches the client to relax muscles through a two-step process.

In session, the client will be taught the process of tensing and relaxing specific muscle groups (see Table 4.2). The client will be instructed that he/she will be working on all the major muscle groups in his/her body, systematically progressing from his/her feet upwards. In the first phase, the client will be asked to tense the specific muscle group, holding the tension for approximately eight seconds, before releasing and relaxing. Often the instructions are provided in written or tape format so that the client can practice the procedure at home in order to become proficient. While this strategy has extensive support in the research, the counselor needs to be alert to those clients who find such an approach ineffective. Clients who for neuromuscular reasons find it difficult to tense and release, or clients who have difficulty focusing on their breathing, may need alternative approaches to accomplishing this first step.

Step 2: Creating anxiety hierarchy. When constructing the fear hierarchy, the counselor helps the client describe scenes or scenarios that he/she feels would cause them varying degrees of anxiety. The situations are described in sufficient detail to enable the client to vividly imagine each one. For example, when working with a client who is afraid of public speaking, it may be sufficient to say, "Getting up to give my oral report," but if described in a bit more detail such as, "Getting up in front of all my classmates in a crowded classroom to give my oral report," the scene once visualized may be more graphic and help the client to experience the event as real. Typically, the counselor will want to create about 18 situations that will be reviewed and reduced to 10 or 15 items. The goal is to create a hierarchy that is fairly well spaced in terms of the progression of anxiety. Through reflection "in" practice, the initial hierarchy may be modified as difficulty in progression up the hierarchy may suggest the steps were not equally spaced and thus additions to the hierarchy need to be made. Case Illustration 4.4 demonstrates how a hierarchy for fear of public speaking may look.

■ ■ ■ ■ ■ ▬▬▬

CASE ILLUSTRATION 4.4
PUBLIC SPEAKING

Counselor: So, Todd, do you have any questions about the process I just described?

Todd: No, I am not sure if it's really going to help, but I'll try anything.

Counselor: Well, I appreciate how important this is to you and as I explained, these techniques have been very beneficial for others who have felt anxious about a number of things or situations—including public speaking. So, if you are ready let's begin.

Todd: Okay.

Counselor: You explained to me how you began to feel your heart beating and felt like your stomach was going to leap out of your throat when you had to get up in social studies class to give your report.

Todd: That was horrible. I thought I would pass out.

Counselor: I'm sure that was really uncomfortable. If we were grading the degree of anxiety that you were feeling at that time, on a scale where 0 equaled absolutely no anxiety and 100 was the most anxiety you have ever experienced, where would this scene of the social science report be?

Todd   It was bad—maybe a 70 or so!

Counselor: Good . . . let me write the event on a card and put a 70 on the other side. So, what do you remember about the event . . . what was going on?

Todd: Okay, Mr. Kahn called my name to come up to the front and I can remember standing up from my desk and walking past Brad, who was smiling. I got to the front of the class and turned around at the podium. I saw Liz, my friend, staring at me a like a deer in headlights!

Counselor: So here's what I wrote—tell me if this reminds you of that specific event. "I heard Mr. Kahn call my name and I got up, walked past Brad, who was smiling, and when I turned to see the class I saw Liz staring at me!"

Todd: Yeah that's it . . . my stomach is upset just talking about it.

The counselor working with Todd used this first scenario as a reference point around which to develop other situations that elicited less anxiety as well as a few that elicited more anxiety. In building this hierarchy, the counselor may employ the data collected during the functional behavioral analyses, especially since the client recorded SUDS (subjective units of discomfort) scores for each antecedent event. The resulting hierarchy is presented in Table 4.2.

TABLE 4.2   Todd's Fear Hierarchy

Being called up to the front of student assembly to sing a song.	100
Having to sing a solo in music class when I am required to sight-read the music.	90
Practicing my Christmas solo in front of my music class.	80
Providing an oral report in class with Liz (the girl I like) sitting staring at me.	70
As president of the student government, introducing the principal at student assemblies.	60
Being on stage as part of the student government when the students are invited to observe one of our meetings.	50
Participating in a mock debate in social studies class as a member of the "affirmative" team.	40
Practicing my social studies speech in front of my mom and dad.	30
Having my mom listen to my Christmas solo.	20
Presenting the sales script that I use in my part-time job as a telephone solicitor.	10

In the illustration, the counselor and client created a hierarchy using imaginal scenes. However, reflecting "on" practice and the specifics of the client's fear stimuli, the counselor may decide to actually present the fear signal in session rather than employ imaginal scenes. For example, a person exhibiting intense anxiety when confronted by a dog may first learn to relax to the word "dog," then a picture, then a puppy in a cage, then a puppy being held by the counselor close to the client, etc.

Step 3: Pairing of fear stimuli with relaxation. The process of desensitization involves having the client sit comfortably, employ the relaxation strategy to get relaxed, and once relaxed, signal the counselor, perhaps by simply raising an index finger that they are ready to begin. The counselor will now present an item found on the hierarchy, starting with those items listed as low-anxiety producers. The counselor will introduce the fear signal, *in vivo*, that is in real form (e.g., puppies), or if that is not possible or feasible, the event will be presented in imaginal form, as in the case of Todd. The fear hierarchy that was developed insures that the amount of relaxation experienced at any one time is stronger than the anxiety being elicited by the item on the fear hierarchy. The plan of the intervention is to proceed up the hierarchy only after the items lower on the hierarchy no longer elicit anxiety. The process requires the counselor to be alert to client anxiety and to make adjustments to the presentation sequence to ensure that the experience of the relaxation is stronger than the amount of anxiety elicited by the presenting stimuli. This counselor attention to client response will serve as the data for reflection in practice and adjustment to the intervention plan.

The session, with the exception of the first one, will start with the last item successfully experienced from the previous session. Typically, counselors will not attempt to desensitize the client to more than three items on the hierarchy in any one session. As with all procedures, the actual implementation needs to be tailored to the unique needs and concerns of the client by way of reflection "in" and "on" practice. Case Illustration 4.5 illustrates the counselor's adjustment reflecting "in" practice with Todd.

■ ■ ■ ■ ■ ▄▄▄▄▄

CASE ILLUSTRATION 4.5
REFLECTING "IN" SESSION

Counselor: Okay Todd, let's, continue. Remember, stay focused right now on your breathing—slow, smooth, rhythmic—relaxed. Don't forget, if you find that your anxiety starts to go up, beyond a 5, just raise your finger and we'll return to relaxing.

So, you are walking up on the stage for the student government meeting, and you realize that the only seat left open is the one in the middle of the table facing out to the audience. There you are knowing that you are going to have to call the meeting to order, and right in the first row—right there staring at you—is Liz.

Good, Todd—keep that image. Hold it . . . hold it . . . .

Great, Todd. Let go of the image, focus on your breathing . . . slow, smooth, rhythmic . . . .

Okay, good. So, Todd, here you are walking up on the stage . . . *(Counselor attempting to represent this scenario.)*

(Counselor notices that Todd moved his index finger to signify his anxiety is over 5 on his SUDS scale.)

Okay, Todd. Take a deep cleansing breath, relax your body, focus on slow, rhythmic, relaxing breaths. We'll take a few minutes to relax. Good, slow, rhythmic, relaxing breaths . . . good . . . letting go of the tension in your body . . . just nice, slow, rhythmic breaths.

(With Todd relaxed, the counselor wants to end the session on a success and thus returns Todd to the item right below this one on the hierarchy.)

Todd, before we stop for today, I would like you to imagine that you are in Mr. Kahn's class having a debate and you are on the "affirmative" team. So, there you are with Roz, Robert, and Brad, and Brad is presenting your group's third point. After he speaks it's your turn to summarize your group's position. You start to speak and everyone is looking at you, but you know your group has the best argument.

Now hold that image and keep breathing . . . relaxed, slow, smooth breaths . . . good . . . good. . . .

In this session (Case Illustration 4.5), the counselor needed to stop the process in session and return to an item lower on the hierarchy, a level that Todd had previously been able to desensitize. The counselor may end the session on this successful note and discuss with the client the possibility of refining the hierarchy to include steps between this one situation of the debate and that of the student government meeting.

A summary of the steps typically employed in systematic desensitization are found in Table 4.3. These steps serve as the targets for the behavioral counselor's "on" practice reflections.

THE BEHAVIORAL-FOCUSED COUNSELOR: REFLECTING "IN" AND "ON" PRACTICE

The counselor employing a behavioral-orienting framework approaches the counseling relationship with the same qualities of warmth, acceptance, genuineness, and unconditional positive regard as found in any effective counseling relationship. Unique to this framework is the rather standardized way behavioral-focused counselors reflect "on" practice. Figure 4.1 lists the targets that guide the behavioral counselor's "on" practice reflection.

This process of reflecting "on" and adjusting by way of reflecting "in" practice is highlighted in our final case illustration (Case Illustration 4.6), the case of Mimi.

TABLE 4.3 Systematic Desensitization—Summary Steps

Step 1.   Help client move into his/her relaxation state.

Step 2.   Present the selected scenario/item from the hierarchy. (In the first session, this will be the first item in the hierarchy. In all other sessions, this will be the last item from the previous session.)

Step 3.   Have the client stay with the image or in the presence of the item for a tolerable length of time—typically 8–10 seconds in imagery, with the goal being to increase tolerance to at least 30 seconds of exposure.

Step 4.   Identify subjective unit of discomfort (SUDS) and re-establish your relaxation again. Relax for about 30 seconds.

Step 5.   Repeat the presentation of the fear stimuli.

Step 6.   Stop and again determine the level of anxiety (SUDS). If the client is experiencing anxiety, have him/her relax, and repeat the process. If the client is anxiety free, move up the hierarchy and repeat the procedure.

Step 7.   End each session with a successful presentation and with the client relaxed.

Reflections "on" practice

The following reflections are some "on" practice reflections and considerations that may serve to guide the counselor planning an approach to the session with Mimi.

1. What is the BORC?
2. As identified by the client, can the BORC be observed and measured?
3. Is the identified BORC the real problem of concern?
4. How ready and able is the client to engage in behavioral analyses?
5. What type of data collection appears to be most useful given both the identified BORC and the client's style?
6. Are there other individuals that should be included in this process?

Reflections "in" practice

1. Are my reflections and summaries of client information accurate?
2. Does the client give evidence of feeling heard and understood? If not, how might I communicate better understanding or at least a desire to understand?
3. Does the relationship have signs of becoming one that is trusting and open? What adjustments in my interaction do I need to make?
4. Is there evidence that the client can and wishes to work collaboratively? How might I have to adjust the pace or direction to ensure that the client is feeling comfortable and engaged?
5. Does the client seem to grasp the model being suggested? Do I need to change the pace of the process or provide additional opportunities for client disclosure and questions?
6. Does the client seem to be valuing the approach being taken? If not, are there examples relevant to the client that would help with highlighting the value?
7. Can we proceed at this moment to the next step?

FIGURE 4.4   Reflections "on" and "in" practice for Mimi

As you read the case it may be helpful to put on the lens, the mindset of a behavioral counselor. As a behavioral counselor, the thoughts and questions that may guide your processing of Mimi's data would include items such as that found in Figure 4.4—reflecting "in" and "on" behavioral counseling.

■ ■ ■ ■ ■ ▬▬▬▬▬▬▬▬▬▬▬▬

CASE ILLUSTRATION 4.6

THE CASE OF MIMI—FUTURE SOCCER STAR

Mimi, a 14-year-old high school sophomore, came to the counselor seeking assistance with what she identified as her weight management problem. While being self-described as "chunky" all her life, Mimi noted that her weight is now causing her physical discomfort as well as social embarrassment. Mimi shared that her family physician recommended that she lose weight, since she was, according to the doctor, approximately 20 pounds overweight for her age and height (weighing 138 lbs.).

(continued)

Step 1: Identify who is to be involved in assessment and intervention. During the initial encounter, in addition to facilitating the sharing of the client's story, the counselor explored the possibility of enlisting others in the process.

Counselor: Mimi, I truly appreciate your openness and willingness to talk with me. You mentioned that your family physician suggested that you lose some weight, but I also sense this it is really mostly your idea?

Mimi: Absolutely. I'm pretty independent and I really want to get control over this now.

Counselor: Mimi, that's great. I was wondering as we begin to develop a plan, would you find it helpful if we included your mom and/or dad in the planning?

Mimi: I don't have any reason for them not to know—in fact, I told my mom I was coming to see you . . . but I really think I can do this on my own, if that's okay?

Counselor: Absolutely. I would like to let your mom and dad know we are working on this, but the specifics, at least for now, can be just between you and me, okay?

(In reflecting "on" practice, the counselor recognizes the client's need and interest to approach this as a self-management process and unless it becomes clear that the involvement of others is needed or of value, the counselor is willing to proceed just with the client.)

Step 2: Identify the BORC (behavior of real concern). While Mimi presented with a pretty clear statement of her concern (that is, being 20 pounds overweight), the counselor wants to be sure that this is the BORC, as well as to translate the BORC into a goal. Sometimes what appears to be a goal, for example, lose 20 pounds, may be a strategy toward achieving another goal, such as increasing self-esteem. The counselor wants to be clear about the actual goal and needs to engage the client in order to define the goal of choice.

Counselor: Mimi, you said the doctor suggested that you were overweight, could you tell me a little more about that?

Mimi: When I went for my physical, the doctor had a chart for kids my age and height and I am like in the top 5% in terms of weight. He said that it would be good for me—and my health—especially since I was planning on playing soccer next fall, if I lost some weight.

Counselor: You were at the doctor for a physical?

Mimi: Oh, yeah . . . you have to do that if you want to play sports!

Counselor: Okay, you said the doctor said you were overweight. What do you think?

Mimi: I've always been heavy, but it is starting to bug me . . . my clothes aren't comfortable, and I have lots of friends and nobody ever says anything, but when they're playing I can't keep up with them. I really want to have more energy and wear some other types of clothes besides my sweats and baggy sweaters.

Counselor: So, this desire to lose weight is really coming from you. You have some real ideas about how you would like to be and feel. You would like to be able to keep playing and dancing with your friends, and feeling physically more comfortable in your clothes . . . and maybe get some new, snazzy ones? [smiling]

Mimi: I already have my summer outfits picked out! [smiling]

(Counselor's reflection "in" practice—clearly Mimi is a pretty mature 14-year-old. She seems to have a good sense of self and a very good support mechanism. The concern appears to be as stated, that is, to lose weight.)

Counselor: Well, I think that is a smashing idea . . . a couple of new outfits! Mimi, I know you said you don't want to be as heavy, but I'm wondering what that would look like?

(Counselor attempting to reframe the goal in positive language.)

Mimi: It would be great if I could lose at least 10 pounds by June and then maybe another 5 or 10 by soccer season! That starts in September.

Counselor: So the goal would be to lose 20 pounds over the course of the next 9 months. That seems reasonable, but I'll tell you what I would like to do. I would like to do some homework . . . but I'm going to give you some too!

Mimi: [making a face]

Counselor: No, not that type of homework. More like detective work! I am going to check with the school nurse to see if losing 20 pounds over the course of 9 months is a healthy goal, especially if you take it slow, okay? That's my homework . . . and now for yours.

Step 3: Data collection—Functional-behavioral analysis.

Counselor: Mimi, have you kept a diary or a log?

Mimi: Both. I love to keep a personal diary . . . you're not going to ask to see that are you?

Counselor: No, of course not. You don't have to share anything that you don't want to.

Mimi: Oh . . . okay . . . but I've also done a log one time on the way I spent time after school. It was for a project we were doing in social science.

Counselor: That's super. That's the kind of thing I was going to suggest that you do for us. I would like you to start today and, as much as possible, I would like you to keep a log simply by writing down all of the following information regarding your eating and exercising. There's no right or wrong way to do this, and you can't get a bad grade, but the more information you can record the better we can be detectives! We'll use the information to figure out a really good plan for losing your weight. How does that sound?

Mimi: I like doing science stuff, so I'm sure it will be fine, but what exactly am I writing?

(continued)

Counselor: Here's a book . . . free of charge! See, you're already getting things from counseling [smiling]! I would like you to write down the following—let's write in the book:

1. The date and time when you ate something.
2. Where you ate it and with whom.
3. What you ate, using as much detail as possible, like how much.

Mimi: [interrupting]

I have a calorie book. Would it be good for me to estimate calories?

Counselor:

(Reflecting "in" practice: Mimi is really engaged and a good collaborator.)

That's perfect. Again, the more information we have the more we can make some good plans. Okay, so let's see, number 3 you are writing down what you ate, calories, etc. Now:

4. What you were doing right before you ate?
5. What happened right after you ate? How did you feel, what did you do? That kind of information.

How's that?

Mimi: I think I can do this, but how's it going to help?

(Counselor reflection "in" practice—I think she is really a curious, bright student and would most likely enjoy understanding the theory.)

Counselor: Well, it's actually kind of cool. We know that people often do things and act in certain ways because of the type of stimulation they receive. Think about trying to whistle and then seeing someone eat a lemon. Maybe the sight of the lemon will make us have a reaction that makes our mouth dry and therefore hard to whistle. If somebody wanted to understand why the person was having such a problem, they may look to the stimulation or event that happened right before they puckered? Does that make any sense?

Mimi: Is it like when I see something sweet, I start to feel like my stomach is growling?

Counselor: Fantastic! So if we find that your mom has all kinds of sweet things around the house and they are all easy to get, then maybe that's something we want to look at in order to help you lose weight? That's why we need the data to help us figure that out!

Mimi: Oh . . . I can tell . . . she does!!!

Counselor: Well, what's cool is that there may be other things that go on that you are not aware of right now and when we look at your log, we may find a bunch of things that seem to be inviting you to eat and gain weight.

Mimi: Got it! But I should warn you . . . I can be pretty detailed about stuff like this . . . so you may be sorry you asked.

(Counselor reflection "in" session—She is on board and appears very capable of serving as self-manager. It was a good decision to work just with her right now . . . she seems empowered.)

Counselor: I can't wait . . . bring on that log!

Step 4: Contract—Set goals. Following the week of data collection, Mimi and the counselor meet. The counselor's "on" practice reflection led to the setting of the following goals for the session: (1) invite Mimi to share on her experience and anything else she wanted to share, (2) affirm the value of her data collection and her willingness to be actively involved, (3) review the data in order to establish reasonable goals, and (4) begin to identify targets for manipulation. The exchange that follows picks up mid-session.

Counselor: Okay, so when we look at everything you ate, it appears that you are averaging about 4,000 calories a day, with about 50% of these coming from sweets (candy, cookies).

Mimi: Yikes!

Counselor: No, no reason to say yikes. You have great information here and we can use it to develop a good plan and strategy to get to where we want to go. Okay?

Mimi: Okay.

Counselor: If we look at these times [pointing to the data], it appears that you tend to eat much of your sweets as soon as you come home from school, as you are watching television.

Mimi: It helps me relax!

Counselor: Relax? It seems that after you eat the sweets you tend to fall asleep until dinner. Is that correct?

Mimi: Yeah, sometimes my mom freaks out about that. She wants me to walk the dogs but I just seem to pass out. I guess a sugar high leads to a sugar low?

Counselor: Well, did you notice that on Monday you weighed yourself and you were 145, and then by Sunday you were actually down 2 pounds to 143?

Mimi: I think that was because I was writing information about what I ate down in my log. I was being good! [laughs]

Counselor: Yes you were . . . [laughs] . . . but you know that happens. Sometimes just being aware helps us. So I am thinking that maybe we could try a couple of things. First, rather than worry so much about weight loss, right now, how about if we focus on reducing your calorie intake each day and limiting the frequency and amount of candy eating that you do?

Mimi: Okay, but I don't want to give up on the weight.

(continued)

Step 5: Develop/implement intervention strategies to facilitate change.
(Counselor reflecting "in" practice—need to help Mimi understand that is still the goal.)

> **Counselor:**   Absolutely. Sometimes weight reductions take a little time to show up on the scale, and I didn't want you to get discouraged. In addition to weighing yourself each day and placing it in the log, I thought we could see progress by slowly reducing your calorie intake from 4,000 calories a day to 2,800 a day and maybe letting you have 2 cookies a day with one rule: You need to walk the dog for at least 15 minutes and then you could reward yourself with a cookie or two. How does that sound?
>
> **Mimi:**   I think I can do that. That would make my mom happy!
>
> **Counselor:**   Okay, so how about we keep collecting information, since that seems to help, and now you simply use the calorie book to estimate the calories and to keep a running total.
>
> **Mimi:**   Could I make it like a graph? I like doing that!
>
> **Counselor:**   That would be cool. So, you keep a graph of your calorie intake, with an eye to keeping to 2,800 a day. Also, every day you walk the dog for 15 minutes, how about if we "award" you a point? Since that's something your mom wanted, I wonder if we can get her to agree that if you earn a certain number of points that you could exchange those for some summer clothes?
>
> **Mimi:**   I love it!
>
> **Counselor:**   Well, let's start with the graphing of the calories and the agreement to not eat cookies unless you walk the dog . . . and we'll see how that goes for this week, and then maybe we can figure out the point thing next time?
>
> **Mimi:**   I'm psyched!

Step 6: Monitored and adjusted. In the subsequent session, the counselor and client expanded on the dog walking to include weekly exercise; the idea of including a token system leading to a new outfit was discarded by the client. Instead, the client found that graphing her calorie intake and reaching the goal of 2,800 daily calories, as well as graphing her increase in sprint speed (for soccer), were reinforcing enough to maintain the healthy diet that she now employed.

Step 7: Plan for maintenance and relapse prevention. Mimi exceeded her initial goal of losing 10 pounds by the summer, reaching a total weight of 122 pounds by the end of school in mid-June. Prior to leaving for the summer, Mimi met with the counselor one more time.

> **Counselor:**   So, Mimi, are you psyched about summer?
>
> **Mimi:**   Absolutely—I got a part-time job and will be going to the shore on weekends, and in August, I'm going to soccer camp at the University.
>
> **Counselor:**   Well, that sounds great.
>
> **Mimi:**   The best part is that my part-time job is at H&J gym, I just sit and check members in, but they let me use the equipment for free and one of the professional trainers, Marilyn, plays soccer for the University, so she's going to work out a program for me!

Counselor: Mimi, you really sound like you are on top of it. How about the weight?

Mimi: I'm not sure if I'll drop the other 8 or 10 pounds cause I'm actually gaining muscle, but as long as my stamina is up and speed is good and I'm eating healthy I feel great.

Counselor: You should feel good about all the work you did. And I hope when school starts you come down to say "hi" and maybe let me have the soccer schedule, I would love to see a game!

Follow Up: In a 6-month follow up, Mimi reported having lost an additional 5 pounds, now weighing 117 pounds. She played school soccer this past fall and is currently running winter track. She is happy with her current weight and very pleased with her overall physical health.

Finally, before we move on to our last orienting schema, it may be useful for you to try this on for size. Exercise 4.2 provides you an opportunity to step into a behavioral-focused schema as you reflect "on" and "in" a counseling session.

■ ■ ■ ■ ■

EXERCISE 4.2

STEPPING INTO THE MINDSET OF A BEHAVIORAL COUNSELOR

Directions: You are to use the following as a guide to your own application of behavioral counseling principles in the process of self-management. It may help to invite a colleague or classmate to join you in this process. The dialogue may make the application of the principle a bit easier.

Step 1: Identify a behavior of real concern. Perhaps it is your smoking or eating behavior, or perhaps your procrastination, study routine, or anxiety about certain situations or events. Identify the BORC and describe it in concrete, observable, and measurable terms (remember you can use a SUDS scale).

Step 2: Begin to record baseline data.

1. What happens right before the "target" behavior?
   - Time and physical setting and any environmental cues that set you off
   - Your actions, thoughts (self-talk), and feelings
   - Are there any signs of possible consequences (positive or negative) that influence your behavior?
   - Your physical condition (tired, hyper, drunk, etc.)
2. List the stimuli that seem to occur right before the behavior in question.
3. What happens right after the performance of the BORC?

Each habit has its own unique set of positive and negative consequences. It is important to consider many possible consequences to uncover them all; this includes possible extrinsic rewards (material, interpersonal, or symbolic of success) and intrinsic satisfaction (enjoyable feelings, relief, and self-esteem) or even relief you may get from avoiding or escaping a stressful situation.

(continued)

It is important to record every time the target behavior occurs, carefully observing and recording exact conditions that preceded it and followed it.

Step 3: Review and analyze your data (functional-behavioral analysis). List any stimuli that seem to elicit the behavior and the payoffs that result from and possibly reinforce the behavior. Identifying these elements will help you understand why the behavior occurs.

Step 4: Use the self-awareness from the behavioral analysis to exercise better self-control. In looking at your data, decide if the modification of your BORC will be best accomplished by:

- controlling the antecedent stimuli;
- controlling the consequences; or
- shaping and creating an alternative way of responding to the stimuli.

It may be useful to check the research to see what strategies have been used in modifying BORCs similar to your own. With this information at hand, develop a step-by-step intervention process that you could employ to reach your target goal.

REFERENCES

Beck, A.T., Rush, A.J., Shaw, B.F., & Emery, G. (1979). *Cognitive therapy of depression.* New York: Guilford Press.

Chambless D.L. & Goldstein, A.J. (1982). *Agoraphobia: Multiple perspectives on theory and treatment.* New York: John Wiley & Sons.

Eysenck, H.J. (1958). The continuity of abnormal and normal behavior. *Psychological Bulletin, 55*(6), 429–432.

Foa, E.B., Steketee, G.S., & Oazrow, B.J. (1985). Behavior therapy with obsessive-compulsives: From theory to treatment. In M. Mavissakeliam, S.M. Turner, & L. Michelson (Eds.), *Obsessive-compulsive disorder: Psychological and pharmacological treatments* (pp. 49–120). New York: Plenum Press.

Kohlenberg, R.J. & Tsai, M. (1991). *Functional analytic psychotherapy: Creating intense and curative therapeutic relationships.* New York: Plenum Press.

Martell, C.R., Addis, M.E., & Jacobson, N.S. (2001). *Depression in context: Strategies for guided action.* New York: W.W. Norton.

Pavlov, I. (1960). *Conditoned Reflexes.* In G. V. Anrep (trans. and ed.), New York: Dover Publications, Inc.

Skinner, B. F.(1953). *Science and human behavior.* New York: Macmillan Company.

Wolpe, J. (1958). *Psychotherapy by reciprocal inhibition.* Stanford: Stanford University Press.

Wolpe, J. (1981). Reciprocal inhibition and therapeutic change. *Journal of Behavior Therapy and Experimental Psychiatry, 12*(3), 185–188.

SUGGESTED RESOURCES

Kahn, W.J. (1999). *The A-B-C's of the Human Experience.* Belmont. CA: Brooks/Cole Publishers.

Kazdin, A.E. (2000). *Behavior modification in applied settings.* Belmont, CA: Wadsworth.

Kazdin, A.E. (2005). *Parent management training: Treatment for oppositional, aggressive, and antisocial behavior in children and adolescents.* New York: Oxford University Press.

Maag, J.W. (2003). *Behavior management: From theoretical implications to practical applications.* Belmont, CA: Thomson Learning.

Mather, N. & Goldstein, S. (2001). *Learning disabilities and challenging behaviors: A guide to intervention and classroom management.* Baltimore,: Paul H. Brooks Publishing.

CHAPTER 5

SCHEMAS: COGNITIVE FOCUS

In the movie *Forrest Gump* (Paramount Pictures, 1994), Forrest, the main character, is heard pronouncing that his "momma" always said that "stupid is as stupid does." Those taking a cognitive approach to counseling may disagree slightly with Forrest's momma. The amendment that the cognitive counselor may add might go something like: "Stupid is as stupid thinks, and this thinking results in stupid feels and stupid does!" While slightly less than articulate, the intent of the "Gumpism" was to convey the fact that those operating from a cognitive-orienting framework believe that focusing treatment on clients' thoughts and cognitions serves as the primary avenue to change.

The current chapter will provide a window to the mind and practice of counselors who employ a cognitive-orienting framework to guide their reflections "on" and "in" practice. The operative assumptions underlying this approach, along with detailed illustrations of the way these principles guide a counselor's reflection "on" and "in" practice, will be provided. It should be noted, as has been done in the previous chapters, that the focus within this chapter is on highlighting the way a cognitive schema guides the counselor's view of a client, his/her presenting concerns, and the counseling process. Those seeking a more detailed presentation of the history, rationale, and research supporting a cognitive model are referred to the "Suggested Resources" cited at the end of this chapter.

The goal of this chapter is to provide the reader with the opportunity to experience counseling through the lens of a cognitive-orienting framework. Specifically, after reading this chapter you will be able to:

- describe the basic tenets of a cognitive model of counseling;
- explain how the utilization of constructs such as schemata, cognitive distortions, and cognitive dissonance are employed as guides to the counselor's reflection on and in practice and result in the creation and implementation of specific intervention strategies; and
- employ a cognitive-orienting framework to engage with a personal exercise in application.

FIRST—ONE CAVEAT!

It could be argued that the current chapter presents a rather narrow view of cognitive counseling. Modern cognitive therapy is truly an integrative therapy, utilizing techniques from behavioral modification, problem-solving therapies, and other therapies in order to bring about cognitive, behavioral, and emotional change. While much of the current research joins behavioral and cognitive strategies into cognitive-behavioral therapy, the goal of this chapter is to present the cognitive-orienting framework as a distinct approach. The chapter reflects the position presented by Judith Beck (1995) that cognitive therapy is not defined by the types of techniques the therapist uses but rather *"it is defined by the therapists' planning and implementing treatment according to a cognitive formulation and conceptualization."*

THE PHILOSOPHICAL UNDERPINNINGS OF COGNITIVE THEORY

Cognitive therapy operates under the assumption that thoughts, beliefs, attitudes, and perceptual biases influence what emotions will be experienced as well as the intensity of those emotions. That is, an individual's affect and behavior are largely determined by the way in which he/she structures or gives meaning to his/her experiences. The process is as simple as A-B-C (Prochaska & Norcross, 1994). At point A are the activating events of life, such as receiving a notice of employment termination or the announcement of low SAT score. Point B represents the beliefs that persons use in order to process and make meaning out of these activating events and all events in their lives. These beliefs (schemas) are developed over the course of one's life experiences and manifest in our verbal or pictorial representations in our stream of consciousness (i.e., cognitions). The beliefs can be rational and functional, and thus result in emotional and behavioral consequences (at point C) that seem to help people respond to the activating events in useful and helpful ways. For example, in the case of the student receiving notice of poor SAT scores, while perhaps sad and a bit nervous, he/she may find that these emotions serve as good motivation for: (1) taking the SAT preparation course and (2) writing a letter to the college admissions office asking for a personal interview—since both behaviors may increase his/her chances of being accepted. However, the beliefs at point B can also be irrational and dysfunctional and may result in nonhelpful feelings and behaviors at point C (consequences). Consider the case of the man receiving the termination of employment notice. If this notice is interpreted as: (1) all is lost and his life is over and (2) his boss is truly evil and out to destroy him, then this man may respond with intense anger and may take threatening actions against his boss. Neither one of these consequences is useful in helping the man gain employment and in fact may prove more detrimental to his health and happiness than the original loss of job. In addition to this fundamental philosophical position that feelings are the result of thoughts and beliefs, there are a number of other operative assumptions commonly held by those embracing a cognitive-orienting framework.

Humans as Meaning Makers (the Use of Schemata and Assumptive Systems)

Humans attempt to create meaning and adapt to life experiences by creating assumptive systems and schemata about self, others, and the world (Piaget, 1983, 1985). These schemata and assumptive systems become organized into attitudes with cognitive, affective, and behavioral components (Rokeach, 1968). These cognitions constitute a person's "stream of consciousness," which reflects the way a person configures self, the world, the past and future (Beck, Rush, Shaw, & Emery, 1979).

To successfully function and adapt to the demands of one's life, a person's assumptive world must correspond to conditions as they actually are and/or clearly provide a sense of reality that is functional for the client. But as will become clear, the assumptive systems that a person employs are not always adaptive and functional. For example, consider a child who learns through early life experience and feedback from others that she is not very smart and often fails at specific types of tasks. This child may develop an organizing system or schema that has two very significant impacts. First, as an adult, this child may approach life events with the self-perception of being inadequate and likely to fail. Under these conditions, this person will have an increased sensitivity to and awareness of data that fits this schema while filtering out or distorting contradictory data. She may have gone through the day making many successful decisions, but with this schema she is likely to remember only those failures that she encounters while dismissing the successes as something anyone could do. This process continues to strengthen the operational assumptive schema. A second outcome of having such an operative schema is that this assumptive system sets up feelings and expectations of failure, which in turn stimulate behaviors (e.g., nonachieving, failure avoiding actions) and feelings (e.g., depression, anxiety) that may actually interfere with her success. In this case, the assumptive system doesn't just filter reality, it serves as a base for a self-fulfilling prophecy in which the prophecy is made by the person and then enacted, thus creating reality.

As may be obvious, the goal in this situation would be for the cognitive-oriented counselor to assist the client to modify his/her assumptive systems, transforming the meaning so that it results in increased adaptability and functionality.

Cognitions Can Be Functional and Dysfunctional

Whether it is by the nature of our design or the creation of our cultures, human cognition can be functional, serving the purpose desired by the individual (and society), or dysfunctional, blocking or at least failing to support one's function and adaptation. In trying to discern the functionality and/or rationality of a client's thinking, Maultsby (1984) proposed the following criteria.

1. Rational thinking is based on obvious facts.
2. Rational thinking helps people protect their lives and health.
3. Rational thinking helps people achieve their own short- and long-term goals.

4. Rational thinking helps people avoid their most unwanted conflicts with other people.

5. Rational thinking helps people feel emotionally the way they want to feel without using alcohol or other drugs.

Schemata Are Resistant to Change

A person's assumptive system has and continues to serve as the mechanisms through which he/she makes sense of experience. Once established, a person's schemata and assumptions are difficult to change, even when change is desired by the client. This is an important point to remember.

Jean Piaget (1983, 1985) highlighted the process by which humans take new experiences and make meaning by either incorporating the new experience into an existing schema (i.e., assimilation) or by creating an entirely new structure (a new schema) or by dramatically adjusting an existing one (i.e., accommodation) in order to make meaning of the situation. Clearly, this second process of modifying an old schema or creating a new one requires more psychic energy; as such it is not the first choice as we try to adapt to new circumstances. In fact, we tend to resist accommodating to new experiences, instead embracing information that confirms our assumptions and schema and either ignoring or distorting those data that are nonconfirmatory. Consider the infant who learns to associate certain features with the construct "bow-wow" (or dog). When first encountering another furry, small animal, that child may process the new experience through the schema of dog and refer to the animal as a "bow-wow." However, perhaps future experiences will highlight features of this new animal that do not neatly fit into the dog schema and cannot be simply overlooked or ignored. Under these conditions, the child will experience cognitive tension and it is this tension, this cognitive dissonance, that will motivate the creation of a new schema for interpreting this experience with this new, non-dog animal. The same is true of a depressed client who sees himself as hopeless, helpless, and worthless. If a friend attempts to point out data that is nonconfirming of the clients self-percepts (such as by saying, "Look Tom, you successfully put your children through college."), the depressed person may attempt to distort the message rather than accept this information as evidence that his belief in being worthless is not valid. Thus, the person may respond, "Are you kidding? Look, I only paid for part of their education, the kids will be strapped with loans for the rest of their lives because I couldn't make enough money to send them. You call that being a provider?" It is important to understand that the client, in this case, doesn't want to be depressed or retain depressive schema, but that a human's natural tendency is to defend his/her beliefs and schemata against nonconfirming experiences, even when these schemata cause pain.

It is clear that achieving significant change in one's assumptive world will almost always be met with some resistance, and when achieved, occurs with concomitant emotional reactions. It is also clear that emotional distress in and of itself is insufficient for modifying these assumptions. We appear more motivated to adjust "reality" in order to have it fit our schemata—our assumptive filters—rather than adjust those assumptions to more adequately reflect our reality.

Cognitions Can Be Modified

There are theories and research (Dattilio, 2006; Ellis, 2002, 1983) that suggest that individuals work hard not to change schemata and cognitions, but choose rather to modify experience so that it fits (assimilates) existing schemata. The truth is that cognitions can be modified. If the client is unable to simply adjust the world to fit the assumption, he/she will be motivated by the cognitive dissonance (tension) he/she experiences to reexamine his/her basic assumptions and embrace more reliable and functional guides.

The counselor operating from a cognitive-orienting framework believes:

1. clients can be taught to shift from self-defeating, dysfunctional thoughts and attitudes to self-enhancing, functional thoughts;
2. through psychological therapy/counseling, a client can become aware of his/her dysfunctional thoughts and cognitive distortions; and
3. correction of these faulty dysfunctional constructs can lead to clinical improvements.

Cognitive Change Requires Work!

When looking at the A-B-Cs of a cognitive approach, one may conclude that this is easy. It is not unusual to find clients and some counselors who believe those operating with a cognitive-orienting framework simply help clients say nice, positive things to themselves as a way of attacking depression. Wrong! Cognitive change requires work; the counselor with a cognitive orientation is continuously active and deliberately interactive with the client.

While the position that thoughts cause feelings is quite elementary, the actual information processing biases that occur in clients who present as angry, anxious, or depressed are really quite complex. Research has demonstrated how bias in a client's memory retrieval, attention, and processing structures are activated in support of the presenting concern. As such, just thinking positively is not going to permanently affect change in self and world views; thus, any benefits will be short lived. For example, a depressed person may be encouraged to say self-affirming comments, but for the depression to be attacked, the negative thoughts, beliefs, and assumptions that perpetuate depressed mood need to be reformed.

Cognitive therapy/counseling takes work. The focus of the counseling is "here-and-now," with the major thrust given toward investigating the clients thinking and feeling "in" practice as well as between sessions (Beck et al., 1979). The client must be helped to identify his/her dysfunctional thoughts, processing bias, and beliefs; actively debate these as simply unsupported; and embrace the reformulation that results from challenging the original schema with new nonconfirmatory data. This process may require that the client learn new skills and strategies that help him/her monitor his/her stream of thought, identify beliefs and attitudes, and subject him/her to the laws of reason. It truly is the learning of a new internal language—a new way of processing information—a new fundamental philosophy of life. And this takes work!

FUNDAMENTALS OF A COGNITIVE ORIENTATION

While each counselor employing a cognitive orientation to guide reflections "on" practice may have his/her own pattern and approach, most—if not all—will employ each of the following as markers of practice progress. The stages, while appearing linear, are less so in the reality of practice. While the overall progression of a counseling contract will move from the point of the client's awareness and acceptance of the cognitive-affective connection through debating dysfunctional beliefs and the resulting reformulation of functional schemata, any one session may exhibit movement back and forth across these markers (see Figure 5.1).

Build a working alliance

Milestone/Target 1:

Raising awareness and acceptance of the thought-feeling connection

Milestone/Target 2:

Becoming conscious of personal dysfunctional cognitive patterns

Milestone/Target 3:

Re-educating/Re-placement of dysfunction with functional cognitive patterns

FIGURE 5.1   General Milestones and Targets for Counseling Progression: A cognitive orientation

How a counselor moves his/her client through each milestone is a function of the counselor's skill and creativity and the client's unique style and ability. A number of specific strategies employed by the cognitive counselor are discussed in the following section.

STRATEGIES AND INTERVENTIONS

The counselor employing a cognitive-orienting framework will employ a number of specific strategies tailored to the uniqueness of each client's concerns, resources, and goals. Further, as with other approaches to counseling, the counselor with a cognitive framework values the need to develop a working alliance and thus employs the fundamental interpersonal relationship-building skills noted as core to the therapeutic relationship. But, as noted, the primary focus of this approach is on employing techniques that facilitate the clients identifying, reality testing, and correcting of distorted conceptualizations and the dysfunctional beliefs (schemata) underlying these cognitions (Beck et al., 1979). The cognitive counselor may employ directive or reflective modes; implement scientific-didactic principles or empathic, nondirective methods; and can call on a variety of educational materials, including readings and videos, all geared to assist the client correct faulty thinking.

The framework of the counselor's reflection "on" practice includes the milestones or targets listed in Figure 5.1, including: (1) assisting the client to understand and embrace the reality of the connection between thoughts and feelings; (2) monitoring and recognizing specific forms of cognitive distortion and/or dysfunctional thinking employed by the client; (3) testing the logic, validity, and adaptiveness of the identified cognitions; and (4) reformulating of cognitions and underlying beliefs so that he/she results in more functional, adaptive processing of life experiences (Beck et al., 1979). While these may serve as markers to guide progression through the counseling process, within process, the cognitive counselor is alert to any specific device or process that may prove useful in assisting the client to gain these insights. The "what" and "how" of reaching these milestones are detailed below.

Target 1: Understanding and Embracing the Reality of the Connection of Thought to Feeling and Action

Once a working alliance has been established, the cognitive counselor will turn attention to assisting the client to reframe the presenting concerns in order to separate that which is fact versus that which is the client's interpretation of those facts. Given any presenting concern, the counselor will assist the client to identify the situations or conditions that appear to elicit the emotional experience and through attentive, reflecting dialogue, identify the beliefs, the "interpretive perspective" that the client brings to the situation and that in fact creates the emotional and behavioral response.

TABLE 5.1   Highlighting the Connection of Thought to Feeling

Situation: You are having a bad day. The teachers have been "on your back," and as you walk out to your car, you pass two friends who seem to ignore you.

Thoughts: Ways one could give meaning to this event.

1. I can't believe they are blowing me off!
2. Great . . . I never get support.
3. Who the hell do they think they are?
4. What is wrong with me? Teachers don't like me, I have no friends, I'm such a loser.
5. Wow, they look like they are into something. I hope they are okay.
6. That looks pretty intense—I'm glad I'm not involved.

Emotions/Feelings: Each of the above interpretations could result in different emotional consequences. For example, each thought identified by number is tied to the feelings listed below.

1. Angry
2. Sad, alone
3. Hostile
4. Depressed
5. Concerned
6. Relieved

The goal is to assist the client to understand and embrace the reality that the way he/she thinks about the situation affects how he/she feels emotionally and physically in response to it. Cognitive counselors may employ a variety of strategies and tools to achieve this insight. Some may present a graphic such as that found in Table 5.1 as a way to demonstrate how thinking about a situation can prove helpful or unhelpful.

For most clients, the concept that it is one's thoughts that cause feelings is contradictory to what they have grown to believe and hold true. The cognitive counselor will go slowly and employ multiple strategies to make this point clear and undeniable. It is important that the client not only understand the connection but actually own the reality that any situation can result in different feelings and actions as a function of the way these events (situations) are interpreted.

During this first phase, the counselor will be looking for evidence that the client experiences a true "ah-ha" as he/she embraces and assimilates this principle. Consider the Case Illustration 5.1 and the visual and verbal techniques employed by this counselor to facilitate this insightful "ah-ha" and the acceptance on the part of the client.

■ ■ ■ ■ ■ ▬▬▬▬

CASE ILLUSTRATION 5.1

THERE'S A MONSTER IN MY ROOM

Counselor: Ruth, I'm very sorry that you are feeling so anxious but I believe there is something we can do that will help.

Ruth: Yeah, just get me out of that class so I don't have to stand up there and give that stupid presentation.

Counselor: Well, while I could see that getting you out of class would result in you not having to do the presentation—in terms of your anxiety and the difficulty you have had sleeping, eating, relaxing—it seems to me that these are experiences you have had in other situations . . . not just this class.

Ruth: Yeah, there's a lot of things that cause me anxiety. This is a busy time of the year and all the tests and projects really get me upset.

Counselor: You know it sounds like you think about things like the class presentation or the prom coming up and you feel these events make you nervous?

Ruth: Yeah, of course they do. I mean they are big deals.

Counselor: Yeah, they can be important, but I wonder . . . if you don't mind, could I show you something that may help?

Ruth: Sure.

Counselor: Now, this may seem a bit silly and you can tell me if it isn't making any sense, but just maybe we can discover something. Okay?

Ruth: Okay.

Counselor: [taking a sheet of paper and beginning to draw]

Ruth, I know you babysit your little 4-year-old brother Jason, so let's use Jason as an example of something. See these three columns, I'm going to label the first column as "A"—activating event. Now imagine that you are babysitting and you place Jason to bed. Okay, so let's write this down. The activating event is:

"A"—activating event		
4-yr-old Jason is in bed. It's nighttime and therefore dark. And let's make it a rainy, noisy night.		

Ruth: Yeah . . . like last night, I was babysitting and it was windy and rainy.

Counselor: That's great. Now, let's imagine that after you placed him in bed and said good night you went downstairs and within 10 minutes, all of a sudden you hear him screaming and when you go up to his room you see he is crying and really, really scared!

Ruth: I don't have to imagine, that actually happened.   *(continued)*

Counselor: Wow—this is something! Okay, so let's look at our columns and all the things we just described. I will put in this third column called "C"—consequences.

"A"—activating event		"C"—consequences
4-yr-old Jason is in bed.		Screaming
It's nighttime and therefore dark.		Scared
And let's make it a rainy, noisy night.		

Ruth: Okay.

Counselor: You see these things in the two columns? These are real events. They are factual! It is dark and it is rainy and noisy and Jason is screaming and afraid. But I wonder why? What is causing his fear?

Ruth: Well, I asked him and he said he was afraid of the dark.

Counselor: Oh, so Jason feels that this event (pointing to "dark" in column "A") is causing his feelings?

Ruth: Yeah . . . but that's normal, right? Kids are afraid of the dark.

Counselor: Ruth, now here's the cool part. I bet if you ask your mom and dad and everyone else you know, "Are little 4-year-old kids afraid of the dark?" I bet most will say, "Yes of course!" But you know what? They're wrong.

Ruth: [looking confused]

Counselor: I know this seems confusing, but stay with me. Do you know how you talk to yourself . . . it's okay . . . that's not crazy! We have to talk to ourselves. That's the way the brain is wired. We experience something and then we have to interpret or give it meaning, and then we know how we want to react to it. So let's see if we can get into Jason's brain as he is drifting off to sleep. So he's lying there. It's dark and as he drifts off to sleep he hears a noise (remember it's noisy). What do you think he says in his head?

Ruth: [not responding]

Counselor: Do you think he might say something like, "What's that?"

Ruth: Oh . . . yeah, I wasn't sure what you meant.

Counselor: Okay. But let's see if we can get into being Jason. Here we are falling asleep, 4 years old, and we hear a noise and our brain goes, "What's that?"

Well, that's a great question, but I bet he answered it. What do you think Jason said to himself in response to the question, "What's that?" It's a . . .

Ruth: A monster?

Counselor: Right on! I bet he may have. But now look what happens [going back to the chart]. See this middle column? I'm going to label that one "beliefs" or "self-talk" or "meaning making," this is how we interpret the things that are happening. So for Jason column "A" describes what is happening and most people think that causes the fear in column "C". But now look: if the noise of

"A" is interpreted as evidence that there is a monster in the room (that's in "B"), then guess what? It is this interpretation that causes the fear, not the event—the dark.

"A"—activating event	"B"—belief, meaning making, self-talk	"C"—consequences
4-yr-old Jason is in bed. It's nighttime and therefore dark. And let's make it a rainy, noisy night.	What's that? It's a monster!	Screaming Scared

And you know what? If there was a monster in the room—in this room—I bet you and I would be afraid. Sadly, there is no monster in the room for Jason, just in Jason's head, and so it is really him that is causing himself the anxiety.

Ruth: I think I get it.

Counselor: Well, let's see . . . let me test you [laughing].

Okay, so Jason is going to bed, it's dark, noisy . . . how does he feel?

Ruth: [starting to say "Afraid"]

Counselor: [interrupting] Wait, wait, wait. How about if it is dark and noisy, but it's December 24th? Now what might he be feeling?

Ruth: [smiling] Excited?

Counselor: Why?

Ruth: 'Cause he would think the noise is Santa and then he would be excited.

Counselor: Isn't that wild? If we believe a noise in the dark is a monster, then we make ourselves afraid, and if we interpret it as Santa, we make ourselves excited. What do you think? Do you see? It's not the events or people in our lives that make us nervous or mad or sad, but how we "see" or interpret these things.

Ruth: My head hurts [laughing] . . . but it's cool.

Counselor: Yes it is.

In the illustration, the counselor not only wanted Ruth, the client, to understand the process but wanted to set the condition that would facilitate her acceptance of this new philosophy. As depicted, it would appear that the client's smiling in anticipation of the impact of believing it was Santa might suggest that she is starting to understand and embrace this insight. But this was about her brother Jason, and the counselor needs to begin to help Ruth see that the same process applies to her and her issue of concern. Having the client truly embrace this A-B-C connection may take multiple sessions and multiple illustrations. Consider the exchange that happened in the next session with Ruth (Case Illustration 5.2).

■ ■ ■ ■ ■

CASE ILLUSTRATION 5.2

RUTH, BUT THIS IS DIFFERENT

Ruth: You know I told my friends about the monster thing . . . and they all think you're nuts.

Counselor: You mean they really believe that the dark makes people afraid?

Ruth: Yeah.

Counselor: Well you know that is understandable. I mean, we seem to teach each other this kind of thinking that our feelings are caused by others. You know, I bet your friends have said things like "You piss me off!"

Ruth: My . . . friends? That's one of my favorite phrases!

Counselor: Well, if you really believe this, then you are saying other people cause my anger rather than that it is me causing my anger by what I say to myself about what is happening to me.

Ruth: I actually get this . . . but when it comes to, like, my presentation or taking the advanced placement tests . . . I mean these things make me anxious.

Counselor: It is hard to challenge our own beliefs because that's how we see things. It is easier to see how Jason is distorting the reality of his bedroom to make it more threatening by adding a monster; or maybe you can see how your friend is making some comment a bigger deal than it needs to be and as a result is causing herself a lot of anger . . . but to see that we are causing our own emotional upset is sometimes hard.

Ruth: Yeah but these things are important and if I screw up it would be horrible.

Counselor: Horrible?

Ruth: Well, like it is really a big deal.

Counselor: Really a big deal?

Ruth: [*getting a little annoyed*] Yes. I want to go to college and this is important.

Counselor: So Ruth, if I use my A-B-C columns, it looks like you are saying that when we have an event—taking the AP test—and a consequence, you are really anxious and having trouble sleeping and eating . . . and while the AP test is something that you want to do well on . . . it seems that maybe you are giving it a lot more importance in your belief section . . . maybe something like . . . [writing in the "B" column]

"A"—activating event	"B"—belief	"C"—consequence
I am taking my AP test Saturday.	I'm going to fail. If I fail I won't go to college. If I don't go to college my life would be ruined.	(Given the life and death nature of my view of the test) I am extremely anxious . . . can't sleep or eat.

Ruth: I know it's not the end of the world. But I think you are right, I sometimes get myself all worked up about it. I think, "Oh my God, it would be embarrassing if I'm the only one not getting the credit . . . I couldn't face my friends."

Counselor: So you see, it's not the test but the way you are interpreting taking it. You are believing that you will be the only one of all your friends who doesn't earn college credit and therefore you would no longer be able to face them. Wow! If that were true, I understand why the AP test has much more importance than simply getting college credit. The way you are describing it, it becomes the determiner of all of your future social interactions!

Ruth: Seems kind of silly when you say it that way.

Counselor: But it doesn't feel silly when you believe . . . does it?

Counselors working from this cognitive orientation typically invite clients to gather data that reflect their own lived experience, with the specific directive for them to try to be attentive to the self-talk (interpretation and meaning making) that occurs during these times. The specific strategies employed can be informal, such as simply asking clients as homework to take notes and remember what they were thinking during times when they were experiencing the emotions and/or behaviors of concern. More typically, the counselor operating with a cognitive orientation will approach the task of data collection with a bit more structure and systematization (see Figure 5.2).

Of course, the form of such data collection needs to meet not only the needs of the counselor for collecting useful data, but also the comfort, resources, and interest of the client. Consider Case Illustration 5.3, which illustrates a counselor's reflection in practice that results in a modified, more client-friendly method for collecting this valuable information.

■ ■ ■ ■ ■ ▬▬▬▬▬▬▬▬

CASE ILLUSTRATION 5.3
A SIMPLE JOURNAL

Roger: I'm not sure. That chart looks like a lot of work. I'm not real good at doing things like that.

Counselor: *(Reflecting "in" practice moves toward a more informal method of data collection.)* I guess when you first see something like this it does seem like it may take some time to use. How about this? Are there times in the day—perhaps in the morning before classes or later in the evening—when you could sit and simply think about your day?

(continued)

Roger: Yeah . . . actually . . . every afternoon I usually go to the coffee shop and just sit and zone out with some coffee.

Counselor: A good way to unwind? Is that something you do with your friends?

Roger: Not usually. I like having some time by myself to listen to tunes, maybe scan the Internet or work on writing songs . . . things like that.

Counselor: That's super. Would it be possible, since you have your laptop, if maybe before you got too much into your music that you could think about your day and see if there was any time that you found yourself getting angry or irritated?

Roger: That's every day.

Counselor: Well, maybe it would help if you could think of one time during the day that you were angry, just one, and then just jot a note to yourself about how angry you were during that time. You know, use a scale, like, of say 0–10 where 0 is major mellow, not stressed, and not irritated, and 10 is almost becoming postal, like the worst anger you have ever had.

Roger: Yeah I could do that.

Counselor: Well, could you also jot down a brief description of what was happening at the time—you know, what was going on? You don't have to write a lot, just enough so that when we get together you can look at your notes and really remember the situation.

Roger: Like all the people and stuff going on . . .

Counselor: Well, as much as you can—the more the better.

Roger: Okay, I can try—like once a day?

Counselor: That would be great. And obviously the more examples you can provide the better—but once a day would be super.

Now that I have you on a roll, how about if after writing down a description of what was happening and how you were feeling, you take a moment and maybe reread what you wrote? But this time try to pay attention to what is going through your mind as you think about the situation, you know, how we talk to ourselves about these things? See if you can hear what you are are thinking and just write whatever is going on in your mind. You don't have to worry about editing or anything, just write it down as it goes through your mind.

Roger: That's kind of how I write my songs . . . just like what comes to my mind. I let go on the paper. So I could do that, but I'm not sure how this will help.

Counselor: Well, I guess that is something we can decide when we look at what you wrote. My hope is that you may begin to see a pattern to your thinking and recognize certain types of thoughts that seem to be connected to your feelings of anger and irritation.

Roger: Oh, that A-B-C stuff. Sure I'm game.

Date	Event or situation	Feelings (Score with 100 being the maximum)	Self-talk (cognitions)	Other possible interpretations
Tuesday	I was going to lunch and Marie, Ellen, Isha, and Natalie were sitting at the table. When they saw me coming they got quiet and started giggling.	Anxious 80%	What are they doing? Are they making fun of me? Why don't they like me? This is horrible. I wish I could just become invisible.	Maybe they were cutting up on something else and I was just walking by at the time. Maybe they are laughing about something I'm wearing? Maybe they are insecure and need to find faults with other people.

FIGURE 5.2   Thought Log

While the counselor in Case Illustration 5.3 may have preferred that the client use the structured technique found in Figure 5.2, the reflection "in" practice led the counselor to be willing to use a less-structured form of data collection (journaling) at least as a starting point.

Target 2: Recognition of Specific Forms of Cognitive Distortion and/or Dysfunctional Thinking Employed by the Client

Once the client has begun to embrace the connection of thought to feeling (Target 1), and has gathered data reflecting his/her cognitive processing and typical forms of interpreting situations of concern, the reflection "on" practice shifts to the identification of the nature of the dysfunctional processing and cognitive distortions employed by the client. Assisting the client to recognize the unevidential nature of these beliefs and their dysfunctionality serves as the next step toward modifying them (Target 3).

It must be again highlighted that even though these beliefs often result in the client's life being filled with painful emotional experiences such as panic or depression, they are the core beliefs that served as the client's philosophical foundation for perceiving and adapting in life. As such, regardless of how silly or farfetched they appear to the counselor, the counselor must remember that these seem reasonable to the client. These beliefs—although clearly dysfunctional—are not easily surrendered or even recognized as "dysfunctional." In fact, as noted previously, the client may actually reshape an experience in order to fit that experience into the existing, even dysfunctional schema, rather than changing that schema. Case Illustration 5.4 highlights this process.

■ ■ ■ ■ ■

CASE ILLUSTRATION 5.4
I'M INCOMPETENT

Counselor: Well Charles, you certainly have built up quite a case to support your notion that you are a failure, totally incompetent.

Charles: I'm not building a case. I'm just stating the facts. Look, my parents sent me to the best private school, and I spent most of my time playing and partying. I barely got into college.

Counselor: But that's a point of confusion for me. I mean, even though you didn't give it your all, you still did well enough at a very competitive prep school to be able to graduate and get accepted to college.

Charles: *(Ignoring the evidence of graduating from an academically competitive environment, and devaluing the acceptance into college.)*

You've bought the PR for this school—any idiot can graduate if mom and dad have money, and really, the "college" I'm going to is like an open-door institute for losers. Certainly wasn't any accomplishment to write home about.

The counselor employing a cognitive-orienting framework appreciates that a client such as Charles (Case Illustration 5.4) would rather not hold on to these damaging beliefs and yet continues to embrace them, not as dysfunction, but as accurate reflections of his reality. Since we are wired to retain our beliefs even in the face of contradictory information, the task for the counselor is to be alert to information that is contradictory to the client's dysfunctional schema, and then to effectively present these data in ways that the client is unable to escape the need to challenge and reformulate his/her dysfunctional beliefs (see Target 3).

During this second phase of counseling, the counselor with a cognitive orientation will employ various techniques to educate the client about forms of dysfunctional thinking (see Table 5.2), including assigning readings, direct instruction, and most importantly, the analyses of the client's raw data reflecting his/her own life experience. The counselor working in collaboration with the client will develop ways to collect these data, which will then be analyzed in session. These data may be elicited during an interview with the client as he/she shares examples of the situations in which they experienced the emotions and/or behaviors of concern, or perhaps the client and counselor will employ a more structured strategy, such as keeping a "thought log" to collect examples of problematic situations. As the counselor reviews the client's data (thought log), he/she may employ well-timed and carefully phrased questions that are structured to invite the client to reflect on specific situations in a way that may open new ways of seeing the event. For example, consider the effectiveness of the questioning posed by the counselor in Case Illustration 5.5.

TABLE 5.2 Listing of Dysfunctional Thinking Processes

All-or-Nothing Thinking: A person sees things as only black or white. If someone points out that I made a mistake and thus am less than perfect, I see myself as a total failure.

Overgeneralization: In this case, a person takes a single negative event and concludes that all others will be the same. If I am rejected by one person whom I invited out and conclude that all people I invite will reject me, then I am employing an overgeneralization.

Mental Filter: When using this form of dysfunctional thinking, a person pulls out only the bad events in his/her life, overlooking the positives. It is like we have a filter that allows some things in (negative details) and excludes any contradictory positive information. The result is that our view of all reality becomes negative.

Disqualifying the Positive: In this case, the person rejects positive experiences, finding reasons to simply dismiss or discount these positives. This is the process that allows one to hold onto negative beliefs when contradicted by a positive experience.

Jumping to Conclusions: This cognitive process results in a person making negative interpretations, even though there are no definite facts that convincingly support this conclusion. It is what leads a person to say, "Why bother? I know I'll fail, or be rejected, or not get the position . . . " without even attempting the task at hand.

Magnification (Catastrophizing) or Minimization: With this form of distortion, a person either exaggerates the importance of things (such as your goof-up or someone else's achievement), or he/she reduces something like a positive personal trait until it appears tiny and perhaps relatively meaningless.

Emotional Reasoning: This occurs when a person uses his/her emotions (feelings) as a basis to draw conclusions about reality. For example, when someone experiences anxiety and concludes there must be something dangerous happening or when he/she feels overwhelmed with a work assignment, concluding that it is therefore hopeless and will never be completed.

Personalization: This occurs whenever we take responsibility for events (most often negative events) for which we have had no primary responsibility.

■ ■ ■ ■ ■

CASE ILLUSTRATION 5.5

WHAT WOULD CHRIST SAY?

The following interaction occurred during a session with a 16-year-old girl who was feeling extreme guilt and despondency because of her "sinfulness." The counselor had previously identified that the client's sense of guilt had been supported by her friend, Louise, who commented that Maura's making out with a boy was damnable.

> **Counselor:**   So Maura, if I understand correctly, you feel so "sinful" because you made out with a boy after the dance?

> **Maura:**   Well it was more than that. This was the church dance and we had youth group right before and they told us how we should avoid the sins of the flesh . . . and here I go and get into it.

(continued)

Counselor: So getting into it means making out?

Maura: Yes, that's all I did, but when I told Louise she told me that I was immoral and sinful and that I was giving in to the sins of the flesh and clearly not loving of Jesus, my Lord and Savior . . . this is unforgivable!

Counselor: Maura, I know you and your family are very much involved with your church, but I'm a little confused. I mean, if Louise were here sitting on your left-hand side, saying to you, "You are a sinner. You have committed an unforgivable sin by making out with this boy.", how would you feel?

Maura: Well, that's what she said and I believe her and I feel scared I'm going to go to Hell.

Counselor: I'm sure that's upsetting, but here's my confusion. Let's pretend that Louise is here saying these things, but on your right side, let's pretend that Jesus is sitting there. And if I understand your faith, you feel that Jesus is the son of God and that Jesus chose to die for you because of his love for you? So what do you think Jesus would say about you making out with this boy?

Maura: [beginning to cry] He would say that I shouldn't do that!

Counselor: Perhaps. But what might he say about you going to Hell?

Maura: No, he would say he loves me and that he forgave me and that I need to be careful about my worldly desires.

Counselor: So I guess I am not sure who you want to listen to. Louise? Or Jesus?

Maura: [smiling] I guess Louise is wrong?

While the counselor was able to employ his own understanding of the client's orienting framework (i.e., Christian theology), it was the gentle questioning employed by the counselor that opened the client's thinking about the issue of her "sinfulness" in a way that allowed her to challenge her initial beliefs and reframe it in a way that would be more adaptive and functional to living life as she wishes. While the cognitive counselor will use a variety of techniques to confront and dispute a client's distorted cognitions, the creative use of questions may be one of the most effective strategies (Beck et al., 1979).

Target 3: Reeducating and Reformulating Personal Cognitions and Interpretive Schemata

As the client identifies those thoughts, interpretive schemata, and core beliefs that are at the root of his/her dysfunctional feelings and actions, the counselor begins to focus on facilitating changes at all levels of cognition. Table 5.3 provides a sampling of the types of interventions that could be employed to challenge and reframe specific forms of cognitive distortion.

TABLE 5.3 Intervention Targeting Specific Distortion

COGNITIVE DISTORTION	UNDERLYING FUNDAMENTAL BELIEFS	TARGETS AND STRATEGIES FOR INTERVENTION
Catastrophizing	Unless things are the way I want them to be it is a disaster, an unbearable situation.	Begin to identify the real, the most probable worst-case scenario. What is the worst thing likely to happen? With this definition of outcome, ways of reducing negative outcome and/or developing a tolerance can be targeted.
Selective abstraction	Only certain data are important to perceive and retain—those things that do not fit my self-percept or view of the world are irrelevant and should be ignored or modified.	Have client engage in mini-experiments in which he/she logs all that happened so you can point out successes that have been discounted.
Dichotomous thinking	Very rigid views of the world as either one extreme or another (black or white).	Have client attempt to view situations from another's perspective as a way of introducing events as evaluated along continuum.
Shoulds and musts	A absolute sense of duty and right and wrong. The view that our way is the only way.	Invite the client to analyze the impact of replacing shoulds and musts with wishes, wants, and preferences. In addition, invite the client to reframe beliefs of what others should—or should not to do. "If I made the rules for the world then others . . ."

This is not a simple invitation to the client to think nice, pleasant thoughts. The counselor will encourage the client to evaluate his/her beliefs in an objective manner. The client will be helped to see his/her cognitions as reflections of actual circumstances or possibly distortions of those circumstances. As such, the counselor will assist the client to assess the degree to which his/her inferences and conclusions correspond to what other objective individuals may conclude. For example, a counselor employing a cognitive orientation may ask the client to consider applying his/her assumptions to other people as a way of inviting them to recognize the potentially idiosyncratic views they hold just for themselves. In this case, a client who believes she must be totally competent to be acceptable to another may be confronted with the fact that she does not hold the same standards for her friends. In fact, she may realize that she would most likely argue with a friend who presented the statement: "I made a mistake . . . no one will like me!" And yet, she may now realize that she uses that same type of thinking when evaluating her own acceptability.

This stage of cognitive restructuring requires work and hopefully will result in the client learning increased cognitive flexibility. Counselors may employ direct instruction or assignment of reading materials in an attempt to facilitate a change in the way the client makes meaning. Most often, counselors will model the process of "disputing" beliefs and invite the client to dispute and debate his/her beliefs, looking for supportive evidence and reshaping the belief so that it is more reflective of the facts. Case Illustration 5.6 highlights this process of disputing a dysfunctional belief.

■ ■ ■ ■ ■ ▬▬▬▬▬▬▬▬▬▬▬▬▬▬▬▬▬▬▬▬▬▬▬▬▬▬▬▬▬

CASE ILLUSTRATION 5.6

NICOLE

Counselor: So Nicole, you did a really good job at keeping your thought log.

Nicole: Thanks, but I'm not sure how it's going to help, it only proves I'm a loser!

Counselor: Well, as we discussed last time, those feelings that you have of being very sad and worthless stem from your belief that you are not loveable and that you will be alone all of your life.

Nicole: But that's true.

Counselor: I know it feels true but let me ask you a question. If we look at your beliefs as hypotheses rather than absolute facts then it would be useful to "test" these against the evidence.

Nicole: Yeah I did. Look at this [pointing to a log date]. Brad called me and told me that he no longer wanted to go out and that he was going to date Mimi. See . . . loser!

Counselor: I bet that was really unexpected and disappointing?

Nicole: Disappointing? Try devastating!

Counselor: But I'm not sure I understand. It was devastating to hear that Brad, a guy you had dated for three weeks, no longer wanted to go out with you?

Nicole: No . . . not just that. I mean if Brad doesn't want me? I doubt anyone will!

Counselor: Oh, so it wasn't the actual event that made you so sad?

Nicole: Not really. Brad's a bit of a jerk and he smokes and I don't like that.

Counselor: So, if we are focusing just on the event, you know what you wrote here in column A, "Brad called and said he didn't want to go out anymore." If we just focused on that, how would you feel?

Nicole: Probably surprised, 'cause I thought we were hitting it off. But you know what? As we are talking about it I kind of feel relieved. I really wasn't enjoying going out with him, but I guess it was better than nothing.

Counselor: Okay, so if you had that thought that it was a surprise but actually, it wasn't the relationship you really wanted, then you wouldn't have felt like you wrote here in "C"—"devastating, horrible, hated myself, scared of being alone for the rest of my life."

Nicole: No . . . but that's how it felt.

Counselor: Well Nicole, it felt that way because if you look here at "B" (belief), you wrote down that you interpreted the situation to mean: "I'm such a loser, no one will ever be interested in being with me. I'm going to be alone all my life. No one could love me." And truthfully, I guess that if this were true that out of all the humans that existed you were the only one who no one, not your mom, or grand-mom, or best friend, would ever love, I guess that would be painful. But if the belief was just a hypothesis and not a statement of fact, could you find evidence to dispute it?

Nicole: Well you already did. My mom does love me, actually my family really cares about me, and as you were talking I remembered all the friends I have and even poor Jeremy—he's a guy who has been dying to go out with me. So yeah, I could find a lot of facts that I guess says some people love me.

Counselor: Nicole, that's great. And if you used your evidence to create a new belief, what do you think it would look like?

Nicole: Well I guess I would have thought, "Damn. I didn't see this coming, but hey, I couldn't handle his smoking and to be honest I'm never real comfortable ending relationships. So okay, I'm probably not going out on a date this week, but there are other guys out there."

Counselor: That's super!

Nicole: Yeah, but that's now . . . not then! How am I ever going to learn?

Counselor: Well, I think there are two parts to that. First, you have to keep practicing hearing your interpretations and your beliefs and learning to treat them like hypotheses that need to be tested before you buy them as truth. The second thing is to just think of this like learning a new language. When you first learned the Spanish word for the color white you probably had to look it up, then write it down, and then read it. But the more you used it, you may have found that while you first thought "white," you may have quickly translated into "blanco" and if you kept using the Spanish word and you saw a picture of something white, you would immediately go to the new language and think "blanco." Well, the same is true here. Maybe at first you have to reformulate your thought well after the event. But eventually, with practice, you will be reformulating as you are in the experience, and eventually you will begin to approach events with this new perspective.

Nicole: That makes sense. So I guess it's practice, practice, practice . . . and I guess that means I should keep my trusty journal next to me? [laughing]

(continued)

Counselor: Maybe not next to you, but it's a great way to keep challenging your thinking. Also, it doesn't hurt to maybe remind yourself by writing a little note or Post-it that your thoughts are hypotheses about you and your world and should be tested for supportive evidence.

Nicole: Got it . . . hypotheses!!!

Most often, the therapy isn't confined to the hour within the office; rather, the counselor with a cognitive orientation will invite the client to engage in practice outside the office. Homework is an intervention associated with cognitive-behavioral therapy (Beck et al., 1979), including homework in the form of disputing irrational beliefs (Ellis & Dryden, 1997). In addition, once the client has developed healthy substitutes for dysfunctional core beliefs, he/she may be encouraged to experiment with using these new beliefs in a specific situation. The hope is that if the client enters a situation acting as if the new belief were true, he/she will experience outcomes that further support the validity of this new way of viewing themself and the world. Consider the brief exchange found in Case Illustration 5.7.

■ ■ ■ ■ ■

CASE ILLUSTRATION 5.7
ACTING AS IF

Counselor: Now remember, this is supposed to be "fun."

Bill: Oh, yeah, fun.

Counselor: Well try it. When you go to the dance tonight and decide to ask Roseanne to dance and you start to walk across the gym floor to ask her, remember to walk as if you were about to do something fun and positive. And as you walk, remind yourself "It's just an invite to the dance—no big deal!"

Bill: Hey, nothing ventured . . . nothing gained!!

Counselor: That's the attitude.

(Next session)

Counselor: How did our experiment go?

Bill: [smiling] Well actually I was able to do it. She said "no" and for some reason I just said "thanks" and then asked Linda, who was standing next to her, "How about you?" And she said "yes"!

It was wild. I just felt like, no big deal! I like to dance and that's all it is and the weirdest thing is that after that happened I danced all night, it was great.

Counselor: That's super! So you felt like it was no big deal, because that's what you believed and it was true?

As the counselor explained to Nicole, the more the client employs cognitive disputing and replaces dysfunctional beliefs with more functional thinking, the more automatic it will become. As noted, it is like learning a new language—one that may at first feel artificial, but with practice may become the language of choice!

THE COGNITIVE COUNSELOR REFLECTING "IN" AND "ON" PRACTICE

As previously noted, cognitive-oriented counseling is an action-oriented form of counseling that assumes maladaptive, or faulty, thinking patterns cause maladaptive behavior and negative emotions. The treatment focuses on changing an individual's thoughts (cognitive patterns) in order to change his/her behavior and emotional state. As such, the counselor employing a cognitive orientation is sensitive to the need to first inform and educate the client about the connection of thought to feeling, be alert to manifestations of dysfunctional thinking, and employ techniques that will facilitate the client's reformulation of faulty, dysfunctional beliefs. In one form or another, these three targets serve as milestones for a counselor operating with a cognitive orientation as he/she reflects in and on practice. Further, as noted throughout this chapter, changing one's beliefs is not an easy task, even when one is highly motivated. The counselor working with a cognitive orientation is mindful and respectful of the work required to develop new schemata and the value of creating conditions of cognitive dissonance to facilitate this change process.

The unique way in which a counselor with a cognitive-orienting framework reflects on and in practice is depicted in our final Case Illustration—the case of Justin. As you will note, the counselor enters the sessions with ideas of what she would like to accomplish, goals established as a result of her reflection "on" practice. However, as you read through the interchange you will see the numerous times the counselor needed to adjust the initial strategy in order to approach the goal from a slightly different angle. This is the adjustment that comes from reflection "in" practice.

As with the previous chapters, it may be helpful for you to review the fundamental principles that serve as the base for this particular counseling orientation. More specifically, it may prove helpful to review the types of cognitive distortions listed in Table 5.2 so that as you read through the case material you will be able to identify Justin's cognitive distortions and perhaps be able to anticipate the counselor's response and in-session adjustments. It is this idea of anticipating the counselor's response that will serve as your guide for being able to step into the mindset of a counselor with a cognitive orientation.

■ ■ ■ ■ ■ ▬▬▬▬▬▬▬▬▬▬▬▬▬▬▬▬▬▬▬▬▬▬▬▬▬▬

CASE ILLUSTRATION 5.8

JUSTIN GOING BALLISTIC!

REFLECTIONS "ON" PRACTICE

Justin was sent to the counselor by the vice principal. It appears that Justin has been flying off the handle at the least provocation and has ended up in the vice principal's office three times in the past week for fighting. As the counselor prepared for the session, a number of assumptions came to mind as she reflected "on" practice in anticipation of the meeting.

The counselor noted the assumption and was careful to remind herself that these were hypotheses—not facts—that needed to be tested. The tentative goals set for the initial session, as well as the underlying assumptions, are listed below.

1. It may be difficult to establish a working, collaborative alliance with the client since the visit is mandated by the vice principal.
2. It will be important to provide the client with the expectation that change is possible without immediately confronting the dysfunctionality of his anger since it is most likely that the anger seems justified.
3. It is important to clarify, at least initially, the reasons for the counseling and the consequences currently being experienced by the client.
4. If possible, try to address Insight 1, the connection of thoughts to feelings.
5. If we have a working relationship, assign homework.

REFLECTIONS "IN" PRACTICE

As Justin entered the counselor's office, it became immediately clear that he did not want to be there. In addition, his approach to life became quickly apparent as he expressed a number of black-and-white absolute beliefs—most often presented in "shoulds" and "musts" as if he made up the rules for the world. This was to be expected, since quite often it is this type of thinking that underlies feelings of anger and hostile outbursts. While tempted to confront this absolute black-and-white view of the world, the counselor is sensitive to the reality that a working, trusting relationship needs to be established before such confrontation would be effective.

Justin: **(Coming through the door.)**

I'm telling you now . . . I don't want to be here! This is bullshit.

Counselor: You sound and appear angry, and I can hear that you don't want to be here. But since you are maybe you would at least have a seat and help me understand what's going on?

(Counselor showing empathy and inviting the client to join in together.)

Justin: [angrily] I'll tell you what's going on. There's a bunch of jerks running this school and Mr. Hathaway is on top of the list!

Counselor: You're mad at Mr. Hathaway?

Justin: He's just one of the jerks. Look, I don't like it when people start telling me what to do. They're not my boss. They have no right coming down on me.

Counselor: Well Justin, I understand that you don't want people to tell you what to do and what not to do, but I'm confused. How does the fact that someone tells you to do something, how does that make you angry?

(While posing the question and seeking clarification, the counselor is also attempting to set the stage for challenging the client's belief that his anger is caused by others. This is laying the foundation for helping the client connect thought to feeling.)

Justin: What do you mean? You tellin' me you don't get pissed off with people bossing you around?

Counselor: Oh, so it's not that they are telling you something to do or not do that makes you mad, it is when you believe they are bossing you around?

(Counselor reframing the client's statement to begin to introduce the concept of meaning making [i.e, bossing] as the source of the emotion.)

Justin: Yeah . . . so?

Counselor: No, no . . . I was trying to understand, I think I get it now.

(Counselor sensing client resistance, backs off from the subtle confrontation.)

So it's really not what he said that made you mad, it's the fact that you're thinking he is trying to boss you around?

Justin: Yeah . . . I can't stand anybody bossing me. They can stick it.

Counselor: I know you say that you can't stand anybody bossing you around, but I bet if your little brother said, "Hey Justin, go get me soda" you wouldn't go ballistic, or would you?

(Counselor again attempting to lay the foundation for introducing the role of thought to feeling creation.)

Justin: Nah . . . not really. I'd just look at him like "what?"

Counselor: So there are times that some people, like your brother, can tell you to do things but you don't get angry?

Justin: Yeah . . . my girlfriend does it all the time and it doesn't make me mad.

Counselor: Wow, that's interesting. Why do you think that is?

Justin: I don't know. I know they don't mean nothing by it, so I just laugh at them . . . thinking like, "Yeah right. Who was your slave last year?"

Counselor: Justin, that's pretty neat. In fact, I bet you that not many of your friends would understand what you just pointed out.

(Counselor attempting to create cognitive dissonance in the client to make him more receptive to a new perspective.)

Justin: Huh?

Counselor: Well, I bet most of your friends really believe that other people really make them mad at times?

Justin: Yeah . . . so?

(continued)

Counselor: Well, look at what you discovered. Look here [pointing to paper writing out the A-B-C] if somebody like your girlfriend or your brother says to you, "Hey you go get me a soda," [writing it down and drawing an arrow across the page] how do you feel?

(Counselor employing A-B-C chart.)

Justin: Like, yeah right! Who was your slave last year? And just ignore them or tell them to get their own and one for me [laughs].

Counselor: So, you don't sound angry?

Justin: Nah . . . it's no big deal.

Counselor: Fantastic, no big deal. Exactly! You laugh because you are thinking *(Counselor now writing this in the middle column, labeled "B" [belief].),* "Yeah right . . . that's funny . . . no big deal," and this thought seems to lead you to *(Counselor writing in the last column labeled "C" [consequence])* just ignore or tell them to get you one while they are up [laughs] . . . not getting angry!

Justin: Yeah.

Counselor: But look at this. Let's write down the same situation, like, let's say, Thomas—the guy you hit at lunch—says the same thing (rewrites the phrase in column "A"). Now how do you feel [pointing to column "C"]?

Justin: I'd smack him or tell him to go, you know what!

Counselor: Okay, that's how you would act. But how would you feel?

Justin: Probably really pissed.

Counselor: Well, that's where I get confused. One time the words make you laugh and another you get so angry you want to hit somebody.

Justin: That's 'cause he has no right bossing me around. Who the hell does he think he is? He's not getting away with that stuff.

Counselor: You do get angry when you think he is, or I guess anyone is, trying to boss you around?

(Counselor responding empathetically yet reframing it from what he did, to what he thought it meant.)

Counselor: So if I was in your head at the time when Thomas said that . . . is this what you would be saying to yourself? Things like, "He has no right telling me what to do, he can't get away with that, I'll show him"?

Justin: Yeah inside and sometimes out loud.

Counselor: Oh, I get it. So it's not the words "go get me a soda" that make you mad, it's when you say to yourself something like, "This is horrible, this is unfair, he's not getting away with this. Somebody's got to show him." Something like this . . . these are thoughts that get you mad?

(Counselor trying to help client make linkage of thoughts to feelings.)

Justin: Yeah . . . I guess.

Counselor: Well let's test the theory. When Mr. Hathaway told you to come see me, you said you got angry. So can you remember what you were thinking?

Justin: Ah . . . yeah, something like "F . . . him! He can't tell me what to do . . . he's not going to boss me around."

Counselor: Justin, look here [pointing to the A-B-C column]. It looks like the same kind of thinking that you did with Thomas. This is what I meant when I said I bet you will know something that lots of other people don't get . . . and that is . . . [pointing to the paper]. It's not the event or the words that make us mad (*pointing to the consequences*) but what we say to ourselves [pointing to B] that make us angry or scared, or sad!

Justin: Yeah . . . but they aren't my boss!

Counselor: You are absolutely correct they aren't your boss, but neither was your brother or your girlfriend, but you allowed them to think they were, even though you ignored them.

Justin: You're right.

Counselor: Wow . . . I guess . . . rather than saying someone else makes me mad, it really is more accurate to say we make ourselves mad about what others do or don't do? You know, rather than thinking you make me so angry . . . the truth is . . . I make me so angry because of what you are doing?

Justin: Yeah, I guess so. But so what?

Counselor: Well if we are the ones making ourselves mad, then we can decide if it makes sense to get mad. It's like we are the boss of ourselves and we can learn not to give the power of our feelings away to another person. In fact, since we are the ones causing our own feelings, we could get to a point where no one or nothing would make us mad.

Justin: Cool . . . like a ninja?

Counselor: I guess . . . but definitely, cool.

Justin: So what now?

Counselor: How do you feel about maybe seeing me a couple of times to see if I can show you some pretty cool stuff about how our brains work and how we really are the source of our own anger, fear, sadness . . . all those emotions. You know, some "ninja" training? [Laughing]

Justin: Sounds okay . . . especially if it also gets Mr. Hathaway off my back.

Counselor: If it's okay with you I'll tell Mr. Hathaway you came and that you and I are going to work together. But, I am going to need your help to make this all work.

Justin: What do I have to do?

Counselor: How about over the next three days you make some observations and write some notes about how you are feeling and acting?

Justin: I'm not sure what you mean.

(continued)

Counselor: Well how about if over the course of the next three days, you try to write down every time you find yourself getting so angry that you may want to punch someone. I hope you don't do that, 'cause I don't want you getting in any more trouble, but maybe . . . if you do feel that angry you could write a real short description of what was happening, and how you were feeling and acting. Could you do that?

Justin: Sure.

Counselor: Great. Now this part may be a little harder. As you read what you write about the event, maybe you also could jot down all the thoughts you were having, you know, that voice in your head, just write down what you are saying to yourself about what was happening.

Justin: Voice in my head . . . hey, Doc, I'm not nuts [laughing].

Counselor: No you're not . . . but it's wild . . . we all have to talk to ourselves when something happens. It's like our brain asks "What's going on?" and then we have to answer . . . you know, interpret what the situation is—what it means—and that, my friend, is where the action begins. 'Cause if we interpret as "He's my little brother acting like a big shot" we react completely different than if we interpret "How dare he talk to me that way. He can't get away with that!!" But, then, you know that.

Justin: Okay I get it. I think I can do that.

Finally, before moving on to our final operational framework, it may be useful for you to try this one on for size. Exercise 5.1 provides you with an opportunity to step into a cognitive-focused schema as you reflect "on" and "in" counseling—where the client is you!

■ ■ ■ ■ ■ ▬▬▬▬▬▬▬▬▬▬▬▬▬▬▬▬▬▬▬▬

EXERCISE 5.1

MY OWN A-B-Cs

As humans, we are by definition less than perfect. So, regardless of your level of education and mental health, it may be fair to assume there are times when we operate with dysfunctional beliefs and schemata. The current exercise is offered as an opportunity to practice the A-B-C-D- and E of cognitive counseling.

Step 1: The first step is to simply identify an emotion that you find may be somewhat problematic for you. For example, maybe you realize you sometimes get irritated at life's circumstances, or a bit too anxious about the demands you encounter, or maybe you even feel some sadness over events for which you have no control. Select the emotion on which you would like to work.

Step 2: The second step is actually a series of steps. For a given timeline, perhaps a week, keep an "A-B-C" log in which you record times when you feel the identified emotion, and place that feeling in column "C." Next, write a brief description of the event or the situation in which this was experienced, placing that in column "A," and finally, write out all of the thoughts that seem to accompany this situation. Be careful! No editing! It would not be unusual to find that as you start to record a thought, you immediately begin to edit, saying to yourself, "Oh, that's silly!" Try not to edit. Only you will see the thoughts, so let's get them out as they first appeared.

Step 3: Review the log and see if you can match any of the cognitive distortions found in Table 5. 2 with the thoughts you listed in column "B."

Step 4: Dispute those thoughts you have identified as dysfunctional. Ask yourself each of the following questions in regards to your thoughts and allow your answers to reshape and reformulate your thoughts so that it is a more adequate reflection of what is. The fundamental idea is to find the evidence that supports the belief, as well as the evidence that fails to support the belief so that a more balanced belief (one incorporating all the evidence) can be formulated. Looking at your thoughts, ask yourself:

Thought(s) listed in Step 3: _____

_____

1. Is this really true? If not, what would be true?
2. Am I jumping to conclusions? If I saw my thoughts as hypotheses rather than facts, would the evidence completely support them?
3. Am I exaggerating or overemphasizing a negative aspect of the situation? What other less negative or even positive elements have I filtered out?
4. Am I catastrophizing? (Am I making it seem worse than it really is?) What is the most reasonable and realistic worse-case scenario?
5. How do I know it will happen? (Am I a mind reader?) Where's the evidence?
6. Is it really as bad as it seems?
7. Is there another way to look at the situation? If my friend was thinking this way, how would I argue with him/her? What would the impact of my arguments be on changing this thinking?

Step 5: Write down your reframed self-talk and carry it on a card or place it on a Post-it where you will see it and be able to remind yourself to use that thought rather than the previously employed distorted thought. Continue to keep your A-B-C log and see if the reframing is effective.

REFERENCES

Beck, A.T., Rush, A.J., Shaw, B.F., & Emery G. (1979). *Cognitive therapy of depression*. New York: The Guildford Press.

Beck, J.S. (1995). *Cognitive therapy: Basics and beyond*. New York: Guilford.

Dattilio, F.M. (2006). Restructuring schemata from family of origin in couple therapy. *Journal of Cognitive Psychotherapy*, 20(4), 359–373.

Ellis, A. (1983). Rational-emotive therapy (RET) approaches to overcoming resistance: II. How RET disputes clients' irrational resistance-creating beliefs. *British Journal of Cognitive Psychotherapy*, 1(2), 1–16.

Ellis, A. (2002). *Overcoming resistance: A rational emotive behavior therapy intergrated approach* (2nd ed.) New York: Springer Publishing Co.

Ellis, A., & Dryden, W. (1997). The practice of rational-emotivebehavior therapy (2nd ed.). New York: Springer.

Maultsby, M.C. Jr., (1984). *Rational behavior therapy.* Englewood Cliffs, NJ: Prentice-Hall.

Piaget, J. (1983). Piaget's theory. In P. Mussen (Ed.), *Handbook of child psychology* (4th ed., Vol. 1. New York: Wiley.

Piaget, J. (1985). *The equilibration of cognitive structures: The central problem of intellectual development.* Chicago: University of Chicago Press.

Prochaska, J.O. & Norcross, J.C.(1994). *Systems of psychotherapy* (3rd ed.). Pacific Grove, CA: Brooks/Cole Publishing Company.

Rokeach, M. (1968). A theory of organization and change within value-attitude systems. *Journal of Social Issues,* 24(1), 13–33.

SUGGESTED RESOURCES

Freeman, A., Pretzer, J., Fleming, B., & Simon, K. (2004). *Clinical applications of cognitive therapy (2nd ed.).* New York: Kluwer Academic/Plenum Publications.

Kazantzis, N., Deane, F., Ronan, K., & L'Abate, L. (Eds.). (2005). *Using homework assignments in cognitive-behavioral therapy.* New York: Routledge.

Nezu, A., Nezu, C.M., Lombardo, E. (2004). *Cognitive-behavioral case formulation and treatment design: A problem-solving approach* .New York: Springer Publishing Co.

Schuyler, D. (2003). *Cognitive therapy: A practical guide.* W. W. Norton and Company.

Wright, J., Basco, M.R., & Thase, M. (2005). *Learning cognitive-behavior therapy: An illustrated guide.* Arlington, VA: American Psychiatric Publishing.

CHAPTER 6

A TRANSTHEORETICAL-ORIENTING FRAMEWORK

Each of the previous models has been demonstrated to be effective in assisting counselors in their pursuit of helping clients. These models were demonstrated to be effective frameworks through which a counselor processed client information, developed hypotheses, moved to "if . . . then" thinking, introduced interventions and observed the impact, and then recycled through the entire process again. The intent of the preceding chapters was not to argue for or against any particular model, but rather to demonstrate the impact and value that an operative schema has for counselors and the counseling process.

Research (see Lambert, 1992, for a review) suggests that different counseling strategies may produce comparable outcomes despite differences in premises, different foundational assumptions, and different intervention strategies. The realization that change may be achieved through a variety of counseling approaches has stimulated the search for integrative principles of change that transcend the boundaries of any one theoretical orientation. A transtheoretical model of change is not a new or alternative theory of counseling—it is actually a bridge between theory and practice.

The current chapter will describe the basic tenets of the **transtheoretical model (TTM) of change** (Prochaska, & DiClemente, 2002; Prochaska, DiClemente, & Norcross, 1992; Prochaska & Velicer, 1997). This orienting framework represents an empirically derived, multistage, sequential model of general change. As has been done with previous chapters, the focus of this chapter will be on highlighting the utility of this model in guiding counselors' reflections "in" and "on" practice. It is the "mindset," this looking glass of the transtheoretical-orienting framework, that serves as focus for this chapter. As you read, you will be encouraged to both understand and employ the transtheoretical framework to develop and test hypotheses about clients and the interventions felt to be needed. Specifically, after reading this chapter you will be able to:

- describe the basic tenets of a transtheoretical model of counseling;
- explain how the utilization of "stages" of change can guide the counselor's reflection on and in practice; and
- employ a transtheoretical framework to respond to simulated case material.

NOT YOUR TYPICAL ORIENTING FRAMEWORK

For many counselors, especially those new to the profession, it is a challenge enough to be able to attend to a client's disclosure, target areas, or elements for change, and to employ their specific orienting framework to develop interventions. Now we add to the mix the realization that perhaps the intervention we employ—the goals that direct our in and on practice reflections and interactions—may need to be filtered through another set of lenses that help counselors understand where each client is poised along a continuum of change.

While a counselor's specific operative framework directs him/her to the form of intervention employed, the awareness of the stages of change and the processes involved in change may guide the counselor to specific timing of those interventions.

Principles of Change Transcend Theoretical Models

The TTM begins with the assumption that cutting across all specific theoretical approaches to counseling are factors that are elemental to the process of change (Prochaska & Norcross, 1994). The factors are assumed to be those that are operative in all circumstances of change, including that which occurs in and out of the formal counseling dynamic. The processes of change relevant to the transtheoretical model are supported substantially with empirical evidence (DiClemente & Prochaska, 1982; Prochaska & DiClemente, 1983, 1984, 1992; Prochaska, DiClemente & Norcross, 1992; Prochaska & Norcross, 1994; Prochaska, Norcross, Fowler, Follick, & Abrams, 1991).

The TTM describes how people modify a problem behavior or acquire a positive behavior and as the name implies, the principles derived are applicable across theoretical boundaries (Prochaska & DiClemente, 1983; Prochaska, DiClemente, & Norcross, 1992; Prochaska & Velicer, 1997).

THE ASSUMPTIONS UNDERLYING THE TRANSTHEORETICAL MODEL

As noted in the introduction, the TTM *is not a theory* of counseling. It is an integrative eclectic perspective that views counseling as a process of change (Proschaska & DiClemente, 1984). It represents an empirically derived, multistage, sequential model of general change based on the following assumptions.

Processes

A second proposition held by proponents of a TTM is that change can be attributed to specific processes; that is, covert or overt activities that a person engages in to alter his/her affect, thinking, behavior, or relationships. Further, proponents of TTM posit that to a large degree, the change that occurs during counseling could

TABLE 6.1   Processes of Change

PROCESS OF CHANGE	DESCRIPTION
Consciousness-raising	Activities that result in increased awareness of the what is and the what could be
Self-liberation	Processes that result in a person's acceptance of personal responsibility, commitment, and power
Social liberation	Seeking new alternatives in response to the social environment
Counterconditioning	Learning to substitute more useful responses in given circumstances
Stimulus control	Restructuring the environment so the problem behavior is less likely
Self-reevaluation	Reappraising the problem
Environmental reevaluation	Reappraising the effect of the problem on others
Contingency management	Rewards by self or others for making changes

be attributed to eight empirically derived separate processes of change (Prochaska, Velicer, DiClemente, & Fava, 1988). Table 6.1 provides a listing of those processes, along with a brief description of each.

The position taken by those adhering to a transtheoretical model of change is that counselors should employ a comprehensive set of change processes and not be restricted to the two or three typically offered by most theories of counseling (e.g., Prochaska & DiClemente, 1986).

Stages

A third operative assumption and a central construct in the transtheoretical model is that in the process of change, people pass through a number of stages. These stages reflect the temporal and motivational aspects of change. Within this model, the concept of stages represents both a period of time as well as a set of tasks or processes needed for movement to the next stage (Prochaska & DiClemente, 1982, p. 160).

The concept of stages is the key organizing construct of the model. Rather than assuming behavioral change is an end-state action, as if only one change occurs when the goal has been attained, TTM sees change as a progression through a series of five stages. Thus, even when the end-state has yet to be achieved, behavioral change could still be well on its way.

Clients Present at Varying Stages of Change

Counselors employing a transtheoretical model assume that not all of the people entering counseling are at the same stage of change. As such, understanding where the client is along the process of change is essential to developing those strategies that will facilitate the client's movement toward a desired end point. Counselors with a TTM schema also understand that while stage theory is presented as a linear sequencing of steps toward a goal, in practice, clients often exhibit a spiraling or cycling back and forth across these stages as they move toward their desired end point.

STAGE AS PRESCRIPTIVE TO PROCESS

Authors such as Norcross, Prochaska, and DiClemente (1986) suggest that knowing a client's stage of change directs the counselor to strategies that can be systematically employed to effect change. In fact, a key assumption of the transtheoretical model is that interventions need to be matched to an individual's specific stage of change to be effective (Prochaska, Redding, & Evers, 2002; Weinstein, Rothman, & Sutton, 1998). The model suggests, for example, that cognitive strategies, including things such as raising awareness, are more useful at the early stages, whereas behavioral strategies appear more appropriate for the later action and maintenance stages. It is further suggested that mismatching of stage to treatment strategy may elicit client resistance to change and actually undermine therapeutic outcome (Prochaska, Redding, & Evers, 2002).

The counselor employing a transtheoretical-orienting framework is skilled at recognizing the client's stage of change both at the time of initial contact and throughout the counseling contract. In addition to focusing on model-specific interventions (e.g., solution focused, behavioral, cognitive, etc.), the counselor operating with this orienting framework identifies where the client is positioned in terms of the stages of change so that processes can be employed to move the client to a stage of change where these model-specific interventions will prove most effective. The counselor's reflection "on" and "in" practice targets not just the stated end goal, but also the processes needed to facilitate the client's movement through the stages of change toward that end goal.

The stages of change include precontemplation (not thinking about changing the problem behavior within the next six months), contemplation (intending to change in the next six months), preparation (planning to change in the next month, typically having already tried unsuccessfully to change at least once in the past year), action (making health-relevant changes in the behavior for as little as one day or as long as six months), and maintenance (having made behavioral changes for longer than six months) (Prochaska, Redding, & Evers, 2002). Each of these stages are presented in detail below, along with illustrations of the processes prescribed for meeting the client at that stage and facilitating movement to the next.

Precontemplation

The initial stage of change is actually one in which the client most likely has no intention to change. While others may see the need for the client to change, the client appears either in denial or simply oblivious to that need. Quite often, clients entering counseling in a precontemplative stage of change are motivated either by an overt coercion, such as being "sent by the teacher" or mandated by the courts;

or perhaps by more subtle forms of pressure, such as when a loved one pressures the client to come to counseling. In either case, the motivation is other-generated, rather than intrinsic to the client.

Lacking personal motivation or ownership of the need and value of the counseling, clients who enter counseling in a precontemplative stage will often dropout prematurely unless the counselor is skilled in ways to facilitate their movement to the next stage. Consider Case Illustration 5.1, Thomas, who is a tenth-grade student sent to the counselor by his English teacher.

■ ■ ■ ■ ■

CASE ILLUSTRATION 6.1
WHO SENT YOU?

Counselor: Thomas, welcome. Have a seat!

Thomas: Here? [sitting]

Counselor: It's nice to see you. What's the special occasion? [smiling]

Thomas: There's nothing special.

Counselor: Is there something I can help you with?

Thomas: I don't know.

Counselor: You don't know?

Thomas: Ask Mrs. Spellman—she sent me!

Counselor: Oh, Mrs. Spellman, your English teacher? Well, I assume she had some reason or some goal for asking you to come to the counselor's office. What do you think it may have been?

Thomas: I don't know.

Counselor: Okay, maybe we can figure it out. What was happening right before Mrs. Spellman asked you to come visit me?

Thomas: Nothing. Just regular class. Some kids were messing around and she was annoyed.

Counselor: Were you one of the people messing around?

Thomas: Not really, I was laughing at them.

Counselor: And how did she react to your laughing?

Thomas: She was really ticked off . . . like I was laughing at her.

Counselor: Okay, so she sent you here because she thought you were being disrespectful?

Thomas: I guess.

(The counselor would attempt to help Thomas make the connection of his behavior and the teacher's response as a way of moving him toward a contemplative stage of change.)

In reviewing Case Illustration 6.1, one might suggest that Thomas was in denial or simply being oppositional with the counselor, but in either case it is clear that even if he knew the reasons for his referral that they were reasons held by his teacher, Mrs. Spellman, and not self-motivating reasons. Further, any attempt to intervene with the presenting complaint would most likely be unsuccessful. Rather, the initial target for change needs to be the facilitation of Thomas' ownership of the problem and the valuing of a counseling relationship.

Too often, counselors operating without this frame of reference rush into confronting the client or attempting to problem solve all for naught. The counselor employing a TTM schema is able to recognize the signs of precontemplation and to allow that data to guide his/her interventions away from the presenting concern to that of building a working alliance.

In this case, as is true for most cases in which the client enters at the precontemplative stage, the counselor may find the use of processes that raise the client's awareness and ownership of the issues and provide some immediate relief to be of value. The use of accurate empathy and reflection (see Case Illustration 6.2) as well as employment of strategies such as the "miracle question" (see Chapter 3) may be particularly helpful in increasing the client's awareness of the problem and ownership of the value of doing something about it.

■ ■ ■ ■ ■ ▬▬▬

CASE ILLUSTRATION 6.2
REFLECTING TO INCREASE AWARENESS

Counselor: But Charles, I am a little confused. You said you don't want to be here, but here you are?

Charles: I told you, if I want my license back I have to see you or somebody!

Counselor: Oh, so you can't have your license unless you come to a counselor? And that's because . . . ?

Charles: They have some stupid rules.

Counselor: A stupid rule?

Charles: I got caught drinking after the dance and got a DUI!

Counselor: So you got caught breaking the law with the DUI. Okay. I know you said it is a stupid rule, but were you aware that there is a law about underage drinking and driving under the influence?

Charles: Yeah . . . of course.

Counselor: Okay. But you felt like you could get away with it?

Charles: Yeah, I usually do!

Counselor: So, you gambled on getting away with it but this time you lost?

Charles: Yeah. I guess I got too wasted and was driving pretty crazy.

Counselor: Wow, I'm glad you didn't hurt yourself.

Charles: Yeah, or screw up my car. I just got it painted!

Counselor: So maybe you feel like the law is stupid and I'm sure the DUI is costing you quite a bit, but the truth is maybe it stopped you from wrecking your car and hurting yourself . . . or maybe someone else?

Charles: I guess.

Counselor: Charles, I know that you "have" to be here if you want your license back, but actually you don't have to be here! In fact, I find that it really is better if the people I work with want to be here.

Charles: I don't know. It's just everybody is on my back.

Counselor: Everybody?

Charles: Well, my parents, my girlfriend . . . they are always telling me I'm going to kill someone or myself if I don't stop drinking.

Counselor: Well it sounds like they care about you and are concerned. Maybe this is something you and I could work on. You know, maybe we could try to figure out what you could do to help them be less concerned?

Charles: I guess.

While Charles (see Case Illustration 6.2) may not be totally convinced of his need for counseling, the counselor's use of attending skills and accurate reflection appear to have at least brought him to the recognition that perhaps working with the counselor may assist in one area of his life; that is, addressing the pressure coming from his parents and girlfriend.

Contemplation

The second stage along this continuum of change is that of **contemplation**. In this stage of change, the client is aware that a problem exists and perhaps has been seriously thinking about addressing these issues for some time. Clients often arrive at this stage because of some event that has increased their awareness of the potential costs to not changing. For example, a student who now understands that he may not graduate with his class unless he completes his science assignments or the person who is now considering engaging in a much-needed weight reduction program given the upcoming class reunion may move from not seeing or owning a problem (i.e., precontemplative) to now embracing this issue as a result of these new events in their lives (i.e., graduation and reunion).

The client in this stage is both aware and desirous of change but has not yet made a serious commitment to take action. Clients could literally be in this stage of contemplation without action for years (DiClemente, Prochaska, & Gibertini, 1985). Perhaps you or someone you know have been seriously considering quitting smoking, changing jobs, joining a gym, or getting into or out of a relationship, but really haven't done much more than talk about it. This is a key indication that you and/or your friend remain in the contemplative stage.

People can be literally stuck in contemplation because they lack the skills and resources necessary to move forward or simply because they are having a difficult time setting manageable, achievable goals. For other clients, moving and taking action is too anxiety provoking, perhaps appearing too challenging and too costly. This is certainly the case in a person who has been in an unsatisfying relationship and yet is afraid to leave it, if leaving it means being all alone!

For clients stuck in contemplation, a counselor can facilitate movement to the action stage by breaking the steps down into smaller units of minimal cost and maximal payoff. Consider Case Illustration 6.3. In this case, the counselor operating from a solution-focused schema (see Chapter 3) helps the client move from contemplation to action by using scaling.

■ ■ ■ ■ ■ ▬▬▬▬▬▬▬▬▬▬▬▬▬▬▬▬▬▬▬▬▬▬▬▬▬▬▬▬▬▬▬▬▬▬

CASE ILLUSTRATION 6.3

JOIN THE CROWD

Counselor: That's super! You did a great job with that miracle question.

Kristen: Yeah, but I'll never be able to do that . . . that's a dream.

Counselor: Well, you are probably correct in saying that it would be really hard to go from where you are now to your ideal. If I understood what you said before, you see yourself at three, where a three is barely being able to look at the girls at the lunch table.

Kristen: Yeah . . . so there's no way I can go from there . . . to simply going up to them, sitting down, and inviting myself into their conversation!

Counselor: I guess that would be a real big step, but how about if we think about it in terms of little steps? Just like if we were trying to go from the ground floor in school to the second floor we wouldn't try it in one big leap . . . ouch!

Kristen: [laughing] Yeah, that could strain your hammies.

Counselor: So what would the next step look like? You know, step four or five?

Kristen: I don't know.

Counselor: Well, let's see, at three you are able to at least make eye contact with the girls as you walk past their table.

Kristen: Yeah, but even that is hard.

Counselor: I'm sure . . . but if making eye contact is a three, what is something smaller you could do that would move you up the scale?

Kristen: Well, I guess I could try to make eye contact and smile as I pass!

Counselor: That's great. Would you be willing to give it a try?

Kristen: As long as I don't strain my hammies. [laughing]

In Case Illustration 6.3, Kristen, the client, truly wanted to take action that would help her initiate social contact with the girls at lunch, but was stuck in contemplation because the action necessary appeared too difficult. Her movement to action was facilitated by the counselor's use of scaling as a strategy that helped to reduce the perceived "cost" of taking action. With this scaling approach in place, the client could now take a series of smaller steps that will eventually move her toward her goal.

Contemplation is a "thinking not doing" stage (Baldwin, 1991, p. 39). Thus, counselors working with clients at this stage need to be very cautious not to try to move the client on too quickly. The client needs time to consider, reflect, and analyze the pros and cons of change. Attempting to move the client too quickly may result in termination of counseling—not because of client resistance but simply due to the fact that the client lacks the readiness for the change being attempted. Case Illustration 6.4 highlights this point.

■ ■ ■ ■ ■ ▬▬▬▬▬▬▬▬▬▬▬▬▬▬▬▬▬▬▬▬▬▬▬▬▬▬▬▬▬▬▬▬▬▬▬▬

CASE ILLUSTRATION 6.4
COMING OUT

Colleen has been working with Mrs. Twisdale, the counselor, for the past three months. While numerous presenting concerns were initially offered, the focus of counseling has now targeted Colleen's desire to tell her parents that she is a lesbian. Colleen presents as a self-assured individual who is comfortable with her sexual orientation. As such, the counselor has begun to strategize with the client about the when and how of disclosing to her parents.

Counselor: Well Colleen, how did it go?

Colleen: You know, I was going to talk with them after dinner, just like we role-played, but then my dad got into his stock papers and I didn't want to bother him.

Counselor: But Colleen, don't you think your disclosure was more important than his review of the stocks?

Colleen: Of course, but I've waited this long . . . what's the big deal?

Counselor: I know you've been wanting to do this for a while and I know how important it is to you, so I just thought you were going to do it.

Colleen: Yeah I will . . . but you know what, the more I think about it . . . I'm okay with being gay and my close friends know and so does my sister, so why do I have to be in my parents' face about it?

Counselor: Colleen, I'm a little confused. I know we talked about this and if I understood what you said before, it was simply that while you didn't want to cause them to have concerns, you felt that it was important to be genuine and who you are, and to not let your parents think that you would someday have a husband like your sister Ellen!

Colleen: Yeah I do. But you know what? The use of the role play was helpful . . . and I think I know what to do. For now, maybe I'll just let it be and maybe do it later when there is less going on.

In reviewing Case Illustration 6.4, it is clear that the client has the skills to make the desired disclosure yet appears unable or unwilling to do so. In this case, the counselor hypothesizes that the resistance is a function of her operating from a contemplation stage. As such, the counselor targets ways to support the client in that stage while attempting to facilitate movement to the next stage (i.e., action stage; see Case Illustration 6.5, Colleen Continued). The counselor, reflecting in practice and employing a TTM-orienting schema was able to be supportive and re-engage Colleen in the counseling relationship, a step that was needed more than pushing the client to disclosure.

■ ■ ■ ■ ■

CASE ILLUSTRATION 6.5
COLLEEN CONTINUED

Counselor: Colleen, you are absolutely correct. I think the things we have discussed and some of the strategies, especially the role play, really have helped you to envision how you wanted to approach this. I really think you know how to do it when you are ready to do it!

Colleen: Yeah, the role play really does help and all the anxiety-reduction skills are great . . . and I am ready, but maybe . . . I don't know . . .

Counselor: Hey, you've worked hard. We don't have to push anything—there's no deadline here. Why don't we just take it off the table right now?

Colleen: Okay.

Counselor: But I'm wondering if it would be helpful to reflect on last night and what was going on at home—and what you were thinking—remember that self-talk?

Colleen: I guess.

Counselor: Well, I was just thinking that maybe by reviewing what was going on with mom and dad and you, last night, we may discover some things that we hadn't previously considered.

Colleen: Oh, okay. That makes sense.

As suggested by Case Illustrations 6.4 and 6.5, those in contemplation are often characterized by ambivalence in which they experience both a fear of change and a fear of staying the same. Any processes that can help the client reduce the fear of change and/or increase the realization of the costs incurred by staying the same will help tip the scale in favor of action. Something as simple as helping the client reevaluate the implications of change and weigh these against the advantages and disadvantages of staying the same may be an effective intervention at this point of the change process. Case Illustration 6.6 demonstrates the counselor's use of a cost-benefit analysis to help the client not just make a decision, but actually make the movement toward the next stage of change—preparation.

■ ■ ■ ■ ■ ▬▬▬▬▬▬▬▬▬▬▬▬▬▬▬▬▬▬▬▬▬▬▬▬▬▬▬▬▬▬▬▬▬

CASE ILLUSTRATION 6.6
COST/BENEFITS

Counselor: So Sarah, it sounds like you really have thought a long time about staying in your relationship with Brad and everyone seems to be giving you advice?

Sarah: Yeah . . . I'm so confused. Some of my friends tell me he's a loser, others think I'm so lucky, I don't know what to do, I don't want to screw this up!

Counselor: [taking out a piece of paper] Well Sarah, what do you see as your options?

Sarah: Well I guess I could ask Brad if we could take a break from the relationship, but I'm not sure what would happen.

Counselor: So one choice would be to ask Brad if you could take a break. What does that mean?

Sarah: Well, you know, like not go steady for a month or so?

Counselor: And during that month, would you both be able to date other people? Go on dates together? Have contact?

Sarah: Yeah, like for a month we could see other people if we wanted and still talk to each other but like only once a day.

Counselor: Okay, so let's write down here as our choice "A." Now what other choices might you have?

Sarah: I guess I could keep it as it is . . . like seeing each other exclusively and having lots of calls and text messages every day.

Counselor: Okay, I'll write that down as choice "B." So how about if we start to list all the possible benefits to each of these choices but also, we need to figure out all the costs to each choice.

Sarah: Costs?

Counselor: Sure, like any choice requires energy on your part, or it may involve not being able to do something else. That's called an opportunity cost. It may even cost you money, like for excessive text messaging?

Sarah: Nah . . . I have unlimited service. [laughing]

Counselor: Okay, so we can scratch that. [smiling] But let's list some benefits to staying with Brad as is and I'll write them here. [pointing to a block on the paper under choice "B"]

Assuming that Sarah and the counselor can identify costs and benefits to both choices of either staying in the relationship or moving to a new form of relating, these data may be enough to facilitate Sarah's commitment to move in one or the other direction.

Preparation

Clients moving from contemplation to preparation often announce this movement. Clients in this preparation stage often decrease their questions about and resistance to the problem or they may increase their statement of resolve. It is not unusual to have clients in this stage share their visions of life after change and even begin to engage in small "experiments" with change (Miller & Rollnick, 1991). For example, Sarah (see Case Illustration 6.6) now verbalizes how choosing to change the relationship would allow her to spend more time with girlfriends and be able to engage in dates that are less intense; both are indications of her preparation to change the current relationship with Brad. With these disclosures as the "ifs" in the counselor's procedural thinking, the counselor will now begin to search for the appropriate intervention (the "thens") that will facilitate Sarah's movement to full-blown action. Being at a stage of preparation doesn't automatically translate into action. At this stage of preparation, a client may appear to be testing the water, showing some action in the desired direction but not yet at the critical level to make the significant commitment. For example, consider the client who comes to counseling just to "see what it's like." This client has made a step in a potentially fruitful direction but has done so cautiously and thus needs to be supported and not pushed. It is important that the counselor spot when this stage is apparent so that strategies used will capitalize on the client's resolve.

At this stage of preparation, the use of goal setting and cost reduction strategies will prove useful. The counselor needs to encourage the client to commit to change even when that action is only preliminary or precursory to the real action. The counselor needs to affirm that all such change, even little "experiments," are steps in the right direction. As such, the counselor who on initial contact with a client hears, "I'm here just to see if this will have any value," may do well to both affirm the initial action and perhaps facilitate commitment to action by being supportive and providing immediate payoff to the step taken. Under these conditions, the counselor may affirm the decision to come as an excellent first step, and help the client identify achievable goals for that specific session in order to ensure a positive experience. The possible rapid transition of a client from precontemplative to preparatory may best be illustrated by the following description of an initial session.

Theodore came to counseling at the insistence of his mother, stating that she is concerned "cause I don't have a ton of friends!" While he initially didn't feel this was a big deal (i.e., precontemplation), the reflections and questioning of the counselor assisted the client to see that perhaps the issue wasn't so much whether he had a ton of friends, but that he was apparently withdrawing from social interaction because of his anxiety about a speech impediment. This redefining of the issue as both persistent anxiety and social withdrawal helped Theodore own the actual costs he encounters (i.e., always anxious) and possible future costs of continued social withdrawal (e.g., difficulty getting a job). Understanding and owning the cost of his current behavior moved Theodore into the contemplation stage.

In subsequent sessions, the client began to share that he could see the benefits of becoming more social and in fact even shared a couple of attempts of mini-experiments that he tried. For example, he noted that on one occasion he approached a classmate and asked if he could copy some notes that he missed. This discussion of what could be and the evidence of his testing the water by way of his mini-experiment indicated that Theodore was moving into the preparation stage. With this as a foundation, the counselor and client were ready to move to full commitment to change, a process facilitated by the creation of reasonable goals of change and the development of strategies, or actions to accomplish this change (action stage).

Action

When it becomes clear that the client is now actively engaged in making changes as a means of addressing concerns or moving toward goals, he/she is in the action stage of change. The action stage is where problematic behavior and circumstances are actually changed and modified. The counselor will know the client is in the action stage because of the clear demonstration of his/her investment of resources into the change process. The client, for example, will risk deeper disclosures, be open to confrontation and therapeutic feedback, be willing to engage in therapeutic homework, and invest in applying strategies discussed and agreed on.

Typically, clients in this stage can point to experiences of success even if the alteration is only for a brief period. Think about the student who excitedly enters the counselor's office with test paper in hand—smiling ear to ear—and exclaiming, "Whew . . . that was hard. But I studied and look . . . an A." This client is in the action stage of change. And while there may be setbacks, the client is committed!

What the client and the counselor choose to do during this stage will most likely be determined by the nature of the client's concerns and goals as well as the counselor's operating framework (e.g., solution focused, behavioral, cognitive, etc.). However, in a generic way, the counselor serves at this stage as a consultant, assisting the client to become more autonomous and to take control over his/her life.

Maintenance

Now that change has taken place and new patterns are becoming established, it is important to implement strategies of maintenance. The final stage of change is that of gain consolidation, generalization, and relapse prevention.

Prochaska and Norcross (1994) stressed the need for clients to be aware of the possible cognitive, behavioral, emotional, and environmental pitfalls that can get in the way of successful action. They point out that awareness is a major factor in preventing lapses from becoming complete relapses. This is not a passive stage, such as simply asking the client to drop in and keep the counselor up to speed with how he/she is doing. This stage of change requires establishment of strategies that facilitate the maintenance of the changes established. Like all other stages of change, maintenance requires reflection in and on practice.

At this point of change, clients may benefit from an education of the relapse dynamic and encouragement for continued actions necessary to prevent relapse of symptoms (Gorski & Miller, 1982)—that is, helping the client understand the external and internal conditions that may elicit a return to a problem behavior as well as strategies that buffer the client from such solicitation. Consider the client who has worked hard to break his habit of smoking. This client may be helped to maintain his new nonsmoking behavior by identifying the times, locations, and people who are most associated with his previous smoking behavior and developing strategies that are geared to either reducing these contacts or buffering him from the possible negative impact of these situations.

In this stage of change, the counselor needs to target the counseling to the identification of more natural supports for the client's change as well as personal strategies to be used to maintain the change now that counseling is ending. Consider the dialogue in Case illustration 6.7.

■ ■ ■ ■ ■ ▬▬▬▬▬▬▬▬▬

CASE ILLUSTRATION 6.7
I'M KEEPING THE PICTURE

Leonard: I've been keeping my log like you showed me. I've been using that 10-point number system to record how anxious I've been and my scores are now always below 3. There was only one time when I was going into my college boards that it went to about a 6!

Counselor: Leonard, I am so happy for you. You've worked hard with learning to use the relaxation tapes and challenging your catastrophic thinking. You truly are controlling your needless anxiety. You should feel good about yourself.

Leonard: I feel great!

Counselor: And needless to say, I am here if you ever want to stop in, or feel a "tune up" is in order. [smiling]

Leonard: I know where you are, trust me. [laughing] But actually, I wanted to let you know that a couple of the things you suggested last month really helped and I am going to continue using them.

Counselor: Really?

Leonard: Well, first I've really gotten into a routine of practicing my relaxation exercises. I do them every night right before I do my homework. It's been great. I've even taught my girlfriend how to do them.

Counselor: That's fantastic.

Leonard: And do you remember the first time you explained to me the idea of the monster in the room? Well I made a little note I put both on my desk at home and on my binder in school that says "Where's the monster?" It's really cool anytime I start to get anxious about being called on or having to go to the front board I just read the note, take a deep breath and bingo—I'm grounded.

Counselor: Leonard, they are great ideas! They really should help you keep your focus and stay away from catastrophizing. You know it may also help to keep your "stinkin' thinking" journal. You know, periodically review situations that cause some anxiety using the A-B-C columns like we did.

Leonard: Oops I forgot to tell you—I am. And I have even gone back to some of the old stuff . . . just to remind me how silly it is!

Counselor: Well we both know it didn't feel silly. It's great that now when you think of all those things you can see they weren't as important as you made them. I really think you have some super ideas for keeping yourself on track. And, anytime you want to just check in, you know where I am!

TTM GUIDING REFECTION "IN" AND "ON" PRACTICE

Imagine a scenario in which a school counselor enters her office only to find Alicia, one of her students, sitting there, looking a bit forlorn and confused. This counselor may call on a specific orienting framework (e.g., solution focused, behavioral, cognitive, etc.) to help her begin to conceptualize this case and to develop a treatment plan. However, if this counselor also employs a TTM of change to guide her reflections on and in practice, her initial reflections on Alicia may include questions such as: Does she own the problem? Has she taken any steps toward her desired goal? In addition, there may be the more traditional questions such as: Why is she here? What does she hope to gain?

This process of employing the lens of TTM to guide a counselor's reflection on practice and adjust, by way of reflection in practice, is highlighted in our final Case Illustration 6.8.

As you read the case, it may be helpful to put on the lens—the mindset of a counselor employing a transtheoretical model of change as his/her orienting schema. With this in place you may be able to anticipate the counselor's response to the material being presented by the client. Responses are guided not just by client concerns or end goal but also by the demands of the stage of change being manifested. Figure 6.1 may serve as a good guide to the processes to be employed at any one time in the counseling interaction to facilitate client movement through the stages of change. It may be useful to make reference to this table as you read the transcript that follows.

FIGURE 6.1 Integrating Stages and Processes of Change

Precontemplation	Contemplation	Preparation	Action	Maintenance
Consciousness raising (observation, confrontation, interpretation, data collection)	Self-reevaluation (of behavior on self-others)	Self-liberation strategies (goal-setting, force field analyses, scaling, shaping, increasing self-efficacy)	Therapy-specific strategies	Managing the environment to increase support, reduce, and control negative influences
Providing dramatic relief (venting, catharsis, crises intervention)	Consciousness raising			Create supports, routines, structures, reminders that assist maintenance of new behavior

■ ■ ■ ■ ■ ▬▬▬▬▬▬▬▬▬▬▬▬▬▬▬▬▬

CASE ILLUSTRATION 6.8
I DON'T CARE

Background: D.J. is a tenth grade student at Jackson-Stones High School. D.J.'s record would indicate that he is a bright, very creative (artistic) boy, who has generally achieved at a "C" level academically. D.J. has been sent to see the school counselor because he is in danger of failing his sophomore year and would have to repeat the entire year. The counselor, Mr. Otis, received the following referral from D.J.'s homeroom teacher.

> Mr. Otis, would you please see D.J.? I have talked with him but to no avail. He appears depressed and not at all concerned about school, grades, or from what I gather, anything. I saw his third-quarter grades and he's in danger of failing every class unless something is done.

Counselor reflections "on" practice (prior to initial contact)

The counselor in this situation will want to assess D.J.'s emotional state and try to understand why he is apparently unmotivated to perform up to his capability. However, in addition, he will also want to assess where this client may be on the continuum of change so that he can use strategies to facilitate movement to the next stage of change.

Reflections:

(I assume since this is coming from the homeroom teacher, D.J. is not in an action stage. I wonder if he sees a problem? Owns the problem? Or perhaps is simply unsure or unable to engage in action?)

(If D.J. is in a precontemplative stage I will need to go slow—I'm sure others have brow-beaten him, so maybe it's best to just be supportive. But if possible, I'd like to share both the reality of his grades and the possible consequences of continuing down this path as well as the fact that we still have an option or two.)

(I need to remember that while I want to jump in and start problem solving with D.J. I need to capitalize on the stage of change-specific problem-solving approaches to prompt a successive pattern of change.)

With these reflections as a guide, Mr. Otis sets the following treatment plan in place.

- Send a request to see D.J. during his study hall.
- Explain to D.J. the basis for the request (i.e., his homeroom teacher's concerns).
- Invite D.J. to share his perspective on the homeroom teacher's concerns and the reality that he may fail.
- Use this invitation to assess D.J.'s position on the continuum of change.
- Employ strategies to move D.J. to the next stage of change.

First meeting with D.J.

Counselor: Thanks, D.J., for coming up to see me. I hope taking you out of study hall was not a big inconvenience?

D.J.: Nah, I don't do anything in there anyway . . . maybe sleep or draw!

Counselor: Well in either case, I really appreciate you coming. Do you have any idea why I asked to see you?

D.J.: Nope . . . I just assume you do this with everyone?

Counselor: Well, actually I do see all the students assigned to me one time or another, but this time I called you in because I received a note from Mrs. Restal.

D.J.: Oh, Mrs. Restal, nice lady, but a pain at times.

(Counselor, reflecting in practice, wanting to encourage D.J.'s awareness and ownership of the problem.)

Counselor: A bit of a pain at times?

D.J.: Don't get me wrong, I really like her, but since the report cards went out it's like I am her own little project.

Counselor: Maybe you can help me. When you say "her own little project," what do you mean?

D.J.: Well, I had all F's on my report card for this marking period and even though I passed last marking period there's a chance that I may have to repeat the year unless I get my butt in gear!

Counselor: Oh, so Mrs. Restal is concerned that you may be failing for the year and would have to repeat?

D.J.: Yeah, but truthfully I don't care!

(Counselor, reflecting in practice, wants to clarify is it that he is unaware? Or finds the alternative too overwhelming?)

Counselor: You don't care if you fail this year?

D.J.: Yeah, I don't care. [sounding defensive]

(Counselor, reflecting in practice, trying to get D.J. to become aware and take ownership, that is, move from precontemplative to contemplative stage of change.)

(continued)

Counselor: D.J., I can hear you say you don't care, but your tone of voice and the way you just looked down seems to suggest you do care at least a little?

D.J.: I mean, nobody wants to repeat a whole year. I mean, my parents would go ballistic and all my friends will be moving on but . . . .

[becomes quiet and a bit upset]

(Counselor, reflecting in practice, D.J. is aware of the problem but is stuck thinking it's either too much or it's too late.)

Counselor: I can see this is actually upsetting to you. Clearly you don't want to start over, or upset your parents or lose your friends.

D.J.: But I failed everything!

Counselor: It sounds like you would like to do something to change this but, at least at this moment, it seems hopeless, unchangeable?

D.J.: It is! I failed everything!!

(Counselor, reflecting in practice, D.J. clearly owns the problem and wants something to change but is stuck in contemplation since he doesn't know what to do. I need to help without rescuing!)

Counselor: That can be scary and truthfully, if it were hopeless, I would say, "Why bother?" But D.J., I don't think it is hopeless.

D.J.: What do you mean?

(Counselor, reflecting in practice, if I can break it down for him, I may get him to take a small step toward preparation!)

Counselor: Well, when I look at your grades, it seems that if you can get C's or better in every class, you will pass for the year and I noticed that in the second marking period you did get at least C's in every class.

D.J.: Getting C's is no big deal. I just have to do the work, you know, the assignments and homework.

Counselor: (*working as facilitator and supporter*) That's super. So you know what to do. But since we are just starting the new marking period, I wonder if it would help if we had a real accurate idea of what the assignments, projects, and tests will be. Maybe if we had that, we could put them in some type of order so it wouldn't feel so overwhelming?

D.J.: I could ask the teachers what we'll be doing. They usually tell us anyway. But it would be a good way to butter them up—[smiling] you know, let them think I am turning over a new leaf!

(Counselor, reflecting in practice, D.J. is in preparatory stage. He needs to be affirmed and encouraged and maybe even structure the task and goals so that they will be successful.)

Counselor: That is fantastic. But let's go slow, we don't have to panic since we are doing this right at the beginning of the marking period. So which course do you feel will be the easiest to get your grade to a C or better?

D.J.:   Probably Mrs. Restal's English class.

Counselor: What would you have to do in that class to improve the grade?

D.J.:   Just study for the vocabularly quiz every Friday and hand in my journal.

Counselor: Would you be willing to try a mini-experiment? *(Testing if the client is in the preparatory stage.)*

D.J.:   I guess. What is it?

Counselor: How about if just as an experiment you study for tomorrow's vocabulary quiz and write something in your journal tonight and hand it in tomorrow. Could you do that?

D.J.:   Sure.

Counselor: Fantastic, I'll check with Ms. Restal on Monday to see what she thinks.

D.J.:   If it works she'll think you're a hero! [smiling]

Counselor: Yep . . . that's what I am . . . a hero! Hey there's the bell. Look, I will call you out of study hall and tell you what I found, if that's okay?

D.J.:   I can just stop down, you don't need to send for me.

Counselor reflections on practice (following initial contact)

Well, it appears that D.J. is concerned but both scared and feeling a bit hopeless. I hope he is able to follow through and experiences some success. We could certainly build on that. I guess the real test of his commitment to action is if he not only studied for the quiz and did his journal but shows up on his own without being called down to the office!

The counselor's reflections suggest that he believes D.J. has moved from precontemplative through to preparation but is open to allow the "data" to support this hypothesis.

Monday: Second session

D.J.:   [knocking on the counselor's door]

Hey, you ready for me? [smiling]

Counselor: Right on time, come on in.

(Counselor, reflecting in practice: Great! D.J. is in preparatory stage. He certainly is more motivated and self-driven than on our first meeting. Maybe we can move to action and strategy planning today?)

Counselor: Why the big grin?

D.J.:   Well, I just saw Mrs. Restal and she gave me a high five—which trust me, looked weird!

Counselor: Why the high five?

D.J.:   Well, apparently I got a 100 on the vocab test and she loved my reflections in my journal . . . you know [with a sarcastic tone and high-pitch voice] I'm just a creative writer!

(continued)

Counselor: [affirming] That's super about the 100! I'm not sure the voice will attract many girls, however. [laughing]

D.J.:   Yeah.

Counselor: But all kidding aside, you are pretty creative—both with your writing and your art work.

D.J.:   Yeah, I was thinking I would like to go to the Art Institute after I graduate.

(Counselor, reflecting in practice, D.J. is clearly giving evidence of his commitment and entering the stage of action.)

Counselor: Whoa, hold on "beany boy"! Graduate and college—let's get you through tenth grade. But I think it's super you're thinking that way and there is absolutely nothing to stop you . . . hmmm . . . except . . .

D.J.:   Me!

Counselor: Yep. But if we can come up with a plan like we did for English for all your other classes and figure out a way to get you to stick with it, then college, here we come! [smiling]

D.J.:   I got some ideas about that, and the only class I'm not sure about is Algebra II. I mean I understand it, but I think that I may have stepped on Dr. Morrison's toes . . . and that can come back to bite me.

Counselor: Wow, it sounds like you have done a lot more over the weekend than I expected. I'd love to hear your ideas about your classes and you and I can maybe put our heads together about Algebra?

(Counselor, reflecting in practice, D.J. is in the action stage and appears to need support, encouragement, and maybe some structuring so that what he decides to do will be successful. As we go through his plans, any adjustments I make will be small and I will reinforce his effort and insights. When it comes to Dr. Morrison, we'll collaborate, brainstorm ideas.)

Counselor reflections on practice following interim reports

Wow, D.J. is shooting for the honor roll. If it wasn't for Algebra's B-, all A's fantastic! Clearly he is engaged and moving in the direction we set. I want to call him down and reinforce this but also strategize with him about how he can stick to it for the next two years.

Maintenance session

Counselor: D.J. come on in. Here's the man! I just saw your interims—fantastic!

D.J.:   [putting on a mocking pout] Yeah, if it wasn't for Algebra I'd be on route to getting first honors. [smiling] Actually, it's cool. Me and Dr. Morrison are on good terms and math just isn't my thing. I'd rather spend time with the writing and music and drawing—you know, my creative side. [laughing]

Counselor: I love it. And yes, I understand the creative side stuff but we want to get your GPA as high as possible, so when it comes time to look at school you'll have lots of options. So creative side or not, keep working on the math.

D.J.:   Actually, I am. Dr. Morrison has been tutoring me during study hall since I don't have to come here! [smiling]

(Counselor, reflecting in practice, it is important to consolidate for D.J. as part of the maintenance plan.)

Counselor: D.J., that's great. You know when you first came in to see me I know it felt hopeless but you did some really neat things. You were able to break it down and look at each class and what was needed, and because you have really good academic skills, once you made your mind up to do it, it was all up hill! Now don't get me wrong, I know it was a lot of work, but you do have the ability as long as you can keep yourself motivated.

D.J.:   Thanks, you really helped when you helped me break it down in small steps. That made it seem doable.

Counselor: Well thank you. But now I'm wondering what can we do to keep your motivation up?

D.J.:   Actually, a couple of things have happened that I think will help. First, my parents took me down to the Art Institute, just to see it. It is so cool. Anyway, I have this picture of the Institute on my desk at home and trust me . . . I see that and bingo—I'm doing homework. Also, I am hanging out with some new people—Niajian, Angelo, Wally, and Carol—and we kind of have a grade competition going on.

(Counselor, reflecting in practice, D.J. is really taking responsibility and has developed both a good support group and a great behavioral cue to motivate his study. Both seem like very good maintenance strategies.)

Counselor: Great ideas! That picture will certainly be a reminder of your goal and the value in doing . . . (yuk) . . . math! But it is also cool that you're hanging with those guys. They are all in the honor's society, but yet are apparently pretty cool.

D.J.:   Yep . . . especially Carol.

Counselor: Okay, Carol, hmmmm. Well maybe that's a point for discussion at some future time? [laughing]

D.J.:   Maybe.

Counselor: Hey, you know where to find me . . . and if you don't . . . I'll catch up with you before the end of the year just to see how things are going . . . you know, with math . . . and . . . Carol? [smiles]

Finally, before we move on to our case applications, it may be useful for you to try this one on for size. Exercise 6.1 provides you with an opportunity to take a look at *your own* goals as reflected in a transtheoretical model of change looking glass.

■ ■ ■ ■ ■

EXERCISE 6.1

NEW YEAR'S RESOLUTIONS

Directions: If you are like most people, you probably use special events like New Year's or your birthday to spend time reviewing where you are, how you have been, and maybe ways you would like to change. Similarly, as you reflect on your past experience with setting these goals and keeping to your resolutions, you may find that for some you were quite successful and others never got off the ground.

This exercise is aimed at the application of a TTM of change to your own life goals.

Step 1: Make a table. On a piece of paper, make four columns with the following headings.

Goals	Progress/stage of change	Recommendation	Review and plan for adjustment

Step 2: Goal identification. Take a few moments to really reflect on you and your life and identify five goals for change. These goals could cover various domains such as health (start exercising, stop smoking, etc.), wealth (save more, stop using charges, earn more money, etc.), relationships (find an intimate partner, make new friends, confront a relationship that isn't working, etc.), self-growth (take classes, read more, participate in yoga, go to church, etc.), and anything that you think you would like to accomplish.

Write these goals down in the table under the heading of "goals."

Step 3: Progress/stage of change assessment. For each of the identified goals, assess your current stage of change or progress toward your end state. In this exercise, let's use the following description of stages.

- Seemed to have forgotten about it . . . was a good idea . . . but (precontemplation)
- It's on my things to do . . . just can't get to it . . . (contemplation)
- I started . . . got a little bogged down . . . but I did start . . . (preparation)
- I'm working on it . . . (action)
- Did it! (maintenance)

List the stage next to the goal in the appropriate column.

Step 4: Selecting processes appropriate to the stage of change for each goal. Now that you have identified where you are along a continuum of change, for each of your goals, write out a specific recommendation that may help move you to the next stage. Use Figure 6.1 as a guide to identifying specific strategies you could employ to assist you to move along the stages of change for each of the goals listed in Step 1. It may help to share your plan with a classmate or colleague to receive their insight and ideas.

List your recommendation in the column labeled "recommendation."

Step 5: Review and adjust/reflecting on practice. In a reasonable amount of time (e.g., 1 week, 1 month, etc.), return to your table and see where you stand with each of the goals. Reassess the stage of change for each goal. Did your recommended change process (Step 3) help? If yes, what could you do to move along the change continuum? If not, was it a matter of not doing the processes described? Was it a matter of an ineffective process? How can you use these data to adjust your plan for change?

It may be helpful to share your data and your insights with a classmate or a colleague.

REFERENCES

Baldwin, S. (1991). Helping the unsure. In R. Davidson, S. Rollnick, & I. MacEwan (Eds.), *Counselling problem drinkers* London: Routledge.

DiClemente, C. C. & Prochaska, J. O. (1982). Self-change and therapy change of smoking behavior: A comparison of processes of change of cessation and maintenance. *Addictive Behaviors, 7,* 133–142.

DiClemente, C. C. Prochaska, J. O., & Gibertini, M. (1985). Self-efficacy and the stages of self change of smoking. *Cognitive Therapy and Research, 9*(2), 181–200.

Gorski, T. T. & Miller, M. (1982). *Counseling for relapse prevention.* Independence, MO: Independence Press.

Lambert, M. J. (1992). Psychotherapy out-come research: Implications for integrative and eclectic therapists. In J. C. Norcross & M. R. Goldfried (Eds.), *Handbook of psychotherapy integration.* New York: Basic.

Miller, W., & Rollnick, S. (1991). *Motivational interviewing: Preparing people to change addictive behavior.* New York: Guilford.

Norcross, J. C., Prochaska, J. O., & DiClemente C. C. (1986). Self-change of psychological distress: Laypersons' vs. psychologists' coping strategies. *Journal of Clinical Psychology, 42*(5), 834–840.

Prochaska, J. O. & DiClemente, C. C. (1982). Transtheoretical therapy: Toward a more integrative model of change. *Psychotherapy: Theory, Research and Pracdtice, 19*(3), 276–288.

Prochaska, J. O. & DiClemente, C. C. (1983). Stages and processes of self-change of smoking: Toward an integrative model of change. *Journal of Consulting and Clinical Psychology, 51,* 390–395.

Prochaska, J. O. & DiClemente, C. C. (1984). *The transtheoretical approach: Crossing the traditional boundaries of therapy.* Homewood, IL: Dow-Jones-Irwin.

Prochaska, J. O. & DiClemente, C. C. (1986). The transtheoretical approach. In J. C. Norcross (Ed.), *Handbook of eclectic psychotherapy* (pp. 163–200). New York: Brunner/Mazel.

Prochaska, J. O. & DiClemente, C. C. (1992). The transtheoretical approach. In J. C. Norcross & M. R. Goldfried (Eds.), *Handbook of psychotherapy integration* (pp. 300–334). New York: Basic Books.

Prochaska, J. O. & DiClemente, C. (2002). Transtheoretical therapy. In F. W. Kaslow (Ed.), *Comprehensive handbook of psychotherapy: Integrative/eclectic* (Vol. 4, pp. 165–183). New York: Wiley.

Prochaska, J. O. DiClemente, C., & Norcross, J. (1992). In search of how people change: Applications to addictive behaviors. *American Psychologist, 47,* 1102–1114.

Prochaska, J. O. & Norcross, J. C. (1994). *Systems of psychotherapy: A transtheoretical analysis* (3rd ed.). Pacific Grove, CA: Brooks/Cole.

Prochaska, J. O. Norcross, J. C., Fowler, J. L., Follick, M. I., & Abrams, D. B. (1991). Attendance and outcome in a work site weight control program: Processes and stages of change as processes and predictor variables. *Addictive Behaviors, 17,* 35–45.

Prochaska, J. O. Redding, C. A., & Evers, K. E. (2002). The transtheoretical model and stages of change. In K. Glanz, B. K. Rimer, & F. M. Lewis (Eds.), *Health behavior and health education: Theory, research and practice* (pp. 60–84). San Francisco: Jossey-Bass.

Prochaska, J. O. & Velicer, W. (1997). The transtheoretical model of health behavior change. *American Journal of Health Promotion, 12,* 38–48.

Prochaska, J. O. Velicer, W. E, DiClemente, C. C., & Fava, J. (1988). Measuring processes of change: Applications to the cessation of smoking. *Journal of Consulting and Clinical Psychology, 56,* 520–528.

Weinstein, N. D. Rothman, A. J., & Sutton, S. R. (1998). Stage theories of health behavior: Conceptual and methodological issues. *Health Psychology, 17,* 290–299.

SUGGESTED RESOURCES

DiClemente, C. C. (2003). *Addiction and change: How addictions develop and addicted people recover.* New York: The Guildford Press.

Miller, W. R. & Rollnick, S. (2002). *Motivational interviewing: Preparing people for change, (2nd ed).* New York: The Guildford Press.

Prochaska, J. M (2005). The transtheoretical model. Taking stock: A Survey on the practice and future of change management. In H. Nauheimer, (Ed.) *The change management toolbook.* http://www.change-management-toolbook.com

Prochaska, J. O. & DiClemente, C. (2002). Transtheoretical therapy. In F. W. Kaslow (Ed.), *Comprehensive handbook of psychotherapy: Integrative/eclectic* (Vol. 4, pp. 165–183). New York: Wiley.

Prochaska, J. O. & Norcross, J. C. (1994). *Systems of psychotherapy: A transtheoretical analysis* (3rd ed.). Pacific Grove, CA: Brooks/Cole.

PART III

PUTTING IT ALL TOGETHER—BECOMING A REFLECTIVE PRACTITIONER

CHAPTER 7

REFLECTIONS "ON" PRACTICE: A VIEW FROM FOUR PERSPECTIVES

As previously noted, the purpose of the text is to assist the reader in seeing how a theoretical perspective or orienting framework guides the behavior of the counselor as he/she attends to client data, develops hypotheses, and then tests these hypotheses through the introduction of specific interventions. The previous chapters have demonstrated how a counselor operating with a specific orienting framework approaches case conceptualization and treatment planning. The current chapter presents a detailed look at a single case as seen through the lens of these four unique orienting frameworks. It is hoped that the presentation of each unique view of a single case will assist the reader in more fully appreciating the value of an operative model as it guides the counselor's reflection "on" and "in" practice. Specifically, after reading this chapter you will be able to:

- identify the presence of specific theoretical concepts/constructs as applied by each of the illustrative counselors as they reflected in and on practice;
- describe the primary differences in the reflections in and on practice as a function of the underlying orienting framework; and
- discuss the unique value of each orienting framework as a guide.

As you read the case, attempt to view the client data through the lens of one of the orienting frameworks previously discussed. As you do, perhaps not only will you be able to identify the salient characteristics that drive the counselor's response but also be able to anticipate the response of the panel member representing that orientation.

INTRODUCTION

The case to be discussed is one involving Drew, a 15-year-old sophomore who is in danger of failing tenth grade. Drew has a history of being a C–C+ student throughout middle school and into his freshman year of high school. But this year, his grades have dropped dramatically and he is on the verge of failing four of his major subjects. In contrast, Drew is an A student in his graphic arts course and music elective.

The counselor in this case illustration attempts to take a nondirective approach. The intent of the counselor's interactions is to: (a) clarify the nature and context of the issue, (b) identify client goals and resources, and (c) present a developed picture of the case to which our four discussants can provide their own theoretical view.

The format for this chapter involves the presentation of a narrative reflecting on the exchange between the counselor and the client, Drew. In Part I of the case, the discussant invites the panel of four counselors to share their reflections on the practice using their unique orienting framework. In Part II, we see the case developing, but this time the discussant invites the panel to "jump in" at any time as a manifestation of their own reflection in practice. The hope is that the panel members can identify the hypotheses that drive their interventions as a reflection of their orienting framework. The panel is composed of counselor "S" (solution focus), "B" (behavioral focus), "C" (cognitive focus), and "TTM" (transtheoretical model).

DREW: A STUDENT ON THE VERGE OF FAILING

Drew is a child with intelligence. He consistently scores in the upper quartile on all standardized achievement tests. However, since middle school, Drew has been a student who is reported to have employed minimal effort in class and has gotten by on his natural abilities. Drew is reported to be a very polite and respectful student and has no notable discipline record.

Part 1: Reflecting "on" Practice

> **Counselor:**   Drew, come on in. Have a seat!
>
> **Drew:**   Thanks.
>
> **Counselor:**   I'm glad you came down. How's it going?
>
> **Drew:**   Okay, I guess?
>
> **Counselor:**   Okay?
>
> **Drew:**   Well, I assume you called me down for a reason, so it must not be going perfectly?
>
> **Counselor:**   That makes sense. In going over your grades I noticed that while you are doing really well in your electives, especially your art class, you are failing your majors this period and could fail for the year.
>
> **Drew:**   Yeah, I guess.
>
> **Counselor:**   Do you have any ideas about what's happening with you in those classes?

Drew: Yeah, I'm just not into them.

Counselor: Not into them?

Drew: Never have been much of a student . . . and I guess I don't put a lot of energy into it.

Counselor: Well, that seems to be what your teachers are saying. They all say you are a nice guy and when you participate in class you most often have something of value to contribute. They seem a bit frustrated because they all think that you could do really well with just a little effort.

Drew: I'll pull it together . . . always do.

Discussant: Any initial thoughts you would like to share, as you reflect on the case during this initial exchange?

> S: *Well – if his goal is to float, he seems like he's doing that. I guess I would like to get off what he isn't doing and shift the conversation to what he is doing and how he sees that working for him. I would like to move the conversation to his goal or at least to investigate how he sees his current school performance as working for him.*

> B: *He seems pretty clear, school work and academic achievement don't have any real value/payoff for him. I guess I would want to test possible alternative hypotheses that there is something more going on. You know, maybe screwing up, or just getting by, has some other type of payoff for him? Perhaps he enjoys frustrating his teachers or his parents? I guess I need a lot more information around what "S" said, "How is this working for him?"*

> C: *He sounds like a pretty solid character. I just wonder if he has a clear idea about the decisions he is making and the impact these may have on his future and future choices. While everyone is saying how well he could do if he just tried, I wonder how he sees it? Does he think he could succeed with effort? Or does he believe that if he tried he would still fail but then everyone would know that?*

> TTM: *I certainly don't disagree with anything that is said, but given the fact that Drew is being called down by the counselor as opposed to a self-referral leads me to question the degree to which he sees this as a problem, his problem. I am not really sure the degree to which he is committed to change.*

Discussant: As you reflect on the case—even this initial stage—are there data that seem to jump out at you and that serves as a springboard for your case conceptualization and treatment planning?

> C: *Drew's lack of concern about the reality of failing makes me wonder about a few things. For example, does he really have a reasonable sense of his ability to pull it together? Or is he distorting reality and reducing anxiety by minimizing the importance of the current situation. My questions at this stage would be geared to test these possibilities.*

B: *Well, he is doing very well in his electives. I would try to begin to identify the conditions that support such differential achievement. What does he do in his electives that he is not doing in his majors and what are the conditions that support these differents? So I guess I would want to focus on some better data collection.*

S: *I guess I would follow up on what "B" is stating. I would like to hear what Drew's goal is in each of his courses. It is clear that he has an "exception" in the way he approaches his electives. Perhaps asking the miracle question here might elicit some goals reflecting a desire to bring his major classes more in line with his electives.*

TTM: *Well, I'm thinking that the teachers' and counselor's problem may not be shared by Drew. His attitude appears to be nonplussed and I would want to see if that is accurate. Is he really unconcerned? Or is he in a state of denial or perhaps simply reacting to a lack of awareness about the implication of the situation. I really want to get a feel for what his read on the problem is and his plan for addressing it, before moving in on developing an action plan.*

Discussant: Thanks, but before we move on to see how the first session develops, maybe you could tell me what you would do next and how you may do that?

S: *I would definitely try to get him to articulate his goal. I think at this point I may say, "Well I can hear that you feel confident you will pull it together. Drew, if you are able to "pull it off," what would that look like? You know, what would you be doing differently and what would be the end result?"*

TTM: *I like the way "S" framed it and I may do the same thing. But I'm a bit torn. I guess I want to see where, if anywhere, he has pain, you know, feels a need? So I may try to get him to articulate his problem. I might say, "Drew it looks like you will have to pull it together, as you say. Is there any down side to waiting this long to do that?"*

C: *I think I may be a little more challenging at this point. I may say "Drew, you sound confident, but given your track record in these classes to date, how can you be so sure you will be able to pull it together?" I don't want to sound like a nonbeliever; I just want him to do a reality check for me.*

B: *I think I would come out pretty directly at this point and say something like, "Let me see if I understand. In some of your classes you do really well, and then in these others there's a chance you are going to go down in flames? What's the difference?" I would love to figure out what's maintaining these differential behaviors.*

Discussant: Thanks. It's clear how you are all thinking and I like the way you would go about testing your hypotheses or gathering the data you need to plan your next steps. Let's see what other information we can discover from the first session.

First Session (continued)

Counselor: Well, you sound confident?

Drew: Been here . . . done that. [smiling]

Counselor: Well, when I looked at your records it doesn't appear you were ever "here." I mean, I can see you haven't blazed any academic trails but you've gotten at least C's in your classes each marking period. This time, you've failed all four majors the last two marking periods.

Drew: I know. I did kind of let things get out of hand. I got behind on some major projects and just bagged them.

Counselor: Is that different than before?

Drew: Yeah, I always did projects. It was the homework I never did and that's why I got C's. My test grades are always pretty good.

Counselor: Major projects? Well, what do you think?

Drew: Truthfully I don't know. I'm really not into school but I also don't want to repeat tenth grade.

Counselor: You know, you say you are not into school but when I look at what you are doing in your electives, you seem to be into them!

Drew: I love art and music, always have.

Discussant: Anything new here? Anything you would do at this point?

TTM: *Actually, some really good stuff. I mean he's sounding a lot more serious and appears to be accepting that he may have a problem. That's a great start. Plus, he does have some strategies he has used in the past. I'm just not sure if he is planning to try to attack the problem or if he feels it is hopeless.*

S: *He is clear about one thing, he doesn't want to repeat tenth grade. I really would like him to develop that goal a bit more. Pass tenth grade, and what else? I would really want him to develop the picture of what he would be doing instead of failing tenth grade.*

B: *Well, we know what he doesn't want—to repeat tenth grade—but I would like to get him to state more concretely and in positive language, what he does want. I would like to take this somewhat vague goal and get him to make it more concrete, more operational. I think that would help us set subgoals and start to strategize on how to move forward.*

C: *I want to get a little more of an understanding of his sense of self-efficacy. I'm not sure if he sees it as hopeless and that would have to be identified if we are going to get him to tackle the problem.*

Discussant: Thanks. Let's return to see how this session ends and then maybe you could share with us your reflections "on" practice as they would guide your planning for the next session.

Counselor: So, since you are obviously into music and art, it is easy for you to do well in those courses?

Drew: Yeah. I am always messing with that stuff, even at home. I think that's something I would like to do with my life.

Counselor: You mean, like your career?

Drew: Yeah. I'm not sure which one or if I could combine them or do something with computer graphics and music. I don't know.

Counselor: That's really neat. I am sure with computer software and game design there is a real need for computer graphics and music engineering, but I bet there are many other jobs being created that call on these talents.

Drew: Yeah, that was on my things-to-do list, come down here and do a career search.

Counselor: That's fantastic. I can't do it today. I've got good news and bad! The good news is we have a great self-search program that I think you would really like and the bad news, and this one I'll bet you a soda on, all the things you find will require at least two years of college! [smiling]

Drew: I know, I know. [smiling]

Counselor: But then you also know failing tenth grade won't cut it?

Drew: I got it, I got it. [smiling]

Counselor: Drew, how about if you get to class. Tomorrow, I'll get you out of study hall to start on the self-search. How does that sound?

Drew: Okay. Thanks.

Discussant: Well that was a bit of a turnaround. It seems like at least for now, Drew's interested in coming to the counselor's office. The question I have for each of you is "Now what?" You have a commitment from him to come back, as you reflect on practice, what would your goals be for the next session?

> *TTM: I like where we are. Maybe I'm reading too much into it but I see Drew as very interested and committed to begin to take steps to guide some career decisions. I think that these steps may be the ones that set the stage for his ownership and commitment to better classroom engagement and achievement. So I think we are beyond the pre-contemplative stage, the stage I think he was in when he came to the office, and are moving rapidly toward an action stage. The computer search will be a good preparatory step. So for me, I want to focus on the career search, targeting the benefits of the various jobs and also the requirements. Hopefully those pointing to the need to get into the college!*

> *B: I like that strategy. I think if we can find the payoff for Drew we can structure it so that performing certain pro-academic behaviors, like doing homework, studying, handing in projects, etc., are all tangibly reinforced with some type of art or music artifact or some type of self-statement regarding his future career. But I really have to help him make the connection between his performance in the*

"majors" and the payoff of his art/music career. I am concerned that the payoff we are talking about—that is his career—is too far off in the future to be really that reinforcing. Even though he's a sophomore and may be a little old for it, I might try to employ the Premack principle in which he would be required to do a little work on his major subjects before he is allowed to work on his electives.

C: *Actually, I am not that far from you all. But I probably would be more likely to have him begin to share his image of what it will look like when he is in his dream job. I would try to use this emotive-imagery as a motivator for engaging the less-enjoyable assignments. I also would want him to begin to hear his evaluation of the major assignments and homework. If he is interpreting them as lacking value (dumb, a waste of time, etc.) these thoughts will be demotivational. I would like to help reframe them as necessary to those things he loves. It's like exercising to get in shape! Or maybe for him, the discipline of practicing and doing music scales, before soloing!*

S: *I still want to get a clearer picture of his goal and I can see using the career search and career discussion as a vehicle to getting him to articulate where he ultimately wants to be. With that in place, I probably would have him do goal scaling so we can begin to see what needs to be done next as we proceed toward his ultimate goal.*

Discussant: That was very helpful, but now we want to make you work a tiny bit harder. What follows is a portion of the second session Drew had with his counselor. It occurred one day after the initial encounter. What I invite you to do, is jump in anytime and as often as you wish. I would like you to step into the dialogue and simply let us know what you would be doing at any one point in time—if different from our counselor. The hope is that you will share what it is you are reacting to (reflecting "in" practice), along with your hypothesis and then your intervention. Let's begin.

Counselor: Hi Drew. Come on in. How's it going today?

Drew: Not bad. Would it be okay if we used the career search/discovery program?

Counselor: Sure, let's go over to the career center and we'll get you started.

S: *His presence at the door plus his request to engage in the self-search are good signs and I would affirm them. As we were going to the center I would say something like: "I'm really happy you came down and remembered about the program, I think you will find it pretty cool."*

TTM: *I see his presence at this meeting as well as his interest in the computer program as evidence of his interest and ownership of a problem. I'm not sure it is the real problem—that is, his lack of achievement in his majors—but it is certainly a step in a direction that may open up his awareness of the situation he has gotten himself into. So I'd be curious to see how enthusiastic he is once we get to the center and I would hope that he starts to see the value/need for education as a precondition to the careers he may find of interest. At this stage, I would just listen*

*and maybe use simple reflections or questions to highlight the educational compo-
nent as we did the search.*

[Moving to career center and beginning the self-search computer program.]

Drew: This is really cool. I can't believe all the things you can do with it.

Counselor: Yep. When we bring the juniors down as part of their career
counseling, most of them are just as impressed. I have found that a good
way to start would be just to play with the program. You can place key
words in like artist, musician and even video game designer, and it will
create a list of related jobs, employment requirements, salary ranges, and
even projections as to future job opportunities.

Drew: That's cool. How about rock star! [laughing]

Counselor: Hey, you could try.

Drew: You said "video game designer." Is that really a job?

Counselor: Why not try typing it in and we'll see?

Drew: [typing in the search block] Whoa! Look at all the other links. Software engineer, video marketing, virtual realities, simulators, and training.
What's that?

Counselor: Click on the link and it should take us there.

Drew: [reading the description] "Engineering and Virtual Realities. A new
area of engineering that creates training simulators operating in virtual
realities. Currently employed in flight simulation training, surgical simu-
lations, drone flight simulators, and many other arenas." Awesome!

Counselor: And look here . . . it is a growth area—meaning that it is going
to be a big area for future employment.

TTM: *Well his interest is certainly peaked and I'm not too sure if it is too early but
you know I may try to begin to move him to articulate a real goal rather than just
play at the computer. So while he is getting acquainted with the computer, I think
I might try to structure some plan for our interaction. I might say something like:
"Drew, I'm really happy you are finding this interesting, you seem like you are
into it. But you know what – it may be a really good idea for us to focus on one or
two areas, not as a decision, but as a starting place to begin to see what type of
education and or training is involved." If I could get that type of commitment as a
preparatory step we may be able to move into a discussion of his current school
performance.*

S: *I am okay with encouraging him to play just as a way of getting him engaged,
but I think before he went back to his classes I would want him to begin to think of
where he wants to be, in terms of his own goals. So I think before he stopped I
might intervene with, "Drew, you really seemed to enjoy that. And I know you
have to get back to class, but how about if you try something for me? Before you
and I get together tomorrow I'd like you to spend a little time thinking about the*

following: 'Imagine that tonight while you are sleeping, a miracle happens and when you come to school tomorrow morning you discover that you are exactly the type of student you really want to be and school is everything you want it to be. If you could play with that idea and really allow yourself to develop that image maybe you and I could meet and begin to figure out ways to make it a reality. What do you think?'"

B: I think we are on the right track. It appears that Drew is capable of being self-motivated if he has an interest in something. I think if we can help identify some future state—goal that he would like to achieve—then we can use that to structure and shape the behaviors required to achieve it. I also think the computer search is an enjoyable activity that maybe I can use as a reinforcement for doing some other things. So I might say something like: "Drew, it looks like you are enjoying this. It is pretty cool! But you know what else I'm seeing? All the careers you are getting excited about require at minimum at least two years of college. It is clear that that would be something you could handle, but not if you continue the way you are going. So, how about if we get together tomorrow and plan an attack on these grades and maybe do a little more of the search?"

C: I would want to highlight the power of his attitude and how it impacts his enthusiasm and behavior. I might say something like: "Drew, you really look like you are enjoying this. You know what I find amazing? Here you are focused, really attending, and eager to learn about careers! Wow, if there would be a way we could bottle that attitude so that you could bring it to your other classes you'd be quite a star!"

(The session continues for 20 minutes with Drew simply searching and experimenting with the program.)

(At the end of the school day, Drew pops into the counselor's office.)

Drew: Hi.

Counselor: Hey Drew. I thought you'd be long gone.

Drew: Nah, I've got to hang until 4—we start tryouts for the musical today.

Counselor: That's great, but we may have a slight problem.

Drew: Problem?

Counselor: Yep. You know the school policy restricts extracurricular participation if you are academically ineligible, and with four failures you are definitely ineligible.

C: Oops . . . now I don't know how that comment came across but I don't want to set him up with a hopeless attitude. I think I might have said something like, "So there you go again, just like this afternoon when you want something you really are willing to put out the time and energy. Boy, we have to figure out how to bottle that!" I would maybe introduce the idea of ineligibility after he talked a bit more. I might ask a few questions to see if today was just informational or if he may be *"cut" because of the grades. If the latter were possible, I may confront him with that reality. If this were just an initial meeting I might let him go and discuss the potential eligibility problem next time.*

S: *I want to affirm his presence. It's great he came down again, even if it was just to say hi!*

TTM: *I definitely agree. This is a sign of engagement and commitment to at least work with the counselor on something, but I think we need to move from relating to resolving and that will require us focusing on a specific problem and goal.*

B: *Well I'm not sure what the policy is regarding being part of the musical but I might be thinking about finding alternative ways we could use that to shape his academic behaviors. Maybe if we can get his teachers to write notes of progress that may be sufficient to make him eligible? But for now I think I would simply reinforce him for stopping in, like, "Drew, great to see you," or invite him to talk about the musical and support that.*

[continuing]

Drew: But the play is not until the middle of May and that's two marking periods away!

B: *Thank you Drew! I think we have something that we really can work with in terms of shaping his academic performance. The play is much more of an immediate payoff than a future career. So at our next meeting I would want to develop some subgoals like homework completion, quiz grades, projects, etc. for each of the four majors and get Drew to record and graph his performance. Hopefully, graphing his progress along with my verbal praise and even reminders about the musical would all serve to reinforce the completion of his assignments.*

C: *What I heard in his reaction was a belief that he can pull it together before May. I like that but I would want to challenge him to see how well developed and reasonable it is. I might say, "Drew you sound confident that you can get the grades up before the play. Would you tell me how you plan to do that and how you will know if your plan is working?"*

TTM: *Yep! Drew's statement says to me he is committed to being in the play and thus indirectly committed to improving his grades. So I might use a similar strategy as "C" to invite him to share his preparatory steps, like developing a plan, and then maybe going one step more into action and ask him: "How about if we really look at your plan and see how maybe I could be incorporated to keep you on track?"*

[continuing]

Counselor: Well, if we could get your grades up so that you are passing this marking period, it may be okay.

Drew: Actually, that's what I was stopping in for. I was talking to Samantha at lunch.

Counselor: Samantha?

Drew: Yeah. Samantha Higgins, she's also in the drama club, and she was the one telling me that I better get it together if I want to be able to be in the play. So, I know all that virtual reality stuff is neat but I guess for now I'd be happy just to be able to get off ineligibility and be in the play!

TTM: *In terms of stages of change, I think he has really moved to an action stage. He owns the real problem of his poor grades, seeing their consequences in terms of the musical and future careers and he is even being supported by his friend, and in sharing it with his friend gives evidence of his preparatory commitment. So I think we are ready to contract for action and might simply say something like: "That's great. Not only is Samantha correct but the fact that you clearly see how your grades could affect not just your participation in the musical but also your career options says to me you have really made some great insights. How about if we get serious about developing our plan of attack? Maybe we could get together tomorrow?"*

S: *I like the fact that he is talking about musicals and careers and I agree that he appears committed. For me, I think I would want to reframe the goal to grades in his majors more specifically and begin goal scaling and looking for exceptions. In the next session I would ask him: "Drew, what would you think were realistic goals for grades in each of your four majors during this third marking period?"*

B: *I think we are moving in the right direction, but at this stage I am focusing more on what is the specific, concrete, observable goal that he may want to set for himself. So I might say: "Drew that's great. How about if we get together tomorrow and really set some goals for this upcoming marking period? Not just grades in your majors but maybe behaviors you want to start to employ?"*

C: *I would like to reinforce his positive attitude. "Drew I am thrilled you are really thinking about doing something about this. That attitude is really going to be an important part of the puzzle, so I need you to keep it. You know, just like you are determined to make the musical we need to get 'psyched' and determined to get the grades you need in your majors."*

[continuing]

Counselor: That's great. I think working on the eligibility issue is a super place to start. We have plenty of time to do some career planning, so maybe our first task is to see what we can do about the current marking period? We could check with your teachers in the next couple of days and find out your current status and what they suggest you need to do to improve your grades for this period.

Drew: I think I know, but I could talk with them. Would it be okay if I came in to see you during study hall on Friday? I'll tell you what I found out.

Counselor: That would be perfect!

REFLECTIONS "ON" PRACTICE

Discussant: I am sure we are not over the hump or by any means have this issue resolved, but it seems you all agree that Drew appears to own the problem and is now positioned to be a collaborator in his own treatment. So as we end this section, maybe you could share your vision of an initial treatment plan or approach?

> S: *Well, picking up on "B's" last comment, I would also ask him to translate those grades into actions that he would have to be doing, like handing in all homework, getting a specific minimal grade in each assignment, etc. With this as our end point, I would invite Drew to goal scale, asking him to identify where he is at the moment in terms of each of these actions and what he needs to do to move up one or two steps. Throughout the process I would keep referring to the skills, the attitudes, and the specific behaviors he employs to be successful in his electives as the resources we want to come to bear on the majors. I think using the same type of skills and attitudes that get him to plan and stay focused on doing major art projects can be applied to the projects he has to do for science and social studies, etc. So that would be the plan of attack.*

> B: *I feel that Drew simply got himself in a hole and that his old strategies of "kicking it in gear at the last moment" simply didn't work this time. My plan would be to:*
>
> a. *have him set target grades for each of his majors for this third marking period;*
>
> b. *identify specific behaviors like completing homework, studying for a specific amount of time each night, developing time lines for assignment completions, and even asking and answering questions in class; and*
>
> c. *develop a method for Drew to monitor his performance of the identified behaviors as well as recording of his grades. I think it is important to not only have him chart grades for each class, but also to chart time given to studying or working on projects. Monitoring his behavior provides more immediate feedback and maybe we can provide reinforcement for these independent of the grades. I am thinking that the charting and the verbal feedback from his teachers (and me), along with the recording of his improved grades, may be sufficient reinforcement, but that's something that he and I would have to discuss.*

> C: *I think the behavioral structure and approach is very useful. I would want him to look at the power of his thinking as it came to bear on the situation. At one point he was thinking "it will all work out" even when the data were clearly pointing to the fact that it wasn't working out. Also, when we first met I got the feeling that he was convincing himself that it was hopeless and as such was defensively developing an "I don't care attitude." That attitude clearly became self-fulfilling.*

While we were working on reversing this situation, I would also like to take it as an opportunity to encourage him to be a bit more diligent in monitoring his thinking to avoid artificial confidence or dysfunctional hopelessness. I think I would try to get him to identify his self-defeating thoughts and their impact on his tendency to avoid engagement in his assignments and help him reframe things so that he was able to focus and engage in these projects and assignments. I would want to set up a thought monitoring process with him targeting thoughts such as "Why bother?", "This is stupid", "I can't do this", or even "I'll do it later" and help him see the negative effects these thoughts have on his behaviors and as such, his grades. Once this insight is gained, I would want him to learn to challenge his thoughts and reframe them so that he sees his assignments as either opportunities to employ his artistic eye and skill (e.g., with a cover page or poster) or at worst as simply hoops that he must jump through, or as a minor cost of admission to those things (i.e., the play, a future career, etc.) that he prizes.

TTM: *I see this as pretty much a matter of motivational deficit since he appears to have the knowledge and skills necessary to succeed. As a result, now that we are in the action stage with Drew owning the problem and showing signs of beginning to take some steps to correct things, I probably would use a strategy similar to that described by "B." In addition to employing shaping and reinforcement to increase his academic achievement behaviors, I would want to plan with Drew some strategies that would support maintenance of these changes. I think that Samantha or perhaps some of his other friends might be a good support. Also, his interest in the career search can be a good resource for helping to maintain his motivation. So as things improved I would want to follow up with Drew, using the career search as a focus so that the interaction was more future-goal oriented, rather than simply problem focused.*

Discussant: Well, thank you for all your reflections.

UPON FURTHER CONSIDERATION

It does appear that Drew would have been served well by any one of these counselors. Before moving on to the next chapter, it may be beneficial for you to engage in Exercise 7.1.

■ ■ ■ ■ ■

EXERCISE 7.1

REFLECTION "IN" AND "ON" PRACTICE

Part I: Identifying Theory in Practice

Directions: The following exercise is best completed in collaboration with a classmate or colleague. Having now observed the "on" practice and "in" practice reflections of counselors operating with four unique perspectives, you are invited to return to the dialogue in an attempt to identify and label the application of concepts and constructs in action. Specifically review the panel members' reflections and attempt to identify evidence of each of the following:

■ ■ ■ ■ ■ ▬▬▬▬▬▬▬▬

EXERCISE 7.1 (CONTINUED)

Solution Focus:
  Positive goal setting
  Scaling
  Affirmation
  Collaborative style
  Exceptions

Behavioral:
  Operationalization
  Shaping
  Functional-behavioral analyses
  Operant conditioning

Cognitive:
  Cognitive dissonance
  Assimilation
  Insight 1– connecting thought to feeling
  Cognitive reframing

Transtheoretical:
  Precontemplative stage
  Contemplation
  Preparatory
  Action
  Maintenance

Part II: Guiding Personal Reflection on Practice

Directions: Along with a classmate or colleague, review the various hypotheses proposed by the panel members as well as the interventions that emerged from these hypotheses. Identify the data that you found relevant and discuss how you would employ these data to guide your hypotheses and the intervention you would employ. Does your approach reflect that of one of our panel members? Or is it more of an eclectic view?

CHAPTER 8

TURNING REFLECTIONS TO PRACTICE DECISIONS— FOUR PERSPECTIVES

In the previous chapter we were able to observe the thinking of four counselors as they reviewed a counseling interaction. The discussion that followed each segment of client-counselor dialogue provided insight into the reflections "on" and "in" practice as they were guided by the unique orienting framework of the discussants.

The current chapter provides another opportunity to step into the mind of a counselor employing a specific orienting framework. A single case of an aggressive middle school student is seen through the lens of each of the four orienting frameworks previously discussed. Unlike the previous chapter in which the specialists were discussing what they would do, the current chapter presents them in action, as if they were the counselor. The goal of this chapter is to provide the reader with the opportunity to observe the processes employed by each of the four counselors operating from a unique perspective. It is hoped that as you read the interactions between client and counselor you will be able to identify the specific concepts or constructs that guide the counselors' responses and interventions. Specifically, after reading this chapter you will be able to:

- identify the presence of specific theoretical concepts/constructs as applied by each of the illustrative counselors as they reflected in and on practice;
- describe the primary differences in the specific reflections in and on practice as illustrated across counselors; and
- discuss the unique value of each orienting framework as a guide for intervening with this client.

LATANYA—TRYING TO FIT IN

Background

LaTanya is a 12-year-old student who is new to W.H. Harding Middle School, having transferred only this year. LaTanya's now been in school for five weeks and has already been sent to the disciplinarian four times, all for fighting incidents.

In the referral to the counselor, the disciplinarian described LaTanya as a child who "exhibited uncontrollable outbursts of aggression, during which time she would kick, scratch, and bite other children. The outburst appeared unprovoked and unpredictable." The observations of her teachers suggested that LaTanya's relationships with peers were nonexistent and she was often excluded from social and group activities. When engaged within a collaborative activity, LaTanya was described as quickly assuming a dominant stance and attempting to boss the others within the group.

The information in her cumulative folder suggests that even with her aggressive behavior and resulting social rejection, LaTanya is achieving at grade level and has an interest and talent for math and science.

Referral

The school counselor has been asked to work with LaTanya, not only to help her gain control over this aggressive behavior, but also to help her develop positive peer relationships.

INITIAL SESSION

Mrs. S (Solution Focused)

Mrs. S: Good morning, LaTanya. I'm Mrs. S, your school counselor. Please come in and have a seat.

LaTanya: I didn't do anything wrong. [defensively]

Mrs. S: Oh, no. I'm sorry that you think that. I know you are new to our school and as your counselor I wanted to meet you and see what, if anything, I could do to help you with fitting in here at Harding.

LaTanya: I don't like Harding. The kids are nasty.

Mrs. S: Nasty?

LaTanya: Yeah, they give me dirty looks.

Mrs. S: That doesn't sound very welcoming.

LaTanya: I don't like it here.

Mrs. S: Well, LaTanya, I could understand why someone wouldn't like being in a place where people are nasty or give dirty looks, but I'm wondering, if school could be the way you would like it to be, how would it look?

LaTanya: I'd be back with my mom in New Jersey and going to my old school.

Mrs. S: And LaTanya, if you were back in your old school, how would that be?

LaTanya: It wouldn't be great but at least I'm not afraid of the people in that school and they would be afraid to give me those looks.

Mrs. S: Oh, so the benefit of being in your old school would be that you would feel safe?

LaTanya: I guess.

Mrs. S: So when I asked, if it could be the way you would like it to be here at Harding, it, sounds like if you felt safe here at Harding that would be better?

LaTanya: I guess.

Mrs. S: LaTanya, would you do me a favor? Would you pretend that you are here at Harding and this is a safe place for you and no one is giving you nasty looks or being mean? Now, if that actually happened what would you be doing?

LaTanya: I don't know. I don't like it here!

Mrs. S: I understand that you don't like being in a place that is mean and unsafe, but if somehow . . . maybe like through magic . . . you discovered that you were safe here, how would you be?

LaTanya: Like everybody else.

Mrs. S: That's super! And what would you be doing? How would you be acting?

LaTanya: Just doing school stuff and hanging out like the other kids do, and maybe I'd be on the softball team . . . stuff like that.

Mrs. S: That's great stuff! Doing school work and hanging out with friends and playing sports. Now if you were doing those things, how would that work for you?

LaTanya: I don't know . . . I guess I would be happier?

Mrs. S: LaTanya, can you remember a time when you found yourself happy—maybe hanging out with school friends?

LaTanya: No.

Mrs. S: No—not even for a small amount of time?

LaTanya: Well, maybe when I first went to St. John's. In first grade I had some friends and I played pee-wee soccer, I was really good.

Mrs. S: That's neat.

LaTanya: Yeah, I liked that! I wish I could go back there.

Mrs. S: So when you have friends and can play sports you seem to be happier? Let's pretend that through some magic, tomorrow you came to school and had a couple of really good friends and had made the softball team. If that happened, how do you think you would be?

LaTanya: I don't know. Maybe I would like it here more or I wouldn't care what other kids not on the team or my friends did or said I guess.

Mrs. S: Well that seems to make sense. LaTanya, I could use your help, maybe you and I could do a little experiment?

LaTanya: Experiment?

Mrs. S: Well, look here. See this line? Over here is how you felt and acted when you were at St. John's. If I understood what you said [writing it down], you were "happy and had friends and played on sports team."

LaTanya: Yeah, and I used to have my papers hung up, too!

Mrs. S: Great! Let's put that down. So you were doing school work and doing well and having papers hung up, and you had friends and you played sports. LaTanya, if we make that a 10 on our scale—you know the best—where do you think you are now?

LaTanya: A zero!

Mrs. S: A zero? But I thought Mrs. L, your homeroom teacher, said you volunteered to take the attendance down to the office. That's school work.

LaTanya: Yeah. I did that and I guess I'm doing some work in classes, like Charlotte and I were the first to complete our labs in science class.

Mrs. S: Wow! So you are doing quite a few things like cooperating in homeroom and working well with a classmate and completing labs.

LaTanya: Yeah, I guess . . . so maybe I'm at a one or two.

Mrs. S: LaTanya, I have an idea. Remember I said we might want to do some experiments kind of like you do in science? Would you be willing to just pay attention for the next two days and try to remember any time that you felt happy during the day or times when you were doing some type of school work and maybe even any time you cooperated with a classmate? If you could do that, then when we get together we could really estimate a lot more accurately where you may be on our line and maybe we would even get some ideas about what we could do to help you move up the line.

LaTanya: Yeah, I could do that. Do I have to write it down?

Mrs. S: You know, you don't have to . . . but if you could write some of it down that would be great. But you can do it any way you want, okay?

LaTanya: Okay.

Mr. B (Behavioral Focused)

Pre-client meeting:

After reviewing the cumulative folder, the counselor, Mr. B, met with LaTanya's homeroom teacher in an attempt to begin to gather data regarding LaTanya's social interactions and her ability to respond to challenge, confrontation, and conflict. According to the homeroom teacher, LaTanya "is no problem in homeroom or science class. She has volunteered to be our attendance volunteer and just seems quiet in class." Mrs. L., the homeroom teacher, is also LaTanya's science teacher and she also noted "in class LaTanya is able to do the work; in fact, we've had two mini-labs and she and Charlotte (her partner) are the first to complete their work and it is well done. LaTanya is a very clear and logical writer. She seems to really enjoy labs."

Mr. B: Good morning, LaTanya. I'm Mr. B, your school counselor. Please come in and have a seat.

LaTanya: I didn't do anything wrong. [defensively]

Mr. B: Oh, no. I'm sorry that you think that. I know you are new to our school and as your counselor I wanted to meet you and see what, if anything, I could do to help you in fitting in here at Harding.

LaTanya: I don't like Harding. The kids are mean and nasty.

Mr. B: Nasty? I'm surprised. You know I was talking to Mrs. L., your teacher, and she said that you and Charlotte are doing really well in science. Is Charlotte nasty?

LaTanya: No. I like her. She's okay. It's just some of the other kids are mean, they give me dirty looks.

Mr. B: I'm sorry to hear that . . . that doesn't sound very welcoming.

LaTanya: I don't like it here.

Mr. B: Well, LaTanya, I could understand why someone wouldn't like being in a place where people are nasty or giving dirty looks. I'm wondering, you mentioned that Charlotte is nice, is there anyone else in class or homeroom that seems nice like Charlotte?

LaTanya: Yeah, I guess.

Mr. B: Could you describe a time, other than when you are with Charlotte doing your labs, that you feel okay and people, at least some, seem nice?

LaTanya: In homeroom when Mrs. L. asks me to call roll and check off the names of students who are absent. Nobody ever acts mean then 'cause they know what would happen!

Mr. B: What would happen?

LaTanya: I would put their name down as absent and they would get in trouble!

Mr. B: Really?

LaTanya: No. But I know Mrs. L. would get on them.

Mr. B: Oh, I see. So when you are reading roll or when you are taking notes and writing them in science class, these are times when you feel happy and people are nice?

LaTanya: Yeah, and sometimes in Math class when I am called on to go to the board to do a problem. Mr. Jenkins says I'm good at math.

Mr. B: Wow. Okay, so LaTanya, it sounds like when you are doing things that you are good at, like math or science or even helping out in homeroom, that these things make you feel good?

LaTanya: Yeah, but it's not like that all the time!

Mr. B: Okay, that's something I would like to hear about. We know some of the situations that help you feel good, now how about those situations where you don't feel as happy? Could you give me an example?

LaTanya: Like yesterday at lunch. I was coming back with my tray and I was going to sit down at the table with Robert and Marquan and I put my tray down and Brittany, who was next to Robert, looked up and said, "What do you want newbie?" and everyone laughed. I told her to shut the "f . . . " up.

Mr. B: So at lunch Brittany was giving you a hard time and you cursed at her?

LaTanya: Yeah, she's lucky I didn't rip her face off.

Mr. B: It sounds like she really made you mad. When you are angry, is that how you respond to it? You know, curse or hit?

LaTanya: If they deserve it.

Mr. B: How does that work for you?

LaTanya: What do you mean?

Mr. B: Well, what happens when you act that way?

LaTanya: I usually get in trouble! But they shut up!

Mr.B: Oh, so now Brittany doesn't give you a hard time?

LaTanya: Yeah right! She's always mean.

Mr. B: So when you get angry and curse or hit, you get in trouble and if Brittany is a good example it seems that these behaviors don't even work to stop the others from being mean?

LaTanya: I guess.

Mr. B: LaTanya, I wonder if you would like to figure out another way of dealing with these people. You know, a way that would stop them from being mean while at the same time keeping you out of trouble?

LaTanya: I guess. But they can't get away with that stuff.

Mr. B: Okay, but maybe there is a way you can stop them and still not get in trouble?

LaTanya: How?

Mr. B: Well that's going to take a little figuring out and I'll need your help. I understand that you are pretty good at science and experiments.

LaTanya: Yeah, I guess.

Mr. B: Would you like to do a little experiment?

LaTanya: What?

Mr. B: How about if for the next two days you kept some notes for me in this little notebook? [handing her a new copy book]

LaTanya: Like what?

Mr. B: Okay. How about if during the next two days if there is a time when you "curse at a classmate" or "feel like you want to hit them" that you just write it down, over here in this column we'll call "B" for behavior.

Just describe what you did. Like if we use the cafeteria example, you would write down, "I told Brittany to . . . !"

Okay? Then if you could, over here in the first column that I have this "A" on, I would love you to write down what happened or what was going on right before you acted this way. Like, if we use the example with Brittany in column "A" you would write, "I was going to sit for lunch and Brittany said 'what do you want newbie?' and everyone laughed," and then over here [pointing to "B"] you wrote, "I said: 'f . . . you' and walked away."

Okay?

LaTanya: Yeah, but what happens if I use a curse word?

Mr. B: Well, it's okay for now. Just try to describe it as it happened. Remember we are being like scientific investigators.

LaTanya: But how about if I was feeling like punching her?

Mr. B: Write it down. The more information, the better! The last thing is to write down what happens right after you did what you did.

LaTanya: You mean like everyone laughed and I walked away, or if I get in trouble, that kind of stuff?

Mr. B: LaTanya, that's super, you really are good at this.

LaTanya: This seems like a lot of work.

Mr. B: Yeah, I guess it does. I don't want you to do too much. But the more you can write down the more helpful it will be. Even if you are only able to write down about one event that will be great!

LaTanya: Okay, I'll try.

Mr. B: Super!

Mrs. C (Cognitive-Orienting Framework)

Mrs. C: Good morning, LaTanya. I'm Mrs. C, your school counselor. Please come in and have a seat.

LaTanya: I didn't do anything wrong. [defensively]

Mrs. C: Oh, no. I'm sorry that you think that. Please have a seat! I bet coming down here thinking you were in trouble made you a little nervous?

LaTanya: I'm always in trouble!

Mrs. C: Really? Always?

LaTanya: Not always, but a lot.

Mrs. C: Well, actually, that is something I wanted to talk with you about. I am a bit confused. When I look at your records you seem to be a person who can do the schoolwork pretty easily, but I also saw that you have seen Dr. Watson (the disciplinarian) quite a few times already this year.

LaTanya: I hate this place. I hate the students. They're nasty!

Mrs. C: Nasty?

LaTanya: Yeah. They give me dirty looks.

Mrs. C: Dirty looks?

LaTanya: Yeah, and they just act mean and nasty.

Mrs. C: That doesn't sound very welcoming. Could give me an example so I can understand better?

LaTanya: Like yesterday at lunch. I was coming back with my tray and I was going to sit down at the table with Robert and Marquan and I put my tray down and Brittany, who was next to Robert, looked up and said, "What do you want newbie?" and everyone laughed. I told her to shut the "f . . . " up.

Mrs. C: So at lunch Brittany called you a newbie, and you became really mad . . . and then cursed at her?

LaTanya: Yeah. She's lucky I didn't rip her face off.

Mrs. C: Wow. It sounds like you were really mad.

LaTanya: Yeah. So if somebody gets all up in your face wouldn't you be pissed? Sorry.

Mrs. C: Well if I were honest, I would have to say no, not really.

LaTanya: Yeah, right. So somebody gives you attitude and calls you a name and you would not get mad? Yeah, right.

Mrs. C: Well LaTanya, let me ask you something. You are a sixth-grader and let's pretend that you walked past the kindergarten classroom. As you pass the classroom a little kid in the front gave you a dirty look and called you "poopy face." How would you feel?

LaTanya: [laughing] I might pretend to give him a hard look, but I'd laugh.

Mrs.C: But, LaTanya, he's giving you a dirty look and calling you a name and you are not angry? I mean he is giving you attitude.

LaTanya: Yeah, but I don't care. He's a dumb ass, I don't care what he thinks!

Mrs. C: Yep . . . that's it!

LaTanya: Huh? What's it?

Mrs. C: Well, you blew him off and you didn't get mad because you just didn't care. So when you asked me if I would get angry with Brittany I said "no" because you know what, I don't care what Brittany thinks of me!

LaTanya: Oh?

Mrs. C: I know it is a little confusing, but if we look at these two things it seems that when you care about what other people say or do, then because you care, you seem to give them control and then you respond to their comments with anger. But if you don't care, then no matter what they say or do it doesn't bother you.

LaTanya: Okay, but she pissed me off.

Mrs. C: Well you and I see it a little differently. I mean, let's pretend you saw Brittany just like you saw that little kindergartener. You know, just a person that you don't care about?

LaTanya: You mean like she's a dumb ass?

Mrs.C: Well, I don't like to call names, but if that means you don't care, then yep.

LaTanya: [laughing] I'm telling!

Mrs. C: [smiling] But remember I don't care!

LaTanya: Okay. So if I didn't care then I wouldn't get angry . . . I guess I get it.

Mrs. C: LaTanya, it is clear to me that you are a young woman who likes to make your own decisions and be in control of your own life.

LaTanya: That's what my mom and grandmom say.

Mrs.C: I could teach you some pretty neat stuff that will help you make sure that you don't give away your feelings or your energy to anyone you don't want to have it. Like if you don't really care about Brittany, wouldn't it be better to give her none of your precious time and energy? Not to give her the control!

Latanya: Yeah, she doesn't deserve it. [smiling]

Mrs. C: Good for you. So I have an idea. Do you ever keep a diary or journal?

LaTanya: Yeah, but I'm not showing you! [smiling]

Mrs. C: Oh, some juicy stuff? I don't need to see that. I was thinking if you could keep a little log or journal for me it would help us. What I would love you to do is find a couple of times during the next few days when you find yourself getting angry. Write down how you feel and how you are acting or what you are saying and if you can describe what happened right before you got angry. Was something said or done? Were you remembering something? Could you do that?

LaTanya: I guess, but I'm not sure why.

Mrs. C: Well maybe I could use it to show you something really special about the way we give our control away and more importantly, how we can learn to stop doing that.

LaTanya: I'll try.

Mr. TT (Transtheoretical-Orienting Framework)

Mr. TT: Good morning, LaTanya. I'm Mr. TT, your school counselor. Please come in and have a seat.

LaTanya: I didn't do anything wrong. [defensively]

Mr. TT: Oh, no. I'm sorry that you think that. LaTanya, do you know why I sent for you?

LaTanya: I don't know, I'm always getting blamed for something.

Mr. TT: So you have been getting blamed for things here at school?

LaTanya: Yeah. I don't like it here. I hate Harding and the kids.

Mr. TT: Well you sound unhappy. What kind of things have you been blamed for?

LaTanya: I don't know, they say I'm always fighting and have a bad attitude, but it's these other kids. They're always up in my face.

Mr. TT: So while you believe the other kids are the ones that are doing the bad things, somehow you get blamed?

LaTanya: Yeah, I just defend myself!

Mr. TT: Okay. LaTanya, could you tell me how this might happen? How do you get blamed for what the other kids are doing?

LaTanya: Well, they know how to do things, like sneaky, and when I yell at them the teachers only hear me.

Mr. TT: I think I understand it. So like you are talking with the kids and then they do something that makes you mad, and then you react by yelling and you are the one that gets caught?

LaTanya: Yeah, it's not fair! I hate this place and Dr. Watson.

Mr. TT: It sounds like you feel it's unfair, but in looking at your record, it looks like you have been in trouble about five times so far. It seems that even if the other kids are doing something, your yelling seems to get you in trouble? Have you tried to do anything to avoid getting in trouble?

LaTanya: Like what? It ain't me. The other kids start it. If they'd get out of my face I wouldn't be in trouble.

Mr. TT: Well that makes sense, but I guess I am wondering if there is something else you could do to either get them out of your face or react differently to them when they do get up in your face so that you don't get in trouble?

LaTanya: I don't know. If I threaten to punch they stop.

Mr. TT: But it looks like when you threaten them or curse at them they may stop temporarily, but in either case you get in trouble?

LaTanya: Yeah.

Mr. TT: So, I bet threatening them or cursing at them feels like it is working, but is it?

LaTanya: I guess it isn't 'cause they just get worse and I'm going to be put in a special class if I don't stop it.

Mr. TT: A special class?

LaTanya: That's what my grandmother said.

Mr. TT: Well I'm not sure about that but am I correct if I say that maybe it would be better for you if you could figure out a way not to get in so much trouble?

LaTanya: Yeah. I've tried, but they piss me off! Sorry!

Mr. TT: Well, I am glad that you've tried it before. I bet if you and I put our heads together we might be able to look at what you tried and figure out what else we could do—that may work a little better?

LaTanya: Maybe . . . I don't know . . . I could just be good.

Mr. TT: Boy that would be great. But I bet you have tried that before. Has it worked?

LaTanya: Well, for a little while, and then somebody gets on me and I freak.

Mr. TT: But LaTanya, even though it has only worked for a little while it's still really good. I mean, that's a great start and maybe we could figure out what else you could do to make it last longer. Would you like that?

LaTanya: Yeah, I guess. What do I have to do?

Mr. TT: How about if you just try to be good for the rest of today and tomorrow and then maybe you and I could meet and see how it worked out and what else we could do. If you would like, we could get together tomorrow afternoon and see what we can do.

LaTanya: Okay. Should I just come down?

Mr. TT: That would be super and I'll let Mrs. L. know that you are coming here after lunch rather than going back to homeroom. So I'll see you tomorrow. By the way, it was really great meeting you!

LaTanya: Thanks . . . see ya.

SECOND SESSION

The second sessions are presented in somewhat abbreviated form and pick up where the initial sessions left off. The dialogue starts with the last exchanges from the first session.

Mrs. S (Solution Focused)

From Session 1

Mrs. S: LaTanya, I have an idea. Remember I said we might want to do some experiments kind of like you do in science? Would you be willing to just pay attention for the next two days and try to remember any time that you felt happy during the day or times when you were doing some type of school work and maybe even any time you cooperated with a classmate? If you could do that, then when we get together we could really estimate a lot more accurately where you may be on our line and maybe even get some ideas about what we could do to help you move up the line.

Reflections "on" Practice (After First Session)

LaTanya appears to be a child with a clear idea of the type of school experience she would like to have, and even illustrations of exceptions where she has experienced some of her goals here at Harding. I want to continue to affirm her ability to deconstruct this area of concern and begin to more clearly develop her goal of being happy and involved and having friends. I want to help her build on those times when this is the type of experience she has had (exceptions) and figure out how to use the attitudes and skills she used in those situations to these new ones.

Session 2 (After Initial Exchanges)

Mrs. S: Well, looking over your notes I can see why Mrs. L says that you and Charlotte are two of her best students. You really wrote a lot down, that's fantastic!

LaTanya: Actually, it was kind of fun. I felt like a reporter on a newspaper. I was really surprised how often I was happy and doing things I liked.

Mrs. S: That's great reporting. Let's look at a couple of these and see if we can figure out how you did them. Wow. Look here today—you have that you were laughing at lunch and having a good time. That's great. That is certainly different than the other day when you were about to "rip a face off." How did you do that?

LaTanya: What do you mean?

Mrs. S: How were you able to have a good time and laugh at lunch today? What was different?

LaTanya: Well, first of all, Brittany wasn't there.

Mrs. S: And how did being there alone help you have a good time?

LaTanya: No I wasn't alone. Robert and Marquan were there. But Brittany—she's the girl I got in a fight with last time—she wasn't there.

Mrs. S: Oh, I get it. So you are there with Robert and Marquan but what were you doing that contributed to you having a good time?

LaTanya: Well, we were talking about music and stuff and I'm really into music, and I was telling Robert all about the band I wanted to start.

Mrs. S: A band . . . how cool!

LaTanya: Yeah, but Robert didn't believe me and he started to tease me, calling me "LaTanya-cool-J."

Mrs. S: So Robert was teasing you but you still had fun? How did you do that?

LaTanya: I don't know, I just teased him back.

Mrs. S: What do you mean?

LaTanya: Well he was calling me "LaTanya-cool-J" and I said he had it wrong, it was just "Lady LT" and I made this pose like I was a starlet. [demonstrating pose]

Mrs. S: That's great. So you just played with him and didn't take offense. Wow, that's super.

LaTanya: It was fun. We started talking about Lady LT clothing . . . and dolls. It was fun!

Mrs. S: So unlike the other day, rather than take offense to somebody making fun you just played along and it seemed to work . . . that's cool.

LaTanya: Yeah.

Mrs. S: I'm wondering if Brittany were there and if you could do the same thing, if anything would have been different than the other day?

LaTanya: I don't know, she doesn't like me.

Mrs. S: But how would Robert and Marquan act if you just played along with Brittany, even if Brittany didn't want to play?

LaTanya: I bet they would have laughed!

Mrs. S: And if they laughed how would that affect you?

LaTanya: Actually, I think I would be okay. I think I would just laugh and play with those guys.

Mrs. S: That's fantastic! LaTanya, do you think you could give that a try tomorrow and maybe check in and let me know how it went? You know, like another mini-experiment?

LaTanya: I can try, but I can't promise it will work.

Mrs. S: Just trying is good enough!

Mr. B (Behavioral-Orienting Framework)

From Session 1

Mr. B: Okay. How about if during the next two days if there is a time when you "curse at a classmate" or "feel like you want to hit them" that you just write it down, over here in this column we'll call "B" for behavior. Just describe what you did. Like if we use the cafeteria example, you would write down, "I told Brittany to . . . !"

Okay? Then if you could, over here in the first column that I have this "A" on, I would love you to write down what happened or what was going on right before you acted this way. Like, if we use the example with Brittany in column "A" you would write, "I was going to sit for lunch and Brittany said 'what do you want newbie?' and everyone laughed," and then over here [pointing to "B"] you wrote, "I said: 'f . . . you' and walked away."

Okay?

Reflections "on" Practice (After First Session)

I'm looking forward to seeing if LaTanya will keep some notes that we can look at. It almost seems like either she has no alternative way of responding to peer criticism, except through verbal or physical aggression; or, if she does, she has problems delaying her immediate reflexive action to engage in a more socially acceptable behavior. I'll need to check to see if the aggression is being reinforced by peer reaction.

Second Session

Mr. B: LaTanya, great job! Look at these notes. You really did a great job reporting. I know you are not happy about these three situations, but the fact that you were willing to write it all down will really help us!

LaTanya: Well actually, I am okay with the three things I wrote down because only one is really bad, the others were little things. Like early today I wrote down that when I couldn't find my special CD that I wanted to bring and show Marquan, I got angry and said the "s" word. And yesterday at lunch, Alex dropped his Jello on me when he tripped on my book bag. I called him an "a-hole" but then I apologized. Really! I told him I was sorry! So they're not real bad! The third one was yesterday. Right after Alex did that, Brittany came by and called me Jello-head and said it looked better than my extensions, so I kicked her!

Mr. B: Well I'm proud of the hard work you did writing all this out for us, and the fact that you were able to apologize to Alex, it showed me that you really are trying. Now let's look at what happened with Brittany. So, in column "A" you wrote Brittany called you a "Jello-head," and in "B" you have that you kicked her. Okay, what happened right after that? Oh, I see you have that Robert and Marquan laughed and Brittany told Mrs. Johnson, the lunch monitor, and you were sent to the assistant principal. Hmmmmm . . . .

LaTanya, what do you think happened here?

LaTanya: I don't know. I just hate her. She thinks she's better than everyone else and I just don't know, she makes me so angry, and before I know it I'm doing something or saying something that gets me in trouble.

Mr. B: That's really good insight. It's like when Brittany makes a statement she is hitting some type of button and you flip on? Boy, if we could figure out how to disconnect that button, or maybe have it attached to a different button that resulted in a different response, that would be great.

LaTanya: Yeah, it would help me stay out of trouble. But I can't do that.

Mr. B: Well, I have a couple of ideas that could help. You know what? If every time Brittany said something you immediately felt real relaxed—mellow—then you wouldn't react with anger.

LaTanya: Yeah . . . me mellow!

Mr. B: Well, I've seen you pretty mellow and laid back when you are listening to your music.

LaTanya: But, that's different.

Mr. B: I know. But I bet you could learn to use that same type of behavior . . . you know, mellowing out . . . even in situations like with Brittany! Boy that would blow everybody's mind!

LaTanya: [smiling] Yeah. I'd be really cool L.T.!

Mrs. C (Cognitive-Orienting Framework)

From Session 1

Mrs. C: Oh, some juicy stuff? I don't need to see that. I was thinking if you could keep a little log or journal for me it would help us. What I would love you to do is find a couple of times during the next few days when you find yourself getting angry. Write down how you feel and how you are acting or what you are saying and if you can describe what happened right before you got angry. Was something said or done? Were you remembering something? Could you do that?

Reflections "on" Practice (from First Session)

LaTanya is certainly a bright and opinionated young woman. She's beginning to get the idea of the thinking–feeling connection, but hopefully if I use her own examples this will become a little clearer. I think with her, I just want to help her reframe Brittany's and others' critical comments as less important, maybe to get her to use the "I don't care framework."

Second Session

Mrs. C: So how did the note-taking work out?

LaTanya: I'm not sure if I did it correctly. I only have three things written down.

Mrs. C: LaTanya, whatever you have will be great. Could I see?

LaTanya: Sure.

Mrs. C: Okay. So here you were rushing to get to the bus stop and you couldn't find your CD and you were cursing a little bit! And then, Alex dropped Jello on you (ouch!) . . . and over here . . . oh, good-old Brittany was back making comments. LaTanya, this is great! Now I'm going to show you something that I would bet none of your friends or even Brittany knows, and it is the secret to keeping all of your power!

LaTanya: Huh?

Mrs. C: Well, I know you have these three things written down and you are saying they made you mad. But you know what? None of these made you mad . . . not the CD you couldn't find or Jello, or even Brittany. None of these made you mad.

LaTanya: Oh yeah? Brittany pisses me off.

Mrs. C: Actually, it's not Brittany that makes you mad, it's you that makes you mad about what Brittany is saying or doing.

LaTanya: Huh? What's the difference?

Mrs. C: Wow . . . it's a huge difference. If Brittany makes you mad that means she's the one with the control. But, if you are the one making you mad then it is you with the control, and any time getting mad isn't working for you or causing problems you are the one with the power and can stop!

LaTanya: Okay. But I'm not sure how she's not making me mad?

Mrs. C: Well, this is really wild and like I said, it's kind of a secret that not many of your friends know, but you know how you speak to yourself . . . like a voice in your head?

LaTanya: Oh, great. So now you are going to tell me I'm nuts.

Mrs. C: No, no. We all do that. We have to. It's like if I'm walking out to my car and I hear a noise, I can hear myself saying, "What's that?" That's normal. We have to talk to ourselves about what we are experiencing. That's how we know how to react. But watch, and this is the cool part. If I'm going to my car and I hear a noise and then in my head I say, "What's that?" how do you think I'll feel if I then answer the question and say, "It's a mugger coming to take my money!"

LaTanya: I don't know about you but I'd be running!

Mrs. C: Me too, and scared. But wait! What happens if I'm wrong? What happens if it is just a cat or a dog and I'm getting myself all upset and scared thinking it's a mugger? Wow, what a waste of my energy. And by the way, what's upsetting me? Is it the noise or my belief that it's a mugger?

LaTanya: The idea that you think you are going to be mugged!

Mrs. C: Fantastic. So it could be said that I am making myself afraid by the way I'm thinking!

LaTanya: I think I get it?

Mrs. C: Well let's try it out. When Alex dropped the Jello, what did you think? What thoughts went through your brain?

LaTanya: I first thought . . . can I use the words that go through my mind?

Mrs.C: Just for now since this is our experiment.

LaTanya: I first thought, "Oh crap!" I cleaned it up and then I thought, "Stupid arse!" What a jerk . . . but then I thought "Oh, he tripped over my bag. It's not his fault."

Mrs. C: Wow, that's fantastic. So initially you were concerned about the Jello—yuk. And then you started feeling angry, but then as soon as you said "It's not his fault," you were able to get calm and even apologize! So see how quickly your thinking went from Alex as a jerk and probably should be punished, to it's not his fault? With this new thought you calmed down quickly and even apologized.

LaTanya: Yeah, I know that now, but I just reacted then!

Mrs. C: I know that's how it seems, but with a little practice I bet you could hear what you are saying and learn to talk to yourself in a way that makes it better for you.

LaTanya: What should I do?

Mrs. C: Well, would you be willing to take more notes like you did last time? But this time, in addition to writing down what happened and how you reacted, maybe you could listen to your self-talk, you know, that voice in your head. And if you would, I would like you to write everything down that you hear, even if it sounds silly. And then the next time we get together we'll go over your notes and see if we can find ways to attack any "stinkin' thinkin'." That's what I call thinking that causes me problems like my thought I was going to be mugged and got myself all afraid and it was just a cat!

LaTanya: I'll try.

Mr. TT (Transtheoretical-Orienting Framework)

From Session 1

Mr. TT: How about if you just try to be "good" for the rest of today and tomorrow and then maybe you and I could meet and see how it worked out and what else we could do. If you would like, we could get together tomorrow afternoon and see what we can do.

Reflections "on" Practice (from First Session)

Well I guess some headway was made. LaTanya seems to have taken some ownership over the situation and is at least contemplating the possibility of making some changes. I'm looking forward to seeing if she comes down on her own since that would show some commitment to change and something I could build on. I think we need to set small goals and just get her to take a few preparatory steps.

Second Session

LaTanya: [knocking] Hi Mr. TT!

Mr. TT: LaTanya, come on in. Great to see you! How did the last couple of days go?

LaTanya: Pretty good.

Mr. TT: Pretty good?

LaTanya: Well, I didn't get any detentions, but I did get into a fight with Brittany in the caf!

Mr. TT: A fight?

LaTanya: Well not a fight-fight. I called her a slut!

Mr. TT: Ouch. How do you feel about that?

LaTanya: She deserved it. She called me something that I can't say to you.

Mr. TT: Well I can understand that you felt attacked by her comment, but I'm still wondering how you felt about using that language with her?

LaTanya: I told my grandmother and she said that I shouldn't use that type of language since I'm a lady. My grandmom is always saying that.

Mr. TT: So your grandmom thinks that type of language is below you?

LaTanya: Yeah. She always says we should show our class!

Mr. TT: Wow. How do you feel about what she says?

LaTanya: My grandmom is the best. She's beautiful and a really good person. I love her and really want her proud of me, but I don't know how she does it, nothing seems to ruffle her. But Brittany just gets me so angry . . . I want to rip her face off.

Mr. TT: But you know what? Just the fact that you would like to be more like your grandmom is a step in the right direction. Maybe we could figure out how she does it and then we could practice being more like her?

LaTanya: That's funny, 'cause that's what I do in church. My grandmom is an elder in our church and everybody calls her Ms. M and she calls everyone darling, and so when we are at church I call her Ms. M and try to compliment people like she does. The people at church always call me Ms. M's princess. I like that!

Mr. TT: Ms. M's princess! Wow, what a compliment. How do you think they would feel if they were in the cafeteria yesterday?

LaTanya: [looking down]

Mr. TT: Sorry, I wasn't trying to make you feel bad, it's just that when you said princess I could see you that way, but I know that's not how you were in the caf. So, maybe we need to bring the "princess" to school? What do you think?

LaTanya: I don't know. That would be hard because the kids aren't like the people at church. They're mean.

Mr. TT: LaTanya, you are right that some of the kids can act pretty mean, but I'm wondering if your grandmom were here what she would say to you?

LaTanya: She'd tell me to walk away. She always says, "Life is too short to waste it on nonsense."

Mr. TT: Wow, your grandmother is really something. So she'd think arguing with Brittany was nonsense and she would just say, "Princess, walk away. Don't waste your time"?

LaTanya: Yeah. [laughing] And she'd turn her back and walk away like this. [demonstrating a swagger]

Mr. TT: [laughing] Well, Ms. Princess, we need to start applying that attitude here at school. I have an idea. You have great handwriting. Why don't you write a little reminder on your binder . . . something like, "life's too short," or "Grandmom says . . . ".

LaTanya: How about, "Ms. M's Princess!" I like that!

Mr. TT: That's fantastic. Do you think if you looked at that throughout the day it would help you act like Ms. M's Princess? You know, be proud, respect others, and don't waste your time and energy on fighting?

LaTanya: Maybe.

Mr. TT: Well I think it's a great idea and really worth testing, if you are up to it!

LaTanya: I think I can even draw a little picture and put it on a couple of my book covers and even in my lunch box!

Mr. TT: Wow, your grandmom would be pretty proud!

Subsequent Session: Mrs. S (Solution Focused)

Reflection "on" Practice

Well, LaTanya is certainly doing really well with the anger—even the teachers are noticing how much more engaged she is with her classmates. Her use of humor has really been an effective means for diffusing criticism.

Mrs. S: LaTanya, come on in. It's been quite awhile. What's new and exciting?

LaTanya: Yeah, with baseball practice and stuff it's been hard to come down after school.

Mrs. S: So you're busy with school and baseball and stuff?

LaTanya: Yeah. Do you remember me telling you about starting a band?

Mrs. S: Sure.

LaTanya: Well we are going to perform in the talent contest and I was hoping you would come and watch us.

Mrs. S: Are you kidding? I wouldn't miss it. [smiling] I was just thinking, "Wow, what a difference." I mean, it was not that long ago that you were in my office saying you were a zero on our scale. Do you remember that?

LaTanya: Yeah. Wait, I thought we changed that to a one or a two. [smiling]

Mrs. S: You're right! Sorry! So, where do you see yourself now?

LaTanya: Hmmmmm . . . maybe close to ten. [smiling]

Mrs. S: LaTanya, that's really super. I was hoping that's how you saw it because I know you have been really active in school, with baseball and now the talent contest, and all of your teachers have told me how much you contribute in class. It is really great!

If someone asked, "How did you do it?" what would you say?

LaTanya: I don't know. I would say I owe it all to my wonderful counselor, Mrs. S. [smiling]

Mrs. S: Why thank you. But really, what's different?

LaTanya: I am just myself. I like to be involved and now I am, so that makes school better.

Mrs. S: Okay. But in addition to being involved, you also don't seem to get as angry when people make comments or faces or . . .

LaTanya: Well, actually I have lots of friends and people really don't get to me. When somebody is up in my face, I just ignore them or make a wise comment that shuts them up.

Mrs. S: So the fact that you are getting involved in things and that you use your humor just to deal with anybody who is being critical, that all seems to work. That's great. LaTanya, I am really proud of you. You've worked hard and I think you are really a super addition to Harding.

LaTanya: Thanks. And since you said that, I need a faculty sponsor if I want to run for student council next year. Would you be my sponsor?

Mrs. S: Absolutely! Let's see, athlete, scholar, humorist, and now politician . . . look out Harding, here comes LaTanya! [laughing]

Subsequent Session: Mr. B (Behavioral Focused)

Reflection "on" Practice

Mr. B and LaTanya develop a list of things that Brittany has done or said that seem to serve as a stimulus eliciting an anger response. They placed these in a hierarchy and now Mr. B. is presenting these to LaTanya while she practices breathing.

Mr. B: Now remember keep your focus, nice smooth, easy, slow breathing. And if you find that you are getting angry, I want you to just wiggle your finger and I'll give you time to get back into your zone.

Let's begin.

So, here you are sitting outside waiting for baseball practice to begin and Brittany is walking by to go to cheerleading. She looks over at you and says, "What's up jock!" Now focus. See her face . . . see your teammates looking at you as if they are waiting for you to respond. Keep that image and keep focusing on slow, smooth, rhythmic breathing . . . hold it. There she is standing there with that grin that she has saying, "What's up jock!" And she's emphasizing the word "jock" and just smiling. See her and yet keep your slow, smooth, rhythmic breathing. Great . . . hold it. hold it.

Now LaTanya, let go of the image and just focus on your breathing, reminding yourself to stop, breath, respond. Say that a couple of times to yourself as you exhale. Go ahead. Good, very good.

LaTanya, open your eyes.

So how did you do?

LaTanya: Great! It was cool. I could see her and I could even see my teammates, but I was like really zoned, just mellow, I could care less.

Mr.B: That's fantastic! What do you think you may have said or done if you were able to stay in that zone and this was actually happening?

LaTanya: That's funny 'cause when I was doing it I was thinking, "Hi there . . . cheerleader" (real sarcastically) and my teammates laughed!

Mr. B: Well that's super. I want you to keep practicing your breathing and we'll do the last three on our list tomorrow, if that's okay?

LaTanya: That's great. I meant to tell you, in practice yesterday, I used my breathing to relax when I was at bat and it really helped.

Mr. B: You really are something! Great job. See you tomorrow!

Reflection "on" Practice

Tomorrow I think we can finish the hierarchy, but I want to make a tape for her to practice at home. I am really happy she is generalizing the relaxation skill outside of the sessions. Maybe it's time to try it in vivo, so maybe tomorrow we can identify a couple of settings— like baseball or going to the board to do a math problem or presenting her group's report, and of course, Brittany—that she could use and then report back.

Subsequent Session: Mrs. C (Cognitive-Orienting Framework)

Reflections on Practice

I am really impressed with LaTanya's insight and ability to grasp the cognitive paradigm. She seems to like that "stinkin' thinkin'" phrase. I need to help her see the need to just keep practicing and continue to challenge her faulty thinking.

Mrs. C: LaTanya, you are becoming the queen of stinkin' thinkin' attackers!

LaTanya: I don't know. I still get mad sometimes. Like yesterday during the game when I struck out. I almost threw the bat!

Mrs. C: Did you hear that? You almost threw the bat! What stopped you?

LaTanya: I don't know.

Mrs. C: Let's see if we can recreate it.

LaTanya: No thanks. [smiling]

Mrs. C: Goof ball. Describe what was happening

LaTanya: Well, it was the third inning and we were tied and Alicia was on third base and I was up and when the pitcher threw the ball I think I looked at Alicia for a split second . . . anyway, I swung and missed and that was the third out.

Mrs. C: Okay, so you strike out and now you turn to the bench to walk back. That's the actual event but what was going on inside your head: What were you thinking?

LaTanya: I remember saying out loud, "Crap!" And I think that's when I started to wind up on the bat.

Mrs. C: But something must have changed? You must have attacked that stinkin' thinkin' and interpreted it differently?

LaTanya: That's funny, as we are talking about it I can remember hearing my teammates yelling, "That's okay LaTanya," and I thought, "Yeah, that's okay . . . I'll get them next time."

Mrs. C: Fantastic! See that? You went from thinking this is the worse thing in the world, that you are a failure, and that you let the team down, to "Hey, no big deal. I'll get them next time." That's super!

LaTanya: Yeah. And you know what I did? I hit a double the next time up!

Mrs. C: LaTanya that's great. Not just the double, but that you really are trying to be aware of your stinkin' thinkin' and working hard to attack it. Now remember I said, just like in baseball you have to keep practicing or your skill will get rusty. Do you think you will use your journal to debate and challenge that thinking if you find yourself jumping track?

LaTanya: Absolutely. But can I still come down . . . coach? [smiling]

Mrs. C: You better . . . or I'll having you doing laps! [smiling]

Subsequent Session: Mr. TT (Transtheoretical-Orienting Framework)

Reflections "on" Practice

LaTanya has really been committed to working on this anger issue. I think making her grandmother proud is extremely important and she certainly wants to be like her grandmom. I think before we stop the formal sessions we should develop some strategies that would help her continue to develop the "Ms. M's Princess" attitude and style.

Mr. TT: Good morning, lady!

LaTanya: Good morning, Mr TT.

Mr. TT: Well, what's new and exciting?

LaTanya: Do you remember me telling you about my band? Well, we signed up for the school talent contest.

Mr. TT: That's great! Good for you!

LaTanya: Well, I got a little problem. You see, my grandmother is going to come to see us.

Mr. TT: That sounds nice. Where's the problem?

LaTanya: I'm not sure she will approve of our music.

Mr. TT: I thought you told me your grandmother was really into music?

LaTanya: Yeah, church stuff. I'm not sure if she'll like what we do.

Mr. TT: Well you are talking to the wrong guy. I am not very hip [laughing] but isn't there some artist that sings nice love songs?

LaTanya: Yes. There is Beyonce, or Ashanti, Destiny's Child . . .

Mr. TT: Help me out here. Would any of those artists qualify on the Ms. M's Princess scale?

LaTanya: My grandmother doesn't like some of the words in Ashanti's songs. She thinks I look like Beyonce, but prettier [smiling], but she likes Destiny's Child and our band does one of their songs, "Survivor"!

Mr. TT: Well?

LaTanya: I could do that!

Mr. TT: You know this Ms. M's Princess scale is a great tool for helping you make all kinds of decisions. What do you think? Can you use it?

LaTanya: Already have! I joined the church youth choir. I even have a solo in the Easter service. Bingo . . . princess scale! [laughing]

Mr. TT: I think we are on to something. I just wish I could package it for other students to use, the LaTanya Princess scale! I am thrilled you are using it and it really is working. Just one last thing, not only is grandmom going to be at the talent contest, but I'll be there. I'll be the really hip guy in the back, cheering. [laughing]

UPON FURTHER CONSIDERATION

As was suggested in the previous chapter, it may be beneficial for you to more closely reflect "on" and "in" practice as applied to this case of LaTanya. Before moving on to our final chapter, it may be beneficial for you to engage in Exercise 8.1.

■ ■ ■ ■ ■ ▬▬▬▬▬▬▬▬▬

EXERCISE 8.1

REFLECTION "IN" AND "ON" PRACTICE

Part I: Identifying Theory in Practice

Directions: The following exercise is best completed in collaboration with a classmate or colleague. Having now observed the "on" practice and "in" practice reflections of counselors operating with four unique perspectives, you are invited to return to the dialogue in an attempt to identify and label the application of concepts and constructs in action. Specifically, review the panel members' reflections and attempt to identify evidence of each of the following.

Solution Focus:
  Positive goal setting
  Scaling
  Affirmation
  Collaborative style
  Exceptions

Behavioral:
  Operationalization
  Shaping
  Functional-behavioral analyses
  Operant conditioning

Cognitive:
  Cognitive dissonance
  Assimilation
  Insight 1—connecting thought to feeling
  Cognitive reframing

Transtheoretical:
  Precontemplative stage
  Contemplation
  Preparatory
  Action
  Maintenance

Part II: Guiding Personal Reflection on Practice

Directions: Along with a classmate or colleague, review the various hypotheses proposed by the panel members as well as the interventions that emerged from these hypotheses. Identify the data that you found relevant and discuss how you would employ these data to guide your hypotheses and the interventions you would employ. Does your approach reflect that of one of our panel members? Or is it more of an eclectic view?

CHAPTER 9

BECOMING A REFLECTIVE PRACTITIONER: PRACTICE "ON" AND "IN" REFLECTION

The importance of reviewing data presented by the client as the basis for formulating the procedural framework from which interventions emerge cannot be overstated. It is this procedural knowledge that distinguishes the expert from the novice counselor.

The processes of reflecting "on" and "in" practice can be developed, but such development requires practice. The current chapter provides two case studies for your review and guided practice. The intent of this chapter is to help move you from being a reader of reflective practice to becoming a doer of reflective practice.

Specifically, after reading this chapter you will able to:

- describe the client data employed to formulate your case conceptualization and treatment plan;
- identify specific in-session interventions you would have applied, following reflection in practice, to test your hypotheses and/or to formulate interventions; and
- describe the effect of viewing the case data from one alternative orienting model.

OVERVIEW

The first case, David, is a case of an eight-year-old third grader who is exhibiting signs of social anxiety. The reader is provided essential client information, and throughout the case is directed to specific considerations for reflection. It is hoped that these directed reflections will assist the reader in developing a conceptualization of the case and a hypothesized treatment plan.

The second case, Loretta, is a case of a junior in high school who feels stuck in the middle of her parents' marital crises. Detailed information about the client, as well as dialogue taken from two specific counseling sessions, is provided. As with the first case, points of reflection will be provided in an attempt to engage the reader as he/she steps into the role of counselor with his/her unique orienting framework.

CASE 1: DAVID—SOCIALLY ANXIOUS

The case to be discussed is one involving David, an eight-year-old third-grade student who has been referred to the school counselor by his teacher, Mr. McCardle. The initial referral stated only that Mr. McCardle wanted the counselor to talk to David because he seems withdrawn and socially isolated from his peers.

The counselor in this case illustration attempts to take a nondirective approach, hoping to simply clarify the nature and context of the issue; identify client goals and resources; and provide a developed picture with which you, the reader, will be able to generate hypotheses regarding the "what is" and "what should be done." As you will note, stimulants for reflections are inserted to guide your own reflections "on" and "in" practice.

Background Information

According to Mr. McCardle, David appears to be very anxious and avoids social contact with his classmates. Mr. McCardle explained that David, who is a recent transfer from out of state, has been having a lot of problems with his peers. Mr. McCardle describes the other boys, both in David's class and those in the upper classes, as often teasing and taunting David, especially at lunch and in the playground. Mr. McCardle expressed a concern, not just about the fact that the other students tease David, but that David appears not to know how to respond to the teasing in a way that may actually help stop it. Specifically, Mr. McCardle noted that when teased, David will either become "enraged with anger and physically attack the other student," or "crumble into tears and run away crying!"

In taking a brief history of this problem, the counselor discovered that it appears that this verbal teasing and taunting started soon after David's admission to school (six weeks ago). Apparently, on the first day of school David dropped his lunch tray walking to his seat in the cafeteria and some of the older boys (sixth graders) began to make fun of him in front of the entire cafeteria. The other kids were yelling taunts such as, "Way to go speed-o" and "Nice hands Allstate!" Upon hearing these comments, David apparently became upset, started to cry, and ran out of the cafeteria. The older boys then began to chant "Run baby, run" and the cafeteria erupted in laughter. The rest of that day, each time David passed one of the older students he was called "cry baby." David eventually went to the nurse's office complaining about being sick to his stomach and his mother came to pick him up and took him home.

Time Out for Reflection

As you read the presenting information, what initial hypotheses have you drawn about the factors or variables operating at this point in David's school life? In reflecting "on" practice, what orientation or combination of orientations do you find yourself using to process these data? Finally, as you prepare to meet with David, what will your goals be for the first session?

Client Session

Counselor: David, come on in. Have a seat!

David: Thanks.

Counselor: I'm glad you came down. Do you know why Mr. McCardle wanted me to speak with you?

David: Yeah, 'cause the kids are picking on me!

Counselor: The kids are picking on you?

David: Yeah, a lot of the boys—mostly those in sixth grade—call me names like cry baby and get the other guys in my class to do the same thing.

Counselor: Wow, I'm sorry to hear that. How does that make you feel?

David: Pretty bad. I hate it.

Counselor: You hate it?

David: Yeah. Sometimes I want to just go up and smash them.

Counselor: Smash them?

David: Hit them with something . . . I'm not afraid of them.

Counselor: Oh, I see. So sometimes it makes you so angry that you want to punch them or hit them with something?

David: Yeah. I mean, everybody makes fun of me . . . it's not fair.

Counselor: Well it certainly sounds as if a number of people are calling you names and that seems to really upset you and really hurt your feelings and even make you angry.

Time Out for Reflection

Using a transtheoretical-orienting framework:

1. Identify David's current stage of change.
2. What evidence do you have to support that?
3. How would you intervene to test these hypothesis?
4. How would you plan to move him to the next stage of change?

Intervention Strategy:

1. What is your hypothesis about the nature of David's problem and the best way to assist him?
2. What data from the above exchange are you using to formulate that hypothesis?
3. Which model or models does your hypothesis most closely reflect?
4. In your continued interaction with David, what would you do to test your hypothesis?

Session Continued

David: I hate it. I don't like it here. I don't want to come to school and I told my mom that.

Counselor: So you've told your mom that you don't like this school. What did your mom say when you said you didn't want to come to school?

David: She told me I had to and that I should just give it back to the bullies!

Counselor: Give it back?

David: Like call them names or punch them.

Counselor: Your mom said you should punch them?

David: Well no, but she said I should just give it back to them.

Counselor: How do you feel about that idea of giving it back to them?

David: I'd like to punch them, but that would just get me in trouble and mom would be really mad.

Counselor: That is true, at least the part about getting into trouble. And I guess your mom might feel, just like I do, that punching probably wouldn't help much.

David: [beginning to cry] But I hate them for teasing.

Counselor: David, I can understand that teasing can really get to you and make you not want to come to school. I am wondering if you and I got together if maybe we could discover something else that maybe I could do . . . or you could do . . . or maybe we could do it together to make it better. What do you think?

Time Out for Reflection

Taking a behavioral-orienting framework to process the information shared up to this point, reflect on the following.

1. What, at this point, would you identify as the behavior of real concern?
2. What triggers appear to be operating or do you assume might be operating?
3. What reinforcement or contingencies may be maintaining the BORC?

Session Continued

David: I think I just want to go back to my old school.

Counselor: Maybe you could tell me a little about that? How was it in your old school?

David: It was great. I had lots of friends. I was even on the basketball team. I'm pretty good!

Counselor: So you like basketball?

David: Yeah, I like all sports. In fact, I was thinking about going out for baseball in two weeks, but I'm not sure. If those other kids are on the team. I don't know.

Counselor: Wow. So you really like sports and you feel pretty good about how well you play, but even with that you are thinking about maybe not going to tryouts because you are afraid about facing the older boys?

David: Yeah. I mean if I show up and they start teasing me I don't want to start to cry.

Counselor: Well that makes sense, I guess. But I feel sad that you are going to give up something you love just because you may get upset. I really think we could figure out something that might help so that you could try out.

Time Out for Reflection

Given the hypothesis you identified during the first "Time out for reflection" what might you have done differently in this segment (reflection "*in*" practice)? Is there information that you would have sought that was missed by this counselor? Are there specific places within the above exchange that you would have done something differently? Where? Why?

Given the data added in this segment, has your hypothesis regarding David's stage of change, the nature of his problem, and the steps to intervention that are desired changed? If so, what specifically has contributed to the adjusting of your hypothesis? If not, what data continue to support your hypothesis and what would you do to try to find further evidence for support?

Session Continued

Counselor: David, I know you are worried and thinking that you may get upset and start to cry, but has that ever happened before? You know, has there ever been a time when you were playing some sport, something you really liked and felt good at, and started to cry when someone teased you?

David: Last year. It was horrible, my whole family was there!

Counselor: Oh, okay. Would you mind telling me about it?

David: I guess. I was playing on our church's team back in my old home. They had teams for t-ballers and then they had minors and majors and I was on the majors with the fourth- and fifth-grade kids.

Counselor: Wow, that's pretty cool. You were—I guess in second grade and you were on the same team as the fourth- and fifth-grade kids. That's something.

David: [smiling] Yeah. I was the youngest boy on the team. But we had this game and they let me play as catcher near the end of the game 'cause we were winning by a lot. This was the first time I ever played catcher. We never did that in t-ball, the coaches always did that. I was doing pretty good catching, but then one of the other team members tried to steal second base and everyone was hollering for me to throw the ball to second and I tried. The problem is I couldn't reach second base. The ball just bounced past the pitcher and everyone started laughing.

Counselor: How were you feeling when that happened?

David: I started to cry. I felt really stupid. But I never played catcher and the chest pad made it hard to throw. But everyone on that team started laughing and calling me "noodle arm." I started crying so hard I had trouble seeing the pitcher throw the ball and I missed the next two pitches and the coach made me come out of the game. I wanted to go home but I couldn't.

Counselor: I can't imagine how hard it was for you experiencing that, especially since you love baseball and I'm sure you felt proud of playing with the older guys. I mean, you were the only second-grader on the team. Wow, that's something.

But I can understand how you might be concerned now that if you have to catch or throw the ball a long away at tryouts that maybe the other kids will laugh.

David: No, not that. I worked really hard and I can really throw the ball now.

Counselor: Well then I'm confused. What do you think they will tease you about?

David: I don't know. I just know that the older guys are always cutting up on each other and teasing and I know that they'll do that to me.

Counselor: Oh I see. So it's not just you they make fun of but they do it to each other?

David: Yeah, but those guys don't cry.

Counselor: That I understand. Oh, David, I see it's time for you to go back to class right now and I really appreciate you coming in and sharing everything with me. I would like to see you tomorrow because I think we may be able to solve this problem so that you will be able to go to tryouts if you want and maybe even figure some things out so that it is nicer for you here at school. Would that be okay?

David: Okay . . . I guess.

Time Out for Reflection

Reflecting "on" practice.   As you reflect on practice, what preliminary conclusions have you drawn in regards to:

1. The nature of David's problem?
2. Reasonable goals for counseling?
3. Intervention model and strategies?

4. What would your specific goal(s) be for the next session and what strategies would you employ to achieve that goal?

A view from an alternative perspective.   Would your responses to the above-listed questions be different if you employed one of the other orienting frameworks? Select one alternative framework and develop responses to each of the above from that perspective. Look at your responses. Are they different? Would you approach the next session differently if you used a different orienting framework?

CASE 2: LORETTA—STUCK IN THE MIDDLE

Background

Loretta is a 16-year-old junior in high school. Loretta stopped in to see her counselor at the end of the day and asked if it would be okay to make an appointment for the following day during her lunch period. The counselor offered to meet with her then, but she stated, "It could wait."

Loretta has been a good student, achieving honors since being in high school. She is active in extracurricular activities and serves on student council as the junior class representative. The counselor, Ms. Schulman, has been Loretta's counselor since her freshman year and they have a very good relationship. All previous contact between Ms. Schulman and Loretta has centered on course selection and some preliminary career counseling.

Session 1

Loretta came to the counseling office during the fifth period (her lunch period) and the counselor anticipated that she would be interested in discussing colleges or careers, as had been the case in the previous two visits.

> **Loretta:**   Hi, Ms. S, are you ready for me?
>
> **Counselor:**   Always . . . come on in.
>
> **Loretta:**   How are you doing?
>
> **Counselor:**   I'm fine, thanks . . . and you?
>
> **Loretta:**   Okay, I guess. [looking down and somewhat tearful]
>
> **Counselor:**   Loretta, I've seen you when you are fine . . . and this doesn't look or sound like you are fine. What's up?
>
> **Loretta:**   Well, you're going to hear about it soon enough but I am really embarrassed.
>
> **Counselor:**   Embarrassed?
>
> **Loretta:**   I went to the dance Saturday and Mrs. Wilkins caught me in the bathroom, throwing up.
>
> **Counselor:**   Throwing up?

Loretta: Well . . . it's a long story. I feel so stupid.

Counselor: Loretta, it's okay. Why don't you tell me what happened?

Loretta: I was drunk . . . now, don't get mad! Mrs. Wilkins just thought I was sick with a stomach virus or something, but I know that everybody else knows that I was drunk. In fact, Tom and Lupe took me home.

Counselor: I am not sure I understand. You were drinking at the dance?

Loretta: No, I was drinking at home and came to the dance. I thought I was fine but when I got in the gym it was hot and I started to really lose it.

Counselor: Loretta I'm not mad, but to be honest I am really surprised. This doesn't sound like you.

Loretta: [starting to cry] I am really worried. I'm afraid somebody at school will say something and I'll get expelled. That would be horrible . . . my mom doesn't need that right now. [crying]

Counselor: I can see you are upset.

Time Out for Reflection

Take a moment to reflect on the dialogue.

1. What elements seem to stand out?
2. What lens or lenses are you using?
3. What initial hypothesis do you have?
4. What would you do next?

Session Continued

Counselor: Loretta, let's see if we can slow down a bit and figure out what happened first and then we can figure out what we want to do next.

Loretta: Okay. [crying]

Counselor: Can you tell me about what was happening before the dance? You said you were drinking?

Loretta: I wasn't going to go to the dance. I just wanted to stay home. But after dinner my parents got into it again and I couldn't take it so I went to my room. But I kept hearing them argue and it was making me really upset and I decided I would just knock myself out and go to bed. So, I snuck down and grabbed a bottle of vodka and 7-Up and went to my room and drank.

Counselor: You grabbed a bottle of vodka?

Loretta: I just couldn't stand listening to them yelling at each other . . . I hate it.

Counselor: So your parents were arguing and that was really upsetting you and the way you responded was by drinking alcohol? Loretta, has this happened before?

Loretta: The last three months it seems like they fight every weekend. The only reason they don't fight on the weekdays is my dad is away on business.

Counselor: Your parents have been having problems for a while. But I guess I was wondering about your drinking? Is this how you have been responding each time you get upset about their fighting?

Loretta: No. This is only the second time I did that, and the first time, which was two weeks ago, I just passed out on my bed and slept the entire night. That's what I thought would happen this time. I'm not sure why I went to the dance.

Counselor: Loretta, I know you are concerned about the dance and the possibility somebody saw you there drunk, but truthfully I'm more concerned about you and your health. It is clear that you are feeling really bad about what's going on with your parents, but the way you are trying to cope with it is not good.

Loretta: I know it's stupid, but I can't take it any more.

Counselor: You sound really overwhelmed, but the drinking is only compounding the problem. Would you like to tell me what's happening at home?

Loretta: [crying]. I know they are going to get a divorce . . . it will be horrible.

Counselor: Have you shared your concerns with either of your parents?

Loretta: No. I think I'm the reason they are arguing.

Counselor: You're the reason?

Loretta: I don't know. I just don't know anything right now. [crying]

Counselor: Loretta I am really confused. You are an honor student and actively involved in school and have been since freshman year. How would you be the reason for their conflict?

Loretta: I don't know. Maybe I should help out more at home. My dad's always mad that the house is messy or that on weekends my mom doesn't like to cook. Maybe if I helped my mom more he wouldn't be so angry. Maybe I should stay in and cook more or do something to make the house perfect!

Counselor: Well I'm sure you would like to help and wished they weren't fighting, but I'm not sure how this is really your responsibility.

Loretta: My mom is really upset that my dad is away so much. She cries and when I ask her what's wrong, she usually tells me "nothing." But I've noticed that she's drinking almost every night during the week when Dad's away and she seems to not be taking care of herself . . . you know, not fixing her hair and putting on makeup. I'm worried about her.

Counselor: Loretta, I know how much you love your mom and it sounds like she is struggling and probably could use some help—some counseling—but I'm not sure how her drinking or the fact that the house is not as tidy as your dad would like . . . how any of this is your fault?

Loretta: I don't know . . . I just want to make it all right. [crying]

Time Out for Reflection

As you reflect on the case to this point, consider the following.

1. Have any of the data supported your initial hypothesis?
2. Have you adjusted your hypothesis and what you felt was a plan of intervention?
3. Did the counselor target the data you were seeking? If not, was that a function of her operating framework?
4. Finally, where you want to go next?

Session Continued

Counselor: Loretta, I can see that what is happening at home is really affecting you. I can see how upset you are and I hear how much you want to help, but I know you can see that your drinking neither helps you nor your parents.

Loretta: I know it was stupid and if I get caught and somebody tells my parents it will be horrible and then it will be my fault! [crying]

Counselor: Loretta, how about if we do a couple of things? First, you have to promise me no drinking! Promise!

Loretta: I won't. Really—I know that was stupid. I don't even like the taste of it and I felt horrible the next day. I won't . . . I promise.

Counselor: Thanks. Later today I'm meeting with the prom committee and I know if the word is out about you and the dance they will all let me know. That way if it is out, I'll see what I can do to intervene before it becomes a major disaster. Now, do you feel like you can go to class?

Loretta: Yes.

Counselor: Good. How about we get together tomorrow during your lunch period to see where we go next. What we are doing now is just a temporary solution.

Loretta: Okay, but I just don't know what to do.

Counselor: Well, we'll begin to figure that out tomorrow. But we both know what you can't do—drink! So promise me you will make good decisions today to take care of yourself and no drinking.

Loretta: I promise!

Time Out for Reflection

As you reflect on this initial encounter consider each of the following.

1. What pieces of information seem to stick out?
2. What types of information do you feel are missing and that you would like to have?
3. What does the type of information you targeted say about the lens or lenses you use to process this client's story?

Now, as you prepare to meet with Loretta in this second session, how would you respond to the following?

1. What are your goals for the next session?
2. How do you plan to achieve these?
3. What, if any, preliminary strategies do you want to share with Loretta?

Session 2

> **Counselor:** Loretta, how are you?
>
> **Loretta:** Better, thanks. I'm sorry about all the crying yesterday.
>
> **Counselor:** You never ever have to apologize for showing emotions. You were very upset. Would you tell me what happened after we ended our time together yesterday?
>
> **Loretta:** Well, I went back to classes. It was a little hard to concentrate. I kept thinking about my mom and dad.
>
> **Counselor:** And how about after you left school?
>
> **Loretta:** When I went home my mom wasn't there—my dad is in Florida on business and won't be back until Friday night. I was a little concerned about the fact that my mom wasn't there but I didn't want to call her cell.
>
> **Counselor:** So you were worried?
>
> **Loretta:** Yeah, she's usually home when I get there so I wasn't sure what was up.
>
> **Counselor:** Oh, I see.
>
> **Loretta:** But she came in just before five and she was fine, she wasn't drinking or anything.
>
> **Counselor:** So she did come home and was okay? That's good. How were you feeling?
>
> **Loretta:** Relieved . . . I hate it when I come home and she's been drinking.

Time Out for Reflection

Given the hypothesis you derived as a result of your reflection on the first session:

1. Is this counselor helping you to test the hypothesis?
2. Are there data here that assist you in narrowing your hypothesis?

3. What other information would you seek?
4. Where, specifically, in the previous exchange would you have introduced a different intervention, perhaps a question, a reflection, etc.?
5. Which lens or lenses are you using to process the client's information?

Session Continued

Counselor: I can understand your concern about your mom and the way she has been drinking. How did you respond to her coming home as she did?

Loretta: I was so relieved I actually told her!

Counselor: Told her?

Loretta: Yes . . . I told her I was really concerned about her drinking.

Counselor: Oh. That sounded like it may have been hard to do?

Loretta: Yeah . . . but it just came out.

Counselor: How did your mom respond?

Loretta: She hugged me and we cried. She said she didn't want to talk about what was going on with her and dad. She didn't want me to be put in the middle. But she assured me she was done with the drinking and she said things would be okay.

Counselor: How was that for you?

Loretta: Well I felt relieved and glad I said something. But I'm not sure if it will be okay.

Counselor: So, even though you feel you made a move in the right direction, that maybe it's not as good as your mom tried to suggest?

Loretta: I don't know. I know we had one of the best nights together that we have had.

Counselor: That's wonderful. What happened?

Loretta: Well after we talked we decided to order dinner and get a movie. After dinner she and I just hung out and watched a movie. Actually, it was nice because we laughed a lot. Nothing major . . . just some time together relaxing. And then I stayed up pretty late working on my research paper.

Counselor: So it sounds like even though you weren't convinced that all will be okay you were able to put your concerns about the dance and your anxiety about your mom and dad to the side and get back to your school work?

Loretta: Yeah.

Counselor: That's great. You know, Loretta, it may help if you could describe how you were able to do that. How were you able to refocus on enjoying the time with your mom and then on doing your school work?

Loretta: I don't know. I guess just seeing her a little up and sober. I don't know. Maybe just the hanging out with the pizza and movie . . . it all helped me feel like it was the way it used to be, even if just for one night.

Counselor: So the way things were helped you focused on the positives rather than concentrate on all the bad possibilities?

Loretta: Yeah, I guess. I think seeing her happy made me less stressed.

Counselor: Okay, your mom was having a pretty good afternoon and when she is happy you seem to be less stressed, more happy yourself. But how does that work? How does her mood impact you and your mood?

Loretta: I don't know. Sometimes when I see her upset or worried I just think that I should do something to help her. I mean, she's my mom. I should help her. But I don't know what to do . . . so then I get upset and angry at myself, and then I begin to worry about all the things that could happen.

Counselor: Clearly you are concerned about your mom, but it sounds like you are putting yourself under a lot of pressure to do things that you really may not have the ability to do. Plus, it seems that you go from that moment to beginning to think about all the possible bad things that could happen.

Loretta: Yeah. I know I do that but I am concerned about what is happening.

Counselor: I believe that. I know you said that you didn't tell your parents about your concerns, but did you share your concerns with your mom last night?

Loretta: Not really. I told her about my concern about her drinking but I was afraid to say anything about she and dad. I'm afraid that if I say something she'll just get more upset and then start to worry about me. She doesn't need any more things to worry about.

Counselor: So you are worried about your mom and you want to help, but then you are too worried to say anything to her. That seems like a bit of a dilemma.

Time Out for Reflection

You most likely have developed a number of hypotheses about what is going on and even what the counselor could do to intervene.

1. How would reviewing the data up to this point, through a behavioral, solution-focused, cognitive or transtheoretical lens affect the way you conceptualize the case? Would using a different lens modify your operative assumptions?
2. What additional information would you like to have at this point and what would you have done as a counselor to acquire that data?

Session Continued

Loretta: I know I really can't do anything. I mean, I don't even know what's going on, not really. But I am really concerned that if they get a divorce— and I know this is going to sound horrible . . . I mean, so selfish—but if they get a divorce I'm not sure if I'll be able to go to college. I am sorry, I know that sounds horrible.

Counselor: Loretta, I understand that you care about your mom and dad and really don't want them to suffer to get a divorce. I also understand how you might be concerned how anything that happens between your mom and dad could impact you. That's not horrible . . . it's to be expected since a major change in their relationship could create a change in the family—including you. But maybe you could help me . . . you feel that you may not be able to go to college even if they got a divorce?

Loretta: I don't know. If they get a divorce maybe I'll have to stay home and support my mom or maybe they won't pay for me to go or . . . I don't know. [starts to cry]

Counselor: Loretta, I can see you are upset but I'm wondering if maybe you are jumping to some conclusions that may not be accurate.

Loretta: What do you mean?

Counselor: Well everything you are concerned about—you know, having to support your mom, or not having their money to support you going to college—I guess could happen, but these are possibilities, not facts, and I'm not sure how strong a possibility they are.

Loretta: But it could happen!

Counselor: Yes I guess, but because of what you have said to me already, I guess I would question whether you mom would want you to stay home with her? It seems that she really wants you to do the best you can do? And I know from college night your dad was so excited about you and your interest in engineering. So, I am having trouble putting that together with the fact that they wouldn't want you to go to college?

Loretta: I guess.

Counselor: And I am even wondering if something like that did happen, you know, that for whatever reason they were unwilling or unable to pay for your college, if there would be no other options open to you?

Loretta: You mean like scholarships?

Counselor: Well, that's one idea, but there are a lot of students who need financial support to go to college. But we are jumping way ahead of ourselves.

Loretta: But how about if my mom wants me to stay with her?

Counselor: Loretta, you know your mom, but a woman who tells you not to worry, and means it, doesn't sound like a woman who would want you to put your life on hold in order to stay with her. Does she?

Loretta: No. actually, even last night when we were watching the movie she was telling me how she's going to have to bring pizza and movies to my dorm once in awhile . . . and we laughed!

Counselor: And I bet she will. [smiling]

Loretta: You're right. I know she wouldn't want that but . . .

Counselor: But maybe the biggest thing of all is here we are talking about supporting your mom through a divorce that we really have no evidence will even occur. Boy, we can really create major problems in our heads without even really trying.

Loretta: I know, but I can't stop thinking this stuff. When I go to bed I find that my thoughts go wild and I can't fall asleep and I dream about being poor and my mom depressed and drinking and me being abandoned.

Counselor: Abandoned?

Loretta: I know it sounds stupid, but it seems so real, so possible. I think that's why when I hear them arguing I just want to escape!

Time Out for Reflection

Loretta has certainly shared quite a bit over the course of these two brief sessions. As you reflect "on" practice:

1. What assumptions do you make regarding the nature of Loretta's problem and the best strategy(ies) to use in helping her?
2. Is there a particular orienting framework that you feel would be most helpful in this case?
3. Given your assumptions about the nature of the problem, the strategies and orienting framework that may prove helpful, what would be your goals for the next session?
4. What specific things might you do to achieve those goals?

FINAL THOUGHTS

The purpose and focus of this text was described in the Preface as assisting those in the early stages of their counseling careers to begin to think and act like an expert. It was also highlighted that this book is just a beginning, and that becoming an *expert* in counseling, as is true for any profession, requires continued training, personal reflection, supervision, and corrective feedback. This text is just the beginning.

We close this chapter and this text with one final exercise (Exercise 9.1). It is an exercise that invites you to work with your colleagues or classmates as you practice reflecting "on" and "in" practice with the lens of each of the orienting models discussed in this text. The goal again is to begin to think like an expert!

■ ■ ■ ■ ■

EXERCISE 9.1

A CLIENT'S STORY SEEN THROUGH VARIED LENSES

Directions: The following multipart exercise will require the participation of five people. One person will serve as the client, the other four participants should assume the role of counselor, each with a specific orientation (i.e., solution-focused, behavioral, cognitive, and transtheoretical).

Part I: Role Play

The context of the session is provided below, as is a brief description of the client and the client's presenting concern. This is an intake session with the goal being the initial formulation of a case conceptualization and treatment plan.

The goal of this exercise is for each of the counselors to truly step into his/her role and engage the client in a way that would be characteristic of a professional viewing the case through that one specific lens. Your task is to engage the client in a way that will help you formulate your initial hypothesis about what is going on and what needs to be done. It is suggested that the interchange between client and counselor(s) be taped or videorecorded for use later within this exercise.

Part II: Case Conceptualization and Treatment Planning

Following the initial intake, discuss how each of the various theoretical perspectives would respond to each of the following:

1. What is the primary issue being presented? What evidence from the intake would you point to as support for this hypothesis?
2. What is the terminal goal?
3. What are the key factors to be considered in formulating a treatment approach?
4. What is the treatment to be employed (from each perspective)?
5. What specific goals would you set (from each perspective) for the next session?

Part III: Review and Reflect in Practice

Review the taperecording (audio or video) of the session, stopping the tape to discuss each of the following.

1. What are the salient characteristics of a particular orienting framework being demonstrated at this particular point?
2. What is the apparent impact of the counselors' use of their unique lens to guide their reflection on and in practice?
3. What alternative counselor response(s) may have proven more effective at this particular point in the interaction? Which orienting framework may have better directed the counselor to that response?

Part IV: The Impact of Multiple Lenses?

As you process the client data through the specific lens of one orienting framework, you may have discovered that while that lens may have focused your vision on some important factors in the case, it may have missed or even obscured others. Review the data that was gleaned by the counselors using other orienting frameworks and discuss the potential value of employing multiple lenses and multiple perspectives when working with a client. What specific concepts, constructs, techniques, or focus points from the models discussed will you embrace as you attempt to develop your own orienting framework?

THE CASE OF JANIE CRANE

Janie Crane was referred by her eighth-grade art teacher, Ms. Jackson, in December. Ms. Jackson discovered satanic drawings in Janie's folder and found carvings of satanic symbols in her art table. Ms. Jackson stated on the referral, "I have no problem with Janie's 'Goth' subculture, but due to the increase in frequency of satanic content in her art projects and the recent carvings in her desk, I have growing concerns for her well-being. My fear escalated when I found Janie's English journal. There were a lot of references to the devil and satanic worship in the journal. I asked Mr. Howard (her English teacher) why he hadn't reported the content of the journal. He said that he felt there was not enough concern to make a referral at this time. I guess that's why I am sending her down to you. I'm not sure if I'm overreacting or not."

The Client

Janie is a white, thirteen-year-old eighth-grader. She is petite and has dyed black straight hair that hangs in her face. She makes limited eye contact when speaking with adults and has a scar on the top of her ear where she has tried to pierce the cartilage. Janie's read on the situation is that it's a big deal about nothing. She noted: "Nobody understands me. They all just want me to be like my brother and sister and I'm not. My sister is a boring priss and my brother is a jock. Why can't I be what I want to be? I'm happy with myself. Why can't people accept that?"

The intake session (begins at the counselor's request to see Janie during her study hall).

INDEX

NOTES